# PEDRO,
## CARLOS, AND OMAR

# PEDRO,
## CARLOS, AND OMAR

### THE STORY OF A SEASON IN THE BIG APPLE AND
### THE PURSUIT OF BASEBALL'S TOP LATINO STARS

## ADAM RUBIN

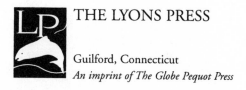

THE LYONS PRESS

Guilford, Connecticut
*An imprint of The Globe Pequot Press*

To buy books in quantity for corporate use
or incentives, call **(800) 962–0973, ext. 4551,**
or e-mail **premiums@GlobePequot.com.**

The Lyons Press is an imprint of The Globe Pequot Press.

10  9  8  7  6  5  4  3  2

Printed in the United States of America

ISBN 1-59228-875-8

Library of Congress Cataloging-in-Publication Data is available on file.

To Sandy, Norman, and Eric

◆

# TABLE OF CONTENTS

# ACKNOWLEDGMENTS

I would like to thank Gary Cohen of SportsNet New York, former Binghamton Mets beat writer Scott Lauber, and MLB.com reporter Kevin Czerwinski for their help proofing this book.

Also, thanks to John Harper of the New York *Daily News* and Tony Massarotti of the *Boston Herald* for recommending me to the publisher and offering insights along the way; and to Rob Kirkpatrick at Lyons Press for guiding me through my first book.

Thanks to the New York Mets organization for their class and cooperation as I covered the team during the 2005 season—specifically, chief operating officer Jeff Wilpon, general manager Omar Minaya, deputies Tony Bernazard, John Ricco and departed Jim Duquette, manager Willie Randolph, and coaches Manny Acta, Sandy Alomar Sr., Rick Down, Jerry Manuel, and Rick Peterson.

Most of all, thanks to the players, who acted professionally amid the intense scrutiny in New York and made the Mets among the easiest clubhouses to cover in baseball.

# INTRODUCTION

The SEASON-TICKET BASE HAD ERODED. The front-office dysfunction had reached a chaotic level. Worst of all, the Mets were in danger of becoming irrelevant in their own market—with the Boston Red Sox garnering more attention in the New York tabloids than the not-so-Amazins, who finished in last place in 2002 and '03, then fourth place the next season.

Desperate to halt the freefall, Mets principal owner Fred Wilpon secretly reached out to Omar Minaya, asking the Montreal Expos GM to return to Flushing, where he had once served as an assistant general manager.

Minaya, the lone Hispanic general manager in Major League Baseball, accepted. He acted ambitiously, too. And not only did the Mets return to the radar in New York, they emerged as a serious postseason contender in 2005 under first-time manager Willie Randolph.

Pedro Martinez—coming off a World Series title with the Red Sox—signed on with the Mets, giving the organization newfound credibility and swagger, not to mention a bona fide ace. Carlos Beltran came on board, too, as Minaya landed the winter's two premier free agents.

The duo gave the Mets a new-found presence in Latin America, where Minaya hoped to build the organization's identity, to entice the region's young talent to sign with the Amazins.

The GM radically shook up the clubhouse, dismissing stalwarts including pitcher Al Leiter.

In his recruiting, the Dominican–born Minaya used his ethnicity as an asset, appealing to the Dominican–born Pedro and Puerto Rican–born Beltran based on a shared Hispanic heritage. The approach worked, even if the bottom line with both players choosing the Mets was, quite literally, the bottom line of Minaya's overwhelming contract offers.

Still, not everyone found Minaya's tactics appealing. Some fans derogatorily referred to the team as *Los Mets*, which Minaya found offensive because of its racial basis. The GM's pursuit of slugger Carlos Delgado, the third player he hoped to land during the 2004–'05 offseason, turned ugly. The free-agent first baseman accused Mets officials of trying to exploit their cultural common ground.

But, oh, how the Mets' karma has changed. Delgado became a Met after the '05 season anyway, when the Florida Marlins—unable to secure funding for a new stadium—held a fire sale and shipped the slugger to Flushing. A year after passing on their four-year, $53 million offer, which happened to have been worth more than the Marlins' bid, even according to Delgado's agent, Delgado glowingly embraced the relocation.

"I'm here because I want to win," Delgado said at his introductory press conference on November 28, 2005, after slipping on a No. 21 jersey as a tribute to fellow Puerto Rican Roberto Clemente. "There's a good opportunity here. They're putting together a good ball club and trying to make it better. That's all a player trying to win can ask for."

Said Minaya: "Players, listen, they know what's going on, especially in the offseason. They look at what team acquired who. . . . The one thing players want to do is they want to win. The fact that you go out and get a big-name guy like a Pedro, that sends a huge message to the other players that these guys are serious about winning."

Minaya merely was ahead of his time in embracing the Hispanic athlete. During the season, Major League Baseball would underscore the importance of marketing to the too-often-overlooked Latin American community. In addition to honoring Clemente at stadiums throughout the country, MLB asked fans to vote for a "Latino Legends Team," remedying the slight of Hispanics six years earlier when an "All-Century Team" included no Latin American ballplayers.

In New York, WFAN—the Mets' flagship radio station—created a show specifically devoted to a Hispanic audience, cognizant of the overlooked demographic. In '05, a record 29.2 percent of the players on Opening Day rosters were born outside the fifty states. Ninety-one players, roughly three per team, hailed from Pedro's native Dominican Republic. Flags from the country were often on display throughout Shea Stadium when the ace took the mound. Thirty-four players hailed from Beltran and Delgado's native Puerto Rico.

Buoyed by Minaya's roster revisions, the Mets finished the '05 season at 83–79, their best winning percentage since their 2000 World Series appearance. They finished tied with the Marlins for third place in the National League East—nothing remarkable on the surface. But the Mets remained mathematically alive in the wild-card race until the season's final week. And had Pedro not surrendered four home runs to the Philadelphia Phillies on August 31, they would have been in a playoff position when the calendar flipped to September—a monumental achievement for an organization that couldn't come close to realizing Wilpon's ambition of "meaningful games in September" the previous season.

Not that anyone faulted Pedro, who pitched through hip, back, and toe discomfort at points during the season, yet still dominated the National League. The ace restored a buzz to Shea Stadium that had been absent since the '00 Subway Series team. His zaniness—whether donning an orange "rally suit" or playing in the sprinklers—served as an energy source for the fans and his teammates alike. The Mets drew 2,829,929 fans to Shea Stadium, their largest home attendance since 1989.

*Pedro, Carlos, and Omar* highlights the contributions of those three men to the rebirth of the Mets organization.

Also, twenty-two-year-old third baseman David Wright emerged as a bona fide major-league star during the season. Mike Cameron dealt with emotional and physical pain, from trade rumblings to a gruesome collision with Beltran that sent both players to the hospital with concussions and broken facial bones. Future Hall of Famer Mike Piazza, in the final season of a seven-year contract as Beltran began a contract of the same length, bid farewell to New York. And Cliff Floyd had an MVP-caliber season, while avoiding the injury problems that had plagued his career.

As 2006 arrived, the organization's relevance in New York had been restored. Things only figured to get brighter, too. The Mets, with partners Time Warner and Comcast, prepared to launch a new regional sports network called SportsNet New York that would provide another revenue stream for the organization. The team also prepared to break ground on a new stadium with an Ebbets Field-type feel, with the 2009 season targeted for its opening.

Minaya had a second straight banner winter during the 2005–'06 offseason, too. With the signing of free-agent closer Billy Wagner and the additions of Delgado and catcher Paul Lo Duca via trades with the Marlins, the Mets became the favorites to win the National League East—even if Randolph tried to temper the expectations by noting that the Atlanta Braves had won fourteen straight division titles.

As Minaya spoke at the podium at the Diamond Club while introducing Delgado, the GM created a lighthearted moment. He turned toward Randolph and told the manager: "Willie, you told me to take care of you, so I'm taking care of you, man, okay? I'm taking care of you. All right? Don't forget that."

"I'm excited," Randolph replied.

Said Randolph: "I expect to win every year. That's just me. I know that's not easy. And it's not like I'm making a bold prediction. I'm a winner. I'm about winning. When I feel that I can have a team that can compete—obviously we have a legitimate chance to compete—then I expect to win. But we'll see. We'll see when we get rolling. It's like everybody else: start from scratch."

Minaya didn't intend to rest on his laurels, either.

"When you believe you have enough, that's when you get comfortable," Minaya said. "I don't believe in getting comfortable."

No matter what they accomplish in the future, the 2005 Mets—The New Mets, as Beltran had dubbed them—set the stage for their achievements.

# THE NEW METS

FRED AND JEFF WILPON HELD their secret rendezvous with Omar Minaya in a conference room at a small airport west of downtown Montreal the morning of September 27, 2004, staying in Canada no longer than the three hours required to conclude their mission.

Three days earlier, a beaten-down Mets ownership had been distraught about the previous week's leak of its decision to fire manager Art Howe at season's end, a PR fiasco that lingered through four tabloid back pages. So, the Wilpons phoned the Montreal Expos GM, declaring their intent to bring him back to Flushing. And on that final Monday of the 2004 season, and of the soon-to-be-relocated Expos' existence, Minaya discreetly accepted, initiating a chain of events that ultimately would bring about The New Mets Pedro Martinez and Carlos Beltran.

Only then, Minaya wasn't thinking about the free-agent bonanzas he'd finally have the financing to pursue, after frugally working in Montreal; nor was he thinking about building the organization for which teenagers throughout Latin America would aspire to play. Instead, Minaya sought only to keep his acceptance quiet. He headed to Olympic Stadium for that night's Expos–Florida Marlins game, played before a crowd of 3,923, and stayed secluded in his office, trying to maintain a low profile despite the media spotlight as Montreal prepared to bid adieu to its Major League Baseball franchise. Only Expos president Tony Tavares, assistant GM Tony Siegle, Minaya's family, and soon, the commissioner's office would be made aware of what had occurred, in addition to incumbent Mets GM Jim Duquette.

"It was kept very private," Minaya said. "And it happened very quickly, too—within seventy-two hours."

Fred Wilpon had tried to rehire Minaya the previous winter in an awkward arrangement with Duquette that left unclear who would have final say, but the principal owner ultimately just shed the "interim" from Duquette's GM title when Minaya balked. Minaya wasn't enamored with the idea of power-sharing in Flushing this time, either, even if MLB officials were making his job difficult in Montreal. After going so far as to prevent any minor-league call-ups when rosters expanded in September 2003—because each player would receive $50,000 for the service time, a bill footed by the other twenty-nine clubs that technically owned the Expos—MLB again forced Minaya's players to split the season between Montreal and San Juan in '04. A clubhouse vote against a divided home schedule had been ignored.

When Fred Wilpon unexpectedly pursued Minaya again, the principal owner this time didn't let Minaya's desire for control undermine the recruiting.

"I'm coming to talk to you," Wilpon stated matter-of-factly.

"About what?" Minaya asked.

"About the general manager's job," Wilpon said.

"Well, what about Jim?" Minaya replied.

"I want you to run my baseball operations."

"Who's going to have full authority?"

"I want you to have full authority."

"*Full* authority of baseball operations?" Minaya asked, just to make sure.

"*Full* authority of baseball operations," Wilpon said.

"Well, let's sit down and talk."

Duquette was a loyal employee who had succeeded the fired Steve Phillips as general manager on an interim basis, two days after Jose Reyes's promotion in July 2003. He had a three-year contract awarded that winter and had been briefed about the possibility of Minaya returning even before the Wilpons' jet took off for Montreal—although he had been led to believe it would be similar to the previously proposed power-sharing arrangement. The sobering news—that Minaya would be fully in charge—came over dinner in Greenwich,

Connecticut, the night the Wilpons returned from Montreal, which happened to be Fred and Judy's forty-sixth wedding anniversary.

Quietly included in Duquette's contract, in the fine print he never really digested, was a stipulation that his GM title and salary could be slashed after one season. The language had been inserted for one overriding reason: The Wilpons had always revered Minaya, who had worked for five years alongside Duquette in Flushing, under Phillips. The fact that Duquette's $450,000 annual salary remained untouched despite the demotion, and his title elevated to senior vice president of baseball operations, served as little consolation.

"Fred made a point of saying how important it was for him to address this with me and how much he wanted for me to stay," Duquette said. "He was stressing the point by saying, 'This is my anniversary. Instead of being home where I should be with my wife, I'm here talking this through with you.' In terms of Omar being the general manager—that was blindsiding, and caught me by surprise, because that wasn't what we had talked about the week before. As I said at the dinner, he's the owner. He has a right to change his mind."

There was a terrible reason for Duquette's ability to put the demotion into perspective. The week before his dinner with Fred Wilpon, Duquette's two-year-old daughter Lindsey had been admitted to The Children's Hospital at Montefiore with a rare kidney disease, one that would keep her hospitalized for nine weeks, nearly to Thanksgiving, before it thankfully had a happy resolution. Duquette's father Jim, who had taught philosophy in Massachusetts, had often told him to find the silver lining in tough times. Duquette remembered that advice as he left Shea Stadium each day at 6 P.M. during the ordeal, bringing dinner to his family at the hospital, where he would remain for three hours. One mother the Duquettes met at Montefiore had lost three children to a rare genetic disorder, and the fourth—who had the same birthday as Lindsey—tragically was afflicted, too.

"I couldn't have done both jobs—be the general manager of the Mets and make sure my daughter was okay," said Duquette, who arranged for Mets players to stop by Montefiore during their winter charity tour in January 2005 in appreciation of the hospital's care. "It took up way too much time. In hindsight, there have been many times when [I've felt] someone was looking down on me."

Duquette dutifully stood by his successor's side at the Thursday news conference that celebrated Minaya's return, held in the old Jets locker room at Shea Stadium.

Minaya, the game's lone Hispanic GM, had used the phrase *full authority* in his phone conversation with Fred Wilpon to describe a power structure that would clearly delineate how honest disagreements with Duquette would be resolved. But when Minaya used this phrase at the media gathering, on an off-day before a season-ending series coincidentally against the Expos, *full authority* took on a different meaning. It was widely misinterpreted as freedom from ownership's purported over-involvement in baseball decisions. This included the excessive meetings and meddling after soliciting input from veterans (including Al Leiter and John Franco) that became widely accepted as gospel among suits around the game, no matter what the legitimacy; industry talk that caused established executives such as Houston's Gerry Hunsicker and Seattle's Pat Gillick to steer clear of the place.

What preceded Minaya's arrival, and swallowed Duquette, were a series of incidents, some too unbelievable to make up and most beyond his control. The dysfunction predated Duquette's ascension and ranged from Phillips's poisonous relationship with 2000 Subway Series manager Bobby Valentine to a college-age photo of reliever Grant Roberts with a bong plastered on the cover of *Newsday*; from Valentine's mimicking of a drugged-up batter at a news conference to address the situation, and claims Roberts was being extorted by a Long Island woman, to Mike Piazza's declaration he was heterosexual, which actually trumped terrorists eyeing the Brooklyn Bridge for attention on one tabloid front page. One incident even involved Duquette's newly hired superscout Bill Singer verbally assaulting Los Angeles Dodgers executive Kim Ng with mock-Chinese gibberish at the GM Meetings in Scottsdale, Arizona.

The distractions reached the critical stage under Duquette's watch with fan uproar over the trade of top pitching prospect Scott Kazmir, a twenty-year-old left-hander who threw in the upper-90s, to the Tampa Bay Devil Rays for Victor Zambrano, balky elbow and all. This swap devolved into finger-pointing, including the leak of pitching coach Rick Peterson's comments on an internal conference call that he could fix Zambrano "in ten minutes." (Peterson vehemently maintained the declaration was understood by team brass to be an expression of confidence that he could help the control-challenged pitcher—not as a literal claim about the time frame.) The final blow to Duquette's tenure came when the *Daily News* ran a headline on the back page that read YER OUT! HOWE A GONER WHEN SEASON ENDS, revealing that Fred Wilpon, the lone hold-out, had been persuaded at a supposedly hush-hush meeting to dump the manager after the 2004 season, eating half of a four-year, $9.4 million contract. Howe, given the option two days after the initial story appeared to either remain through season's end or depart right away, decided to complete the campaign as a lame duck, an uncomfortable position for a gentleman despite any managerial shortcomings.

"I remember following that and saying, 'Man, that sounds like it's all screwed up.' It looked all out of whack," Minaya said. "From the outside, it looked somewhat dysfunctional. There were a lot of people commenting on trade talks. I know Jim, and I've always liked Jim. I felt there wasn't a spokesman. It seemed like everyone was all over the place. And then, even that Art Howe thing . . . You're fired, but you're staying on as an interim? I've never seen anything like that."

Still, at the time of his anointment, Minaya maintains he never had grand visions of an extreme winter makeover that included Pedro and Beltran in Mets uniforms or of the premier free agents allowing the Mets to attempt to become the dominant brand in the Dominican Republic and Venezuela and Puerto Rico. He could not foresee the team's logo splashed all over Manoguayabo, Pedro's hometown, where the World Series champion Red Sox insignia could be found everywhere, including the bodega. Duquette had already done significant groundwork, negotiating contracts with the representatives for Kris Benson and Leiter, and Minaya assumed that the rotation would be set with those two pitchers, plus Tom Glavine, Steve Trachsel, and Zambrano.

Familiar enough with the team because he had been a general manager in the same division—and not all that far removed from assistant GM duties in Flushing—Minaya knew the organization desperately needed a power hitter, ideally at first base, given Piazza's failed conversion to the position. Minaya eventually concluded he would target Carlos Delgado, the free agent who had gained notoriety as a Blue Jay for declining to stand for the singing of "God Bless America." The slugger had a strong commitment against standing for the song based on his opposition to the U.S. Navy's one-time bombing practices in Vieques, an island off the coast of his native Puerto Rico, and subsequent military actions in Afghanistan and Iraq. But Delgado was willing to shelve that behavior to abide by any team's guidelines, even if no one knew exactly how his past practices would play in New York, hardest hit by the terrorist attacks on 9/11.

The GM preferred the lefty-hitting Delgado to Troy Glaus, whom he also liked, and the other available bat at first base, Richie Sexson, fearing those players would make an already righty-dominated lineup too weighted to that side of the plate. Minaya also seriously considered pursuing free agent J.D. Drew for right field, not even considering Beltran, since the Mets had two-time Gold Glove winner Mike Cameron to play centerfield, with two years remaining on his contract. In fact, when Scott Boras presented Minaya with one of the agent's infamous books projecting Beltran's future production at the November GM Meetings in Key Biscayne, Florida, Minaya never opened it. Among the items in the statistics-laden manifesto: the eight home runs that Beltran slugged in the 2004 postseason with the Houston Astros tied Barry Bonds's major-league record; and the fact that Beltran and Ty Cobb were the only two centerfielders ever to have twice recorded 100 RBI, 100 runs, and 40 steals in a season. (While perusing the tome seemed like a waste of time to Minaya, by the end of the Mets' courtship of Beltran, Fred Wilpon had devoured it three times.)

Al Leiter had become a lightning rod for strong emotions among the Shea faithful. On the one hand, he was the Bruce Springsteen–loving New Jersey product who had an All-Star season in 2000 when the Mets met the Yankees in the Subway Series. On the other hand, he was an aspiring Republican politician, seemingly honing the skills that might one day serve him well in Washington, D.C., by acting as clubhouse lawyer, even if he denied it. Close with Jeff Wilpon? Sure, Leiter would agree with that—just as he had been close to Marlins owner/golfing buddy H. Wayne Huizenga during his first stint in South Florida. Nothing sinister about that. And shame on those who relied on Leiter's opinion, not the man himself, if he happened to share his solicited thoughts in casual conversations about the state of the team while speaking as friends with higher-ups. So what if Leiter did express displeasure that Kazmir changed the music to Eminem in a workout room at the Port St. Lucie, Florida, spring-training complex in 2004? Was it really Leiter's fault if that somehow contributed to Kazmir being painted as a wild child—one of the numerous factors that might have led to the flame-throwing first-round pick's departure?

On the field, Leiter went 10–8 with a 3.21 ERA in '04, but his outings averaged only five and two-thirds innings, taxing the bullpen. Yet the Mets organization had been loyal to a fault under the Wilpons, having annually handed John Franco—their aging captain and a Brooklyn native, whose father had been a New York City sanitation worker—one-year extensions at above-market value, even if this time Franco had been informed in August that another contract wouldn't be forthcoming.

Leiter opened the window that allowed Minaya to push him out wider and wider and wider, in fact. Three times he missed deadlines to accept contract proposals, the final offer for a guaranteed $4 million, with the chance to double that amount based on incentives, half easily attainable. Randy and Alan Hendricks, Leiter's agents, agreed with Minaya at the third deadline that both sides would explore other options. The next day—a Saturday, at 10 A.M.—the agents left a voice mail saying Leiter would accept the terms. It was too late. After the weekend, Minaya called back to reiterate he was now looking elsewhere.

"For a guy supposedly running the organization, who had the owner's ear and the general manager's ear, where were those ears in the end?" a bitter Leiter noted to Lee Jenkins of the *New York Times*. Leiter had just signed a one-year contract with the Marlins for $8 million, of which $3 million was deferred without interest and another $1 million went directly to charity. This marriage would end badly in July, when Leiter was handed to the Yankees, who had to assume only $250,000 of the contract.

"*Full* authority of baseball operations?" Minaya had asked during the September phone call with Fred Wilpon.

"*Full* authority of baseball operations," the principal owner had promised, a pledge met with skepticism by the media at the time. The promise now appeared genuine as Minaya unloaded the clubhouse stalwarts—from Leiter and Franco to Mike Stanton and Vance Wilson and Jason Phillips, to even universally liked Joe McEwing by spring training's end—turnover that led to whispers of Minaya building *Los Mets* when coupled with the Hispanic ethnicity of many of the new additions.

The Dominican-born Minaya was free to dream big as he sat at his desk in his second-floor office at Shea Stadium. His storybook path had taken him from the streets of Corona, Queens, to the GM chair only miles away, and even to separate meals with President George W. Bush and Dominican Republic

President Leonel Fernández Reyna during the 2004–05 off-season. Minaya had been ignoring calls from Fernando Cuza, the agent for Pedro, believing that no room existed in the rotation. Now he gave different instructions to new special assistant Tony Bernazard, a well-connected former major-league second baseman of ten seasons. Minaya had hired Bernazard away from the Players Association, where his responsibilities during a thirteen-year stint had included developing a World Cup–style baseball tournament that would be named the World Baseball Classic. Minaya asked Bernazard to inform Cuza that, in fact, the Mets *were* interested in the ace. Minaya reasoned that if Leiter would cost the organization $8 million in '05, there was little harm in boosting that sum to $11 million for Pedro, whom Minaya figured would only command a three-year deal. If Pedro rejected the overture—and initial suspicions were he would, since he was coming off of a historic World Series title with the Boston Red Sox—well, no worries. Minaya was prepared to sign Odalis Perez, another Cuza client, or trade for Anaheim's Ramon Ortiz.

"I thought it was a long shot," Minaya said. "Why would a guy who won a World Series, who's *The Guy* in town—everything is there—why would he want to come to a last-place team, a tough town, not a great hitting team? Why?"

Eventually, Minaya came to think that maybe the proud Pedro wasn't being treated as The Guy anymore; that Curt Schilling and his Cooperstown-bound bloody sock may forever have trumped Pedro in Red Sox lore after Boston's first championship in eighty-six years. Those still in the Mets' front office from the 2002–03 winter were reminded of how the organization had landed Tom Glavine after a messy breakup with the Atlanta Braves, despite similar initial pessimism.

"I said to myself, my thinking was, 'Schilling is The Guy. And I don't care what Schilling does; Pedro is still Pedro.' I think Pedro needed a new challenge," Minaya said. "Fernando Cuza, we have a good relationship. And the fact that we have Tony Bernazard, that helps a lot. Tony had dealt with Pedro many times. I just felt this was not going to be about money for Pedro. This was going to be about a new challenge and about trust. I felt we could provide him the new challenge if he trusted that we were going to go after the players."

To that point, Mets brass had struck out on the free-agent market, even while trying to bulk up the bench. Their credibility was minimal, considering the lack of appeal of the organization after three straight losing seasons, including two last-place finishes, plus the obstacles of a drab ballpark, intense media scrutiny, and unforgiving fans with a lust for booing. Despite higher bids by the Mets, catcher Henry Blanco accepted a two-year, $2.7 million offer from the Chicago Cubs, and infielder Craig Counsell accepted a two-year, $3.1 million offer from the Arizona Diamondbacks.

Pedro's recruitment, which began with Bernazard's call to Cuza, quickly led to Minaya sharing Thanksgiving lunch with the ace at a Santo Domingo restaurant three days after the GM had rejected the Hendrickses' weekend voice mail. During the face-to-face pitch, Minaya's preferred mode of operation (though he especially likes to get into the players' homes), Minaya labeled them both Davids in a David versus Goliath tale. Pedro was a World Series champion after growing up without the fifty cents necessary to take the bus, while huddled under that now-famous mango tree; and the Dominican-born GM was running a New York baseball franchise after growing up on the streets of Corona, Queens.

"We were talking about spiritual things, and we talked about David," Minaya said. "Pedro's very spiritual. We talked about the underdog spirit."

The Red Sox hierarchy—owner John W. Henry and CEO Larry Lucchino—countered Minaya's pursuit by meeting Pedro and Cuza outdoors at the airport in Santo Domingo. They carried with them the World Series trophy, inviting Pedro and his family to pose for photographs with it. In the end, the Sox—whose Bill James–inspired, *Moneyball*-style number crunchers didn't value Pedro as greatly as Minaya did—would guarantee the final season of a three-year, $40.5 million bid. The foot-dragging had turned off Pedro, even if Sox teammate David Ortiz, after Henry and Lucchino's airport visit, confidently proclaimed, "He ain't going to no Mets."

The courtship reached its climax at the December 10–13 winter meetings at the Anaheim Marriott, down the block from Disneyland. Mets and Red Sox brass had suites on the same floor of one tower of the hotel. They had been engaged in simultaneous and serious discussions about sending World Series MVP Manny Ramirez from Boston to Flushing, a salary addition that would prevent the Mets from continuing to pursue Pedro. The Mets decided pitching was the priority and broke off talks with the Red Sox, citing an unbridgeable money gap, which angered Boston officials.

The next day, the Mets all but sealed Pedro.

As Mets brass was closing the deal, Red Sox officials were furiously trying to reach Cuza, making repeated phone calls. The Mets knew it wasn't an agent prank to create a false sense of urgency or pressure, either. Cuza showed them his cell phone, where the all-too-familiar 617 area code kept popping up. Not only that, but the Red Sox also sent over a counterproposal, slipped under the door of the agent's hotel room just as Mets executives were shaking hands with Cuza. At the time, the Red Sox publicly claimed to be out of the bidding.

Lesser issues still needed to be resolved, like the luxury-suite provision at Shea Stadium, which required a phone call from Mets brass to Jeff Wilpon in New York. Minaya, Duquette, and the rest of the brain trust planned to leave Cuza's room to make the call, but the agent suggested he walk into the hallway instead and let them phone from his room. Bernazard, a veteran of several Major League Baseball versus Players Association negotiations, kept checking through the peephole to ensure no one from Cuza's side was eavesdropping, apparently a dirty trick he had encountered during labor talks. The agent acted professionally.

Cuza called his client that night and told Pedro he could close the deal with the Mets with the ace's consent, if he was willing to leave the Red Sox. This was a moment of truth that caused Pedro—as composed as any pitcher on the mound—to experience shortness of breath as he spoke from his backyard in the Dominican Republic. Inside his compound—which includes ten-foot-high yellow walls with razor wire on top, big green double doors at the main entrance, and a man with a shotgun standing guard—Pedro prayed, asking God why the Mets had seemed to show more interest.

The next morning the Mets learned they had an agreement in principle, though they didn't tip their hands as they marched poker-faced through a Marriott side lobby. They departed the winter meetings in a pair of white vans bound for the airport and a cross-country flight on discount carrier JetBlue—an ironic choice of carrier considering their winter spending spree, which included a three-year, $22.5 million contract to Benson. That deal had caused Pittsburgh Pirates managing general partner Kevin McClatchy to rail at the bar being set for starting pitchers—and mediocre ones at that, in McClatchy's biased opinion, having previously employed Benson.

No one from the Mets cared. Pedro had agreed to a four-year, $53 million contract, pending an MRI in New York.

"We high-fived, hugged, whatever, because we were all excited," Duquette said. "But it was all contingent upon the physical. You heard all these whispers, 'Well, he's got a tear' or whatever. Obviously, we were a little concerned."

The Mets held dual news conferences, one at the Diamond Club at Shea Stadium, the other in Santo Domingo. This was a signal of their enhanced international appeal, and something they would mimic once Beltran chose the Mets a month later, when announcements were held in New York and San Juan. (To add to the circus atmosphere, the *Post* sent a four-foot-tall actor named Tim Loomis to Pedro's Flushing media gathering. This stunt was spawned because Pedro had a twenty-eight-inch-tall good-luck charm named Nelson de la Rosa, who had gained notoriety during Boston's World Series run—even to the extent of riding on the championship float with Pedro. "I'm more famous than he is," Loomis told *Page Six* shortly after de la Rosa revealed in the *Daily News* that he had become estranged from Pedro. "I was in Woody Allen's *Shadows and Fog*. I've worked at Radio City's Christmas show. I've appeared on *Saturday Night Live*. And I'm doing the hottest comedy show in the country—Beacher's Comedy Madhouse at the Hard Rock Hotel in Las Vegas. I'm also a lot taller than him.")

Critics had decried how the Mets could hand a pitcher with a supposedly balky shoulder such a lengthy contract. Meanwhile, what failed to be revealed at the time was that the Cardinals had already moved to four years and $50 million with their offer before the Mets ever guaranteed the '08 season.

Regardless, Minaya knew Pedro was exactly the jolt the organization needed, his production in the fourth year of the contract be damned. Pedro would give the Mets an instant swagger, the credibility that would ease the task of attracting others, including the role players who would eventually give the Mets one of the strongest benches in baseball during the 2005 season, with Miguel Cairo, Chris Woodward, Marlon Anderson, and Ramon Castro. The signing would give the Mets visibility in Latin America, where Minaya had begun his career as a scout with the Texas Rangers—signing the likes of Sammy Sosa and Juan Gonzalez— and where the GM knew the Mets would benefit for years, even after Pedro's contract expired. This strategy bore its first major fruit that July, when sixteen-year-old Dominican outfielder Jesus Fernando Martinez signed a $1.4 million contract with the Mets despite higher offers elsewhere. The young slugger cited his affinity for Pedro among the major factors in picking the Mets.

"I was a millionaire since I was twenty-four years old, first of all, to let you know," said Pedro, indicating trust and respect were major criteria, as Minaya had hoped. "When I got to Boston, I was already making millions. I continued to live up to my contract in Boston. So you didn't pick up a bum from the street. Boston wouldn't pull the trigger. I went beyond my efforts to give Boston every opportunity to keep me. Why did they have to wait until the last minute or so? Do I have to sit and wait for someone else to decide what my future is going to be?"

The winter meetings placed the new Mets brass on a stage, even if up to that point their lone roster moves had been re-signing reliever Mike DeJean, cutting loose outfielder Richard Hidalgo and reliever Ricky Bottalico, and shipping Stanton to the Yankees for fellow southpaw Felix Heredia, a move that saved the organization $1 million. This cleared salary room to afford Cairo, but was otherwise a bust for both teams, with Stanton later released and Heredia's season quickly over because of hand numbness and coldness caused by an aneurysm.

Willie Randolph, whose rise paralleled Minaya's (although in Brooklyn rather than Queens), had been hired in November to succeed Howe as manager. This happened despite late and insincere flirtations with Jim Leyland and ex-'86 Met Wally Backman, who lasted all of four days as Arizona Diamondbacks manager because of revelations of a DUI conviction and guilty plea to a misdemeanor harassment charge. Randolph, fifty, grew up in the Brownsville section of the borough, playing punchball, stickball, and stoopball, and starring at Tilden High School. During his first legitimate date, with his childhood-sweetheart-turned-wife Gretchen, he watched the Cubs' Billy Williams slug two homers at Shea Stadium. He rooted for the '69 Mets. And though Randolph played thirteen seasons in Yankee pinstripes, he finished his career with the Mets in 1992. Randolph had not played the final seven weeks of that season because of a broken hand, but manager Jeff Torborg, who had coached Randolph for years in the Bronx, placed him in the lineup on the season's final day. Appropriately enough, since Randolph had 1,243 in his career, his final plate appearance resulted in a walk.

"In this town, whether you're a Yankee or a Met, I think people look at me as one of their own, as a New Yorker," Randolph said.

Seated with the team's beat writers at the annual managers' luncheon at the winter meetings, Randolph proved charming and personable and nothing like the introverted Howe. This was true, even though Randolph generated his first unplanned headline—however harmless—when he revealed he had yet to speak with Piazza since taking the job a month earlier, his one call to the slugger having gone unreturned. The kicker: The previous night, Piazza had appeared on a New Jersey rock station, taking calls from the public.

Not everything went smoothly in Anaheim. Early on, Minaya had identified Delgado as the bat the Mets needed, but their face-to-face meeting in agent David Sloane's room at the Sheraton five minutes away turned decidedly sour, even though Minaya tried to hold it together. With a Dominican–born GM, the Puerto Rican–born Bernazard beside him as special assistant, New York's first African-American manager in Randolph, and a coaching staff that included three minorities—Manny Acta, Sandy Alomar Sr., and Jerry Manuel—the Mets had become a model for staff diversity. Delgado, a Puerto Rican, failed to be impressed, believing the Mets were trying to use Bernazard to play some sort of race card.

When Mets brass showed up at the agent's room with an entourage that included Minaya, Duquette, Bernazard, Randolph, and Peterson, Delgado was immediately turned off. The computer-savvy, leather-jacket-wearing Sloane felt the assembly of Mets execs resembled a Rockettes line. Minaya waited until last to introduce Bernazard. Delgado, feeling he was being played because of their shared Puerto Rican heritage, blurted, "The highest-paid translator on the planet," seemingly a reference to Bernazard's days with the Players Association, when his role partly included communicating with Hispanic ballplayers. Minaya tried to disarm the awkward moment with a laugh, but the Mets never got close to signing Delgado, despite the Marlins' winning bid—four years, $52 million—being $30,000 less in present value than the Mets' offer, using Sloane's own calculations. Florida also lacked the no-trade protection the Mets offered. The deal did put the slugger close to his agent's South Florida home, which Sloane maintained was a non-factor.

The night Delgado picked the Marlins in late January, fifteen days after Beltran had been introduced in Flushing, the Mets traded Class A prospect Ian Bladergroen to the Red Sox for first baseman Doug Mientkiewicz. This seemed like a sound alternative considering his slick fielding, something particularly useful for young infielders David Wright, Jose Reyes, and Kazuo Matsui, who were traumatized by sloppy first-base play the previous season.

Sloane went on to needle the organization into spring training by sending out mass e-mails to the media—some with his own commentary, others with links to articles in which Delgado had been critical of the Mets. One piece even outed Leiter as a co-conspirator by badmouthing his former organization during a Marlins recruiting luncheon.

In a spring-training column appearing in the *Toronto Sun*, in which Sloane delivered a blow-by-blow account of his off-season dealings on Delgado's behalf, Leiter is alleged to have said:

> *Who better to discourage him from going to New York? . . . In New York you have seven or eight competing papers, TV networks and their affiliates and peripheral periodicals. It's fine when you are dealing and kicking butt. It just chip, chip, chip, chips away at your resolve, cracking away your protective toughness. Every bad game, it's like, "Are you worried?" The manager says this . . . "Are you worried?" You begin to doubt yourself. That's why slumps in New York are so elongated. Then, the guys on [talk radio] get on you, move it up another notch, and everyone driving to the game listens. You get to the park and your home fans are booing you, and after the game you say something stupid.*

Leiter distanced himself from the remarks, issuing a borderline denial, though Steve Trachsel—his former Mets teammate—agreed it certainly sounded like something Leiter would say.

Sloane also belittled the Mets, predicting Beltran's signing would have little impact on the Mets' chances in the National League East. "We thought that without Carlos [Beltran], the Mets were a fourth-place club, and we thought that *with* Carlos, they were still a fourth-place club," Sloane said.

The *Toronto Star* ran a column distributed by Sloane that read: "GM Omar Minaya and his assistant Tony Bernazard . . . misplayed the race card. They approached Delgado as a fellow Latino, instead of, first, as a man. Mistake."

The agent maintained even months later that he was merely fulfilling a pledge to reporters to keep them informed about developments, not seeking retribution for anything. What the Mets could never understand about what seemed like a cyber-attack by the agent was that Sloane had been the one at the winter meetings to ask for the entire process to remain quiet, a proposal to which the Mets had readily agreed. Mets brass continued to assert during the season that the Marlins' recruiting party—which included owner Jeffrey Loria, president David Samson, general manager Larry Beinfest, assistant GM Michael Hill, vice president Andre Dawson, and special assistant Tony Perez—which met during a luncheon at Joe's Stone Crab in South Florida, was far larger than the Mets' contingent at the Sheraton in Anaheim that had so irritated Delgado.

With Delgado's negotiations having turned sour, Beltran became a more realistic option. The Wilpons had pushed Duquette to cut the payroll by $36 million in his one winter as GM, resulting in a haul of closer Braden Looper, Cameron, and Matsui. The Wilpons now seemed receptive to spending, understanding that new energy was needed among the fan base before the launch of the Mets' new television network in 2006. They also knew that season-ticket sales were eroding, and the next winter's free-agent class was not nearly as attractive. Still, the organization had not exactly had a positive relationship with Beltran's agent, Scott Boras, dating back to ill-fated dealings over Alex Rodriguez.

Any hostility with Boras had started to thaw in June 2004, when the Mets took a Boras client, right-handed pitcher Matt Durkin from San Jose State, in the second round of the draft. Then came the ultimate olive branch, or more accurately, a shrewd business move, when Boras sent a message to Minaya and Bernazard saying the Pedro signing impressed Beltran.

"Let's forget about the past," Minaya replied. "You know me. I know you. If I'm going to get into the process, I'm going to get into the process to win."

Bernazard had played against Boras when they were minor-leaguers. And Beltran's mother had twice called Bernazard at the Players Association before her son was drafted in 1995, seeking advice about agents.

"When I go after something, I go after something," Bernazard said.

Relentless pursuit proved to be an understatement. Minaya or Bernazard—"the unsung hero," Jeff Wilpon called the special assistant—phoned Boras for thirty-one straight days, a fact the agent could verify because he logs all his calls in a book. A meeting between owner Fred Wilpon and Beltran was finally set for January 3 in San Juan. Boras had wanted the sides to meet in Florida, as Beltran had done with the Astros and Yankees. Minaya insisted otherwise, figuring he could get to Beltran's heart by getting into his living room, though he had to settle for the Ritz-Carlton on the island, minus Beltran's wife Jessica, an absence that concerned Mets brass.

"We knew they were close and that she was going to be a big part of the decision-making process," Duquette said. "We thought it was bad news that she wasn't there. I think she was sick. But we were really hoping she would be there. We even considered going back down there so we could meet with Carlos and Jessica. It never ended up working out."

Still, Beltran came away impressed with the owner's genuineness and fatherly advice, despite a four-decade age gap and their disparate pasts. Wilpon had played high school baseball alongside Sandy Koufax in New York City, while Beltran revered contemporary centerfielders such as the Yankees' Bernie Williams, a fellow Puerto Rican. What struck Beltran most was that Wilpon wasn't selling *against* anyone, including the Yankees. His pitch dealt with the virtues of playing in New York, of the list of Hall of Fame centerfielders who had patrolled Ebbets Field and the Polo Grounds and Yankee Stadium—Duke Snider and Willie Mays and Mickey Mantle.

"He was saying if you wanted to play for a big-market team, New York was the right place to be—Mets or Yankees," Beltran said. "That was something as an owner you don't see happen. You don't see a guy going to Puerto Rico to recruit me and at the same time he's giving me options to go to different places. That sounds funny. But at the same time, that was what he was doing, and that's why I'm here."

Said Duquette: "Fred talked about how Carlos had to do what's best for him no matter what it is. It was classic Fred Wilpon discussing this. He's confident that this is the place, but he's not going to do it at all costs trying to convince him. He treated him like an adult. 'Hey, you've got to make a decision; do what's right for your family.' That seemed to hit home with Carlos."

Before the meeting, Boras had told his client why he ought to consider Flushing. "Carlos, this is not the Mets. This is 'The *New* Mets,'" the agent said. "I think you have to look at them when you meet with Fred."

"This *is* 'The New Mets,'" Beltran confided to Boras afterward, enthusiastically repeating the phrase the agent had planted in his head.

Still, when decision day arrived, and with the Astros set to lose negotiating rights at midnight, Mets brass had several anxious moments. In the early afternoon, Boras phoned Mets officials with bad news.

"We're having second thoughts possibly of coming here," Boras told them, bluntly suggesting they had been eliminated at one point during the conversation.

Team officials suspected it might be a ruse to get them to bid against themselves. Unsure it was final, considering Boras's master negotiating skills, they held out faint hope. Sure enough, Boras called back later in the afternoon and amended his statement, exclaiming, "Okay, you're back in."

"The whole time you're wondering, 'Is this a negotiating ploy or is this really real?'" Duquette said. "It just left you skeptical, because Scott has his negotiating style and you just don't know. He's a bright guy and you just don't know if that's part of his actual style to negotiate and create a sense of urgency."

Eventually, Duquette headed home, where he received a call from a dejected Bernazard at 11:30 P.M.

"We lost him," Bernazard said.

"You've got to be kidding," Duquette replied.

Fifteen minutes later, Mike Fiore, Boras's top lieutenant, called Bernazard and told him: "You guys are the luckiest son of a guns I've ever seen."

A full 180-degree turn.

Bernazard called back Duquette.

"We got him," Bernazard said.

"*What?*" Duquette asked incredulously.

The Astros had refused to give a full no-trade clause. On top of that they offered less money—$105 million.

Boras even tried to engage the Yankees on the final evening to no avail, offering to put Beltran in pinstripes for a six-year, $100 million deal. GM Brian Cashman didn't bite, the organization's money committed to pitching—including the pursuit of Randy Johnson via a trade with the Arizona Diamondbacks, despite the aging Williams in centerfield. While impressed with Beltran, the Yankees had not valued him as a $16 million-a-year player. They didn't want to pay the 40 percent luxury tax on that amount, either, or put Beltran at a salary level comparable to Derek Jeter and Alex Rodriguez.

"They were interested," Beltran said, "but it would have been tough since, I believe, their payroll is over $200 million."

The Mets and Boras's associates worked all night to reach an agreement, with team officials concerned that unpredictable Yankees owner George Steinbrenner might change his mind if he had any chance to reflect and consider Beltran playing for seven years in Flushing. Boras halted discussions with Mets general counsel David Cohen about the final terms at 7 A.M. Pacific Standard

Time that Sunday and slept off a twenty-five-and-a-half-hour day. Minaya, monitoring the situation from his New Jersey home, didn't want Cohen to stop until they were done.

"Once daylight comes, you don't know," said Minaya, reiterating that the Yankees might have become involved had Beltran remained available into the week.

The victorious Minaya then dined with President Bush, his former Rangers boss, at the White House, and even the Commander in Chief, who once had famously traded away Sammy Sosa, had taken notice of the Mets' winter.

"Keep up the good work," Bush told Minaya. "I'll be watching. Pick up some more guys."

Eight days after Fred Wilpon's visit, Beltran, who had solicited endorsements about playing in New York from Astros teammates Roger Clemens and Andy Pettitte, was being introduced as a Met, the first question coming in Spanish, another signal of the organization's new international appeal. A new mantra that would make a Madison Avenue executive proud—"The New Mets"—was born, too, after Beltran smoothly reiterated the phrase at the packed media gathering at the Diamond Club at Shea Stadium, the same location as Pedro's announcement. That is, once Beltran actually reached the Diamond Club. The news conference started a few minutes late as Beltran, his wife Jessica, Boras, Fiore, and nearly the entire Mets brain trust got stuck in a Shea Stadium elevator between the first and second floors en route to the event, though the mishap did not become public knowledge. Executive VP of business operations Dave Howard tried to pry open the doors with his hands as someone joked, "Everybody stop breathing so we don't run out of air."

Moments later, service restored, Beltran, dressed in a pinstriped suit, could utter his famous words: "I feel proud to be part of the new family, the New York Mets. The New Mets. I call it 'The New Mets' because this organization is going to a different direction, the right direction—the direction of winning."

Throughout the season, Mets staffers would answer phones with the greeting, "New Mets." The front of the media guide would carry the slogan, with *New* accentuated in orange and the other words in white. And if you ever got placed on hold while calling Shea Stadium, the recording prominently included Beltran's utterance from the news conference as part of a loop.

Boras really deserved royalties for use of the phrase, but his cut of the seven-year, $119 million contract would have to suffice.

"That was kind of a theme we took in on the day of the press conference, when I said, 'Don't forget what you told me in Puerto Rico—that this is 'The New Mets.' It really came out of our dialogue," Boras said.

Said Beltran: "That came out because this year the Mets went out and added new people; first of all, to the front office, like adding Omar Minaya and Tony Bernazard. And then they went out and hired Willie Randolph and Pedro. So that let me know they were going in a different direction. . . . I really believe now players are going to look at the Mets differently, with more respect."

"I just didn't think we'd be able to sign a Carlos Beltran," Minaya said.

Beltran had grown tired of instability, the annual possibility of being traded while playing for the small-market Kansas City Royals. And while a cynic might suggest the $119 million offer and nothing else prompted Beltran to choose the Mets—perhaps a valid assumption given Boras's track record of sending clients to the highest bidder despite the team's potential for winning, like Pudge Rodriguez's marriage to the Detroit Tigers—Beltran suggested otherwise. Had the Astros come through with a full no-trade clause, a guarantee he would remain in Houston for the length of the seven-year contract, Beltran insisted he very likely would have re-signed with the club he carried to within a game of the World Series in 2004.

"We were close to making a deal with them, but there was some commitment wanted, especially with the no-trade clause," Beltran told Christian Red of the *Daily News*. This interview took place at the outfielder's parents' home in Manatí, Puerto Rico, as Beltran's squirrel-sized pet monkey mingled in the den and consumed human baby food. "That's the difference between the Mets and the Astros. I've been waiting to get to this point, and I didn't want to go through what I went through in Kansas City. I wanted to go to one place for a long time."

Typical of the Yankees, though—they still managed to steal the tabloid covers the day of the announcement. They had swung the long-anticipated deal with Arizona for Johnson, and staged their Big Unit news conference in the Bronx three hours after the Mets' Beltran introduction. In truth, Jeff Wilpon and Yankees counterpart Randy Levine had worked together to avoid conflict and leave both teams happy. But the Yankees got the more prominent attention on the day of the dueling news conferences. After arriving in New York, Johnson created headlines by shoving Channel 2 cameraman Vinny Everett on Madison Avenue en route to his physical. The *Daily News* headline: I WALK, I HIT, I ERROR. And considerably less Mets presence on newsstands as a result.

Of course, Minaya hadn't even considered Beltran early in the winter, in part because the Mets had Cameron. It was Sosa who had generated the early buzz, his time with the Chicago Cubs about to expire because of feuding with manager Dusty Baker. The final straw was when Sosa left Wrigley Field fifteen minutes after the season finale started against the Atlanta Braves on October 3, 2004, something he initially denied, though a surveillance camera in the players' parking lot conclusively proved otherwise. To illustrate the untenable situation, it was Cubs management that revealed the existence of the video to Chicago media.

Minaya, credited with signing a sixteen-year-old Sosa two decades earlier while with the Texas Rangers, fueled the speculation, intentionally or not. In December, Minaya attended the ceremony where Sosa and his wife Sonia renewed their wedding vows. The trade chatter got so loud that Cliff Floyd became convinced he was relocating to his native Windy City. Floyd had even picked out where he would live, near trendy Navy Pier. When Floyd ran into Sosa at a Miami Heat–Indiana Pacers basketball game at the height of the buzz, the Cub quizzed Floyd about playing in New York, figuring they would be teammates, not aware they would be exchanged. Floyd didn't volunteer that information.

"I have agents that pretty much kept me informed with everything," Floyd said. "They would call me, and the phone calls would be '9-1-1 return' calls. I'm thinking, 'Hell, I'm traded.' . . . The talk was Sammy. I was like, 'Well, maybe this is what it's going to be.' How can you hate that, going to Chicago, being my hometown? Around that time I got a couple of calls from Omar and then I just left it alone after that."

In the end, sometimes the best moves are the ones not made. Sosa ended up with the Baltimore Orioles, where he had a .221 average and fourteen homers when he landed on the disabled list August 26 with a toe injury. Soon afterward he departed for his Florida home. The Cubs had picked up $12 million of Sosa's $17 million salary for 2005, plus a $3.5 million severance payment. The Orioles owed Sosa $5 million for '05, plus got an option for '06 at $18 million with a $4.5 million buyout. Baltimore also shipped second baseman Jerry Hairston and minor-leaguers Dave Crouthers and Mike Fontenot to the Windy City.

Floyd would eventually assume Piazza's cleanup role and hear "MVP, MVP" chants at Shea Stadium during the season.

"We couldn't fit him in at the number the Cubs wanted us to pick up," Minaya said. "We could have gotten down to a number that fit for us, but going down, we had to give better prospects. We just couldn't do that. My heart probably would have said, 'Oh yeah, give them the prospects,' but that's not a wise thing to do and in the best interest of the organization."

"He's my friend," Sosa said about Minaya. "A lot of people got confused because he went to my house. They say something negative because he went to my wedding. I invited him to it before. Omar, he's like my father. Omar was one of the guys who signed me when I was a minor-leaguer. . . . He was one of the guys who discovered me. To go back to Omar, it would have been nice, but it didn't happen. We cannot feel bad."

Their winter renovation practically complete, Mets brass still had some unfinished business. Jeff Wilpon had promised Pedro a return trip to the Dominican Republic, and the Mets made good in January, after a stopover in Atlanta where they visited Cameron to allay any concerns about the move to right field to accommodate Beltran.

Cameron, over lunch, never requested a trade, though agent Mike Nicotera had already tactfully let it be known that exploring options which could place Cameron in centerfield elsewhere would be ideal. After all, Cameron was a two-time Gold Glove winner at the position. And though Cameron had offered his blessing to pursue Beltran earlier in the winter, it must have been difficult at the time to conceive that it actually would materialize.

Beltran joining the Mets certainly had seemed a long shot when the organization was pursuing him via a trade during the 2004 season, before Kansas City Royals GM Allard Baird shipped Beltran to the Astros. Yet with the Mets in Kansas City for interleague play before that deal, Cameron, asked about the possibility of Beltran becoming his teammate, barked in reference to his own signing with the organization: "I would have went on to Atlanta. I could have played right field anywhere."

Said a less-than-bubbly Cameron on a conference call with reporters the night of the visit by Mets brass to Atlanta: "I had reservations about it for the simple reason that I've never done it before. The one thing we came to terms with today was, I'm here to do what's in the best interests of the ball club, and try to put this team back on the map."

A whirlwind visit in the Dominican Republic ensued, beginning at the Mets' baseball academy on a sunny, mid-eighties day in Boca de Niqua, thirty miles west of Santo Domingo. It included dinner that evening with President Leonel Fernández Reyna, during which a late-arriving Pedro implored Jeff Wilpon to drink the local brew.

"We made Jeff drink an El Presidente," Pedro recalled. "When you come to the Dominican, you have to drink Presidente. He's like, 'Well, but I'm driving.' 'No, drink a Presidente,' then you go wherever we were going to go."

Pedro had been at the beach, then hanging out with the chief executive's bodyguards, and his tardiness was just viewed as another of his charming personality traits, which Mets bullpen coach Guy Conti noted is something to bear in mind if Pedro should ever arrive late to a ballpark. "People worry about Pedro. He was late for the *President*," said Conti, an eighteen-year-old Pedro's first pitching coach in the United States, in Great Falls, Montana, where Conti taught the future ace his devastating changeup.

What followed was a late-night drive through the downtown streets of the capital, with Jeff Wilpon at the wheel of Pedro's yellow Ferrari and the ace driving the red Ferrari he had bought for his brother Ramon. Pedro purposely ran a red light, alarming the younger Wilpon, who refused to do the same thing and seemingly commit a moving violation, even if word never would have made it back to the New York DMV.

"In the Dominican after like ten, ten-thirty, eleven, you just check on the lights and make sure no one is coming," Pedro said. "I saw the red light. No one was around the street so I just went through it. He was going bananas when he saw I went across a red light."

Jeff Wilpon's thanks for stopping at the red light?

"A Hummer almost ran up my ass," the younger Wilpon said.

Said Pedro: "He's a young man. I figured he's pretty much like me. He's a good driver. I mean, if you can drive in New York, you're certainly capable of driving anywhere else."

They finished the night on Pedro's fifty-two-foot boat, where the ace spends nights during the off-season, eating lobster out of the pool-like waters of nearby islands, which are cooked on the spot.

Soon afterward, Pedro was in New York for the Mets' late-January winter caravan, a weeklong series of stops to benefit charities around the city and gain publicity for the upcoming season. He acted like a model citizen despite his reputation in Boston as a diva needing special treatment.

Well, Pedro was there the first day, at least.

The ace follows a strict off-season training program and believes detours to Manhattan in the middle of the winter can be disruptive. Yet Pedro was charming and bold at the kickoff held in a lower Manhattan art gallery adjacent to the New York Stock Exchange, even as he warned people to not expect him back at the annual event in January 2006. Pedro went so far as to predict the Mets could overtake the Yankees for the hearts and attention of the city—the Yankees who had epically lost to Pedro's Red Sox in the '04 American League Championship Series after leading three games to none, and who were without a World Series title since beating the Mets in the Subway Series in 2000.

"After this season, I don't know if we'll be second," Pedro said.

# ACE IN THE HOLE

WHEN CARLOS BELTRAN CALLED HIS NEW EMPLOYER "The New Mets," who knew that meant a new Pedro Martinez, too?

Pedro had reported to spring training after his fellow Boston Red Sox pitchers six of seven seasons, but there he was on February 8—more than a week before the reporting date for pitchers and catchers—preparing to throw off a mound at the Mets' Port St. Lucie, Florida, complex.

Guy Conti, the Mets' bullpen coach, labeled Pedro's early arrival shocking, and Conti had better insight than many about the ace's inner workings, since their relationship dated back to 1990. Pedro had even referred to the sixty-two-year-old Conti during the winter as his "white daddy." This was a variation on the ace's proclamation during the 2004 season that the Yankees were his daddy, which had grown to larger-than-life proportions when crowds started chanting "*Whoooooo's your daddd-eeeeee?*" first at Yankee Stadium, and then, throughout the country.

Pedro reasoned that he had always done this type of pre-spring training work at home in the Dominican Republic, and that since he had a place in Miami, roughly a two-hour drive on Interstate 95, why not make a statement to his new employer? It was an early, and welcome, sign that Pedro would be a solid citizen for first-time manager Willie Randolph, even if skeptics wondered how long the model behavior would last.

Pedro arrived at the complex at 9 A.M. He went through fielding drills with pitchers Heath Bell, Aaron Heilman, Grant Roberts, and Joe Nelson, all local residents, as well as South Korean Jae Seo. He then did his long-toss program, playing catch at 200 feet with Bell, who had a tough time keeping up at that distance so early in the spring. "*Ooooh*," Conti beamed after monitoring the workout. "He's really in good shape. He's really, really committed. That's the word I keep saying: He's *committed* to the Mets. He's *committed* to the season. He looks so strong."

Said Pedro: "The New Mets are going to have a new attitude. It's going to be a team that went from last place in other years to being a team that's really going to compete and be in the middle of the race."

The Mets had finished in fourth place in the National League East the previous season, mustering only seventy-one wins despite twice being only a game out of first place in July. The underwhelming performance resulted in the firing of manager Art Howe, yet the season still marked an improvement over last-place finishes in 2002 and '03. During these years, the roster was littered with unproductive, injury-prone veterans such as Mo Vaughn, Jeromy Burnitz, and Roger Cedeño, who had name recognition based on their past success, but mostly bloated contracts and waistlines while in Flushing.

Still, the Mets entered the 2005 season with serious question marks, despite an extreme winter makeover spearheaded by general manager Omar Minaya:

◆ Could Jose Reyes and Mike Piazza, who were limited to a combined 675 at-bats in 2004 because of leg injuries—fewer at-bats than Seattle's Ichiro Suzuki (704), Texas's Michael Young (690), or Florida's Juan Pierre (678)—remain healthy?

◆ How would Randolph, previously interviewed and rejected at least a dozen times by teams looking to hire managers—including by the Mets, who considered him two years earlier when they had hired Howe—perform? After all, this wasn't the Yankees, where Randolph served as third-base and then bench coach, and the $200 million roster consisted of perennial All-Stars Derek Jeter, Alex Rodriguez, Gary Sheffield, and Mariano Rivera.

◆ Would Mike Cameron actually be in right field for the Mets on Opening Day? Or with the organization at all? Cameron, a two-time Gold Glove winner, was recovering from December 17 surgery to repair cartilage in his left wrist, and was iffy at best for the April 4 opener in Cincinnati. More importantly, he was being asked to shift to right field from centerfield to accommodate Beltran. The organization was accepting inquiries for his services from other general managers because of his apparent discomfort with the move, even if Minaya all along relished the idea of having Cameron's center-field range in right and didn't want to deal him.

◆ How would the bullpen fare with Felix Heredia and Dae-Sung Koo as its southpaws, and with Mike DeJean slated for eighth-inning setup duty a season after he had been dumped by the Baltimore Orioles?

◆ Would the Mets have enough power in their lineup behind table setters Reyes, Kazuo Matsui, and Beltran? The Mets had missed out on free-agent slugger Carlos Delgado and instead traded for slick-fielding Doug Mientkiewicz, who had no more than eighteen home runs in any of his ten professional seasons, including the minors. No one with the Mets in 2004 had more homers than Cameron's thirty, and that was a career-high total that he might be hard-pressed to duplicate even if completely healthy.

At least Reyes was returning to his natural shortstop position, after the disastrous decision to move him to second base the previous year in order to land Matsui from the Seibu Lions of Japan's Pacific Coast League. Matsui's rookie season in the United States included the National League's worst fielding percentage of any shortstop with a minimum of 100 games (.956), 97 strikeouts in 460 at-bats, and a six-week stint on the disabled list with a lower-back strain. He had played 1,143 straight games before his arrival, the fifth-longest streak in Japanese baseball history.

Randolph felt confident but antsy. The night before addressing his pitchers and catchers, he awoke every hour on the hour, at 1, 2, 3, and 4 A.M. He then laid down the law. Wearing a Mets uniform for the first time since October 4, 1992, the final game of his eighteen-year major-league playing career,

Randolph banned facial hair except for neatly trimmed mustaches during a 9 A.M. address.

Piazza's beard was among the first casualties. Reliever Matt Ginter lost a ZZ Top–looking goatee, too, though he was able to restore the look when he was traded to the Detroit Tigers at the end of spring training for left-handed reliever Steve Colyer.

"I don't want to look like a seventies-style Burt Reynolds. I might just go with the clean-shaven look this year," said Piazza, suggesting his mustache would look awkward sans beard. "It might be the best thing. Maybe I'll look younger and try to trick everybody."

Randolph objected to the suggestion he was bringing the Yankee way to the Mets, even if the corporate culture and sterile, professional clubhouse had worked in the Bronx during a decade of dominance. The manager even objected to calling his demands "rules," preferring the term "standards."

The list of standards—two pages, typed, and waiting on each player's stool in the clubhouse—included a 1 A.M. spring-training curfew and banned alcohol on team buses and planes, cellular phones in the clubhouse, and earrings while playing. There was one note that would really chafe Mets veterans, particularly Cameron when it was later relayed to the position players: No music in the clubhouse without headphones. Silence certainly would seem out of place for a team that blasted OutKast's "The Way You Move" after virtually all of its seventy-one wins in 2004.

"I'm going to tell Willie: 'You always said you have to have rhythm. Hitting is like rhythm,'" Cameron said. "You've got to be able to be respectable, but it would be a long year if we had to go without music."

"Headphones can give you rhythm," countered Randolph, who bent during the season, the music creeping louder and louder as wins mounted. Cell phone rings, including Piazza's odd choice of "Hava Nagila," and later the theme from the *Austin Powers* movies, repeatedly sounded from lockers, too.

Piazza, now the most senior Met and in the final season of a seven-year contract, had arrived fresh off his marriage to former *Playboy* Playmate and *Baywatch* actress Alicia Rickter in a ceremony at St. Jude's Catholic Church in Miami. Auxiliary Bishop Ignatius Catanello from the Diocese of Brooklyn had presided over the service, after which the guests—including former Mets teammates Al Leiter, John Franco, and Todd Zeile, plus fellow perennial All-Star catcher Pudge Rodriguez, but no current teammates—headed to a bash at the exclusive Fisher Island resort where the Vanderbilts used to retreat.

Piazza, who typically kept to himself and had often seemed somber in the past, appeared more upbeat this spring. He got reacquainted with Pedro the first day. Throwing to Piazza for the first time since the 1996 All-Star Game in Philadelphia, Pedro tossed aside his hat, displaying his curly coiffure, and then threw forty pitches to his batterymate, exposing Piazza to the cut fastball the ace had developed since their early days as teammates with the Los Angeles Dodgers.

The thirty-six-year-old Piazza had all but ceded the role as the face of the franchise to The New Mets. Though he had passed Johnny Bench to become the all-time leader for home runs by a catcher during the 2004 season, the grind behind the plate had taken a toll on his body and limited Piazza's production. Now Beltran and Pedro and younger players such as David Wright and Jose Reyes had become the headline attractions of the team, even if Randolph still depended on Piazza's power as the cleanup hitter if the Mets' season was to be a success.

Not that Piazza minded the lack of attention. The symbolism of Beltran in the first season of a seven-year contract, as Piazza was in the final season of a seven-year contract, was not lost on the aging slugger. Piazza, too, admired Beltran's athleticism, portraying himself as a clunky grinder who lacked the centerfielder's grace.

"He's a true athlete," Piazza said. "He looks like he could have run track or played football or basketball or done stuff like that. I watch him and he just attacks the ball so fluidly. The ball jumps off his bat. He's so gifted in a good way. I'm kind of like a lumberjack. He's like a gazelle."

Piazza recalled his time learning to catch in the Dodgers' academy in the Dominican Republic after he was drafted as a nineteen-year-old in the 62nd round. He recalled the skinny flamethrower who came out of the bullpen back then, too.

"He hadn't even come to the States yet," Piazza said about Pedro. "I remember him coming into the game and I was just astounded how hard he threw and the command he had. I was like, 'Holy smoke.' . . . It's funny. Just flash back twelve years and it just seems like yesterday we were both rookies with the Dodgers."

Piazza and Pedro's shared history had not been entirely positive. On June 5, 1998, with the Mets at Fenway Park for an interleague series, Pedro plunked Piazza in the left hand, then offered a profanity-laced tirade directed at the catcher. Piazza, who had issues with Pedro's brother Ramon while they were both Dodgers, barked back at Pedro: "All the money in the world can't really buy any class. . . . He should invest in lessons in etiquette."

Countered Pedro, seemingly fully aware of Piazza's father's ownership of a car dealership and trying to diss the All-Star catcher: "He wants to talk about class? He was a millionaire since he was a kid."

Now, however, they were teammates. And Pedro, during one of the ace's formal news conferences with reporters early in spring training, went so far as to pledge to blow the head off of anybody who wronged Piazza.

With all the buildup to the opening of spring training, the Mets had scheduled a morning news conference with Pedro before the first workout. The only problem? No Pedro, who arrived late for the media session; at least he did show up by the time Randolph had prescribed for players to report.

As Conti had noted, Pedro was late for a dinner with the president of the Dominican Republic during the winter, so the tardiness could be taken with a grain of salt. It was only the media he offended anyway.

"We'll play it by ear," a well-intending but helpless Mets PR director Jay Horwitz told the media, who had assembled expectantly to hear from Pedro.

Five hours and thirty-eight minutes after he was scheduled to address the media, after his workout, Pedro finally spoke, almost comically lecturing reporters about the need for them to treat him with respect.

Randolph, who had been told by cynics since December that Pedro would be a handful—as Red Sox manager Terry Francona would surely verify—indicated he did not intend to prejudge any of his players. And Randolph's initial observations of Pedro's behavior resulted in rave reviews. Pedro even showed up the next day without any stubble on his chin, as the manager had set out in his rules—*uhhh*, standards.

Once archenemies from their Yankees–Red Sox days, Pedro and Randolph had now shared El Presidente beers in the Dominican Republic and dined together in New York, leading the manager to conclude, "He's a really nice guy. It's tough for me saying that. Over the years with the rivalry, you kind of get to where you hate each other a little bit. Just being in his presence, you find out he's a super guy."

Said Pedro: "Willie's a lot more quiet than I thought. He's a very easygoing, very low-key person. I didn't know that much about Willie."

Unlike Pedro, no one ever worried about the squeaky-clean Wright being a disruptive force. He was, after all, the son of a vice and narcotics captain with the Norfolk, Virginia, police department. Jeff Duncan, a one-time minor-league teammate, had even once endorsed his own sister dating Wright. A twenty-two-year-old third baseman, Wright was already among the National League's rising stars and had been working out in Port St. Lucie for a while. Other position players began trickling in over the next few days, among them left fielder Cliff Floyd, Mientkiewicz, and infielder Miguel Cairo, who arrived with a Yankee bag.

Pedro greeted Mientkiewicz, his teammate on the World Champion Red Sox for the second half of the 2004 season, with a hug. Then the razzing began, considering Mientkiewicz had been embroiled in a custody battle over the baseball he caught from closer Keith Foulke at Busch Stadium in St. Louis to complete Game 4 of the World Series as Boston officially ended an eighty-six-year championship drought.

"You got the ball?" equipment manager Charlie Samuels asked.

"Yo, let me get that ball, man," Floyd said.

"It's an icebreaker, I guess," Mientkiewicz concluded.

The next day, Beltran arrived. In fact, much to Randolph's delight, virtually all of the players had reported and were working out before the date the full-squad camp officially opened.

Beltran knew times had changed after he matched Barry Bonds's record for homers in a postseason, then signed a seven-year, $119 million contract. He recalled his typical arrival at the Kansas City Royals camp in Surprise, Arizona, when two reporters had greeted him. Here, there were seven newspapers that had beat writers encamped with the Mets, plus Ed Coleman from flagship radio station WFAN, Kevin Czerwinski from MLB.com, a Japanese media contingent, assorted columnists from the New York papers, and a handful of national writers who bounced around the attractive Florida locales. There were several television cameras, too.

Reminded during his initial meeting with reporters that his role model, Bernie Williams, had four World Series titles with the Yankees, Beltran playfully replied: "We hope in the seven years I'm here that we can get five."

However, Beltran warned not to expect outspokenness, the kind of brashness Pedro could deliver. "I'm not one of those guys who is on the bench yelling, screaming," he said. "I'm very quiet. But when I have to say something, I say it. . . . I know that some of the young guys look at me like a role model. I need to act like that. I need to play the game hard, do things right on the field and off the field."

Ninety minutes after Beltran's chitchat began, Cameron arrived, wearing a floppy hat. Cameron's positive clubhouse presence had been unrivaled in 2004 after he signed a three-year, $19.5 million contract with the Mets. During his first spring training in Port St. Lucie after four seasons as a Seattle Mariner, Cameron had immediately introduced a boom box. This increased the energy level and countered Franco's Frank Sinatra tunes in the easy-listening corner, which had included Leiter, David Weathers, Steve Trachsel, Tom Glavine, and Scott Erickson. (David Cone had labeled that set of lockers "Geritol Row" the previous year, because of the elder statesmen populating the area.) Again in 2005, teammates instantly gravitated to the highly popular Cameron.

"*Midnight!*" reliever Roberto Hernandez called out, using a pet name for Cameron, innocently alluding to the darkness of his skin.

"What's up, Bert?" Cameron replied.

"What's up with you, Loop?" he continued, addressing closer Braden Looper. "Who's got my money?"

Looper handed Cameron the proceeds from the team's fantasy football league.

"*There it is! There it is!*" Cameron shouted.

The good vibes continued.

"Boy, y'all looking like ten years younger," he told newly fresh-faced reliever Mike DeJean. "We've done got everyone shaving their face around here."

"We're going to keep you here, right?" DeJean asked.

"Yeah," Cameron said. "They're going to try to, at least. There's been a lot of talking going on."

Cameron clearly had reservations about moving to right field, whatever his public statements. Late in an otherwise careful Q&A with reporters, he acknowledged thoughts might enter his head during the spring about whether he was wasting time preparing for right field if he's destined to be traded. Cameron expressed concern about how his innate ability to turn his back to the plate and sprint to a spot in the gap before looking for the baseball would translate with the different angles encountered manning right field. Centerfielders like Cameron also had a take-charge tendency on balls in the gap that would have to be suppressed in his new position. Could he, in fact, get comfortable deferring to Beltran on balls catchable by either player? Yet Cameron didn't intend to be disruptive. That wasn't Cameron's way.

"We all know what I am," Cameron said, a thinly veiled allusion to centerfield being in his DNA. "But we're not here for that. I'm not trying to have the lead role in this cast. I'm just trying to do what my body allows me to do. If it was anybody else, maybe they couldn't be able to do that. I'm able to do it. Let's give it a run and see what happens. What we're trying to do is win. If Omar thinks, 'With Mike Cameron in right field I've got a better chance of winning than with somebody else,' then that's what he's going to do."

When asked directly if he could play a better centerfield than Beltran, Cameron wanted no part of the query. "I'm not going to go there with you," he said. "I'm not here to do that. I'm here to help him out."

Asked about possible resentment, Cameron even flashed his sense of humor. "Nah, man. I'm a helluva guy," he playfully replied. "I don't have resentment about anything."

Said Beltran: "If we work together, we can be the two best outfielders in the National League."

After several injury-riddled seasons and a handful of late diagnoses, such as DeJean being allowed to play with an unidentified broken fibula in 2004, the Mets showed they meant business when it came to conditioning. During the winter they had changed hospital affiliations—from the Hospital for Joint Diseases to the Hospital for Special Surgery. They also hired a new head trainer, Ray Ramirez from the Texas Rangers, to replace Scott Lawrenson. The resulting spring workouts included a twenty-five-minute stretching and warm-up period, significantly longer than in past seasons.

The battery of tests before the first official full-squad workout left the sleekest of Mets keeled over in the clubhouse trying to recover from wooziness. The physical included the standing long jump, the vertical jump, a ten-yard sprint, and the one that was the buzz and the bane of players—a 300-yard run. That demanding distance even had minor-league speedster Wayne Lydon—a former track star at Valley View High School in Archibald, Pennsylvania, who had 227 steals over the previous three seasons—falling down face-first at the finish line.

The first few days of workouts went incredibly long, finishing at 3 P.M., as Randolph demonstrated he intended to have a disciplined team, even if golf tee times were disrupted. No squad in Florida remained outdoors even close to that long. Heck, teams training in Arizona may have been in the clubhouse by the time the Mets wrapped up, and the Cactus League camps were two time zones away.

The Mets' first activity as a full squad after warming up involved getting jumps off first base—no coincidence for a team that intended to wreak havoc on the base paths.

No doubt principal owner Fred Wilpon must have been pleased as he arrived in Port St. Lucie with his wife Judy and his two golden retrievers, six-year-old Lefty and fifteen-month-old Tugger, to examine his investment during a three-day visit.

"Hey, Willie!" Wilpon called out.

"Hey, Mr. Wilpon. Good to see you," the manager replied before they hugged, probably something Randolph had not done much with Yankees owner George Steinbrenner, the man known as the Boss, who appears to be an imposing rather than cuddly figure.

"It's a little bit different situation, of course," Randolph agreed. "But I was always real comfortable around George. George and I go way back. I've always felt confident in my skin and who I am, and George has always been good to me."

Fred Wilpon tried to maintain a low profile as he shuttled from diamond to diamond throughout the back fields, trailed by the beat writers. Wilpon had barely uttered a peep over the winter. He didn't even attend all of the major news conferences. He intended to keep the low profile, proclaiming, "Talk to Omar. I'm just an observer."

Wilpon seemingly hoped to remain quiet and in the background as a way of illustrating the autonomy he had promised Minaya. He did not even plan to address the team during his stay. Yet the pleasant, good-natured principal owner broke down and eventually talked to the print reporters in the early evening inside the media workroom adjacent to the clubhouse. He was overly careful to not create a back-page headline, though it would have been difficult to trump Barry Bonds's media session in Arizona that day anyway. The embattled slugger had made his first comments since his testimony—before a grand jury that was investigating the BALCO steroids scandal—had been leaked.

Wilpon tried to avoid a line like the one he had uttered the previous spring, when he'd said the goal for the year was "meaningful games in September." That statement seemed harmless and vague and not overly ambitious at the time, but resulted in endless mocking by season's end, when the Mets endured an eleven-game losing streak that drifted into September as the team continued to spiral downward.

"I will never use the words 'skills sets' either," the principal owner quipped, alluding to his description of Steve Phillips upon his hiring as general manager several years earlier, which similarly became a source of derision once Phillips's tenure went sour.

Eventually, Wilpon offered the most innocuous of goals for 2005, one that could not possibly be used later to deride him or the team. "The goal is winning," Wilpon said, relenting. "Winning games."

Pedro's charm quickly surfaced. He grabbed the head off the baseball equivalent of a football tackling dummy, which is used to stand in the box to mimic a batter, and balanced it on his own head. He reached into a bag, grabbed a baseball, and said to onlookers, "It's good to have more than one," noting how he had used the head from his sister's doll for a baseball while a youngster. When Cameron good-naturedly swiped at Wright's glove during a rundown drill, Pedro declared: "Don't do that. You might look like A-Rod," referring to the grief the Yankees' Alex Rodriguez took for swatting Boston Red Sox reliever Bronson Arroyo's forearm in the 2004 American League Championship Series to illegally dislodge the baseball.

The crowds in Port St. Lucie swelled, thanks to the new energy supplied by Pedro and Beltran, and the renewed optimism about the Mets. By noon during one early workout, 1,700 spectators had descended on the complex, well above average for a location that hasn't been well received by Mets players despite the organization signing a fifteen-year lease. (Though the population is growing up Interstate 95 from West Palm Beach, Port St. Lucie still has mostly chain restaurants, such as Chili's, Outback, and Big Apple Pizza, outside of which outfielders Shane Spencer and Karim Garcia tussled with a deliveryman the previous spring. A half-hour-long drive to Jensen Beach is often necessary for upscale cuisine, with nightlife even farther away. Players sometimes refer to Port St. Lucie as "that hole," a phrase coined by Floyd in 2004, which irks Mets officials to no end because they need the city's cooperation.)

Pedro's only blemish of the early spring involved grabbing his crotch when an aggressive heckler/autograph seeker, who had camped out by the players' parking lot, shouted: "Who's your daddy?"

Inside the clubhouse, Pedro told the story of a fan who had mailed him three live fish at Fenway Park, which he fed and kept alive as his pets for more than three months. Pedro described them as two "Nemos" (goldfish) and a "sucker" (because its lips were always attached to the tank's glass). The next day a bubbly Pedro rode a tractor around the infield while filming a series of commercials with Beltran, the Florida Marlins' Delgado, and the Los Angeles Dodgers' Derek Lowe for the Boys & Girls Clubs of America. Pedro's playful antics continued throughout the spring. One day he entered the clubhouse wearing blue boxing gloves, which he had worn during a Newark *Star-Ledger* photo shoot for the newspaper's season-preview section. Pedro then began innocently jabbing at reliever Bartolome Fortunato. A second set of gloves would show up for a sparring partner in ensuing days.

Later Pedro took out a Bible. "You know I carry a Bible in my bag?" he said, adding: "That's not a good quote?"

Players, particularly the Hispanic players, were energized by him. When Fortunato, a fellow Dominican, threw an up-and-in pitch that forced Floyd to eat dirt, Fortunato joked: "I learned that from Pedro."

Beltran had his own impact in a far quieter fashion—not to mention an impact on fashion. His Louis Vuitton man purse quickly became the rage of the clubhouse, his teammates buying them or getting them as gifts from Beltran. Beltran invited young infielders Wright and Reyes to join him for extra nighttime workouts at Gold's Gym a block down N.W. Peacock Boulevard from the team's complex. No surprise, Wright accepted. The third baseman spent forty minutes one night performing agility drills alongside Beltran, such as standing on a balance-beam-type object while reaching side to side for tossed baseballs. Wright also used a rubber, oval-shaped ball to reproduce difficult hops he would encounter at third base. The hard-working Wright had already been going religiously to Gold's Gym at night for extra training despite Randolph's rigorous daytime training sessions.

The increased cultural diversity in the clubhouse quickly became evident, with Spanish seemingly as commonly spoken as English. When a trainer asked Venezuelan-born pitching prospect Yusmeiro Petit in English to arrive at 7 A.M. for extra conditioning workouts, Dominican-born third-base coach Manny Acta, who was passing by, chimed in, "*Entiendes?*" ("You understand?") Pedro became a storyteller, regaling Reyes and Fortunato and other fellow Dominicans with the tale of St. Louis Cardinals pitcher Jeff Suppan striking him out looking in Game 3 of the World Series, and Red Sox teammate Manny Ramirez's amused reaction in the dugout afterward. Minaya walked by and joined the Spanish conversation.

Minaya had dramatically altered the face of the Mets in one winter, from Leiter and Franco as the visible figures to Pedro and Beltran. As Minaya turned over the roster, however, whispers began—digs about the ethnicity of the general manager's imports. *Los Mets* became a commonly uttered phrase, first quietly or anonymously on fan message boards, then more overtly. Nelson, a journeyman reliever who had been working out at the complex even before Pedro's early arrival, couldn't help but survey the clubhouse and use the term. Nelson didn't mean it in an offensive way, just as an observation, even noting that his own wife is of Cuban descent to ensure his remark wasn't taken in an unintended context.

Minaya did not care for the talk-radio and Internet chatter, believing it was borderline racism. "People who make those comments have a racial bent to their thinking," Minaya said about *Los Mets* utterances. "When you hear that, you ask yourself, 'Do they make those comments when the staffs are all another race?' But look, when you are doing something that has never been done before, people are going to make comments. A lot of times it's part of being a minority."

It seemed perfectly reasonable to accept that if the Mets wanted the number-one starting pitcher and the top position player on the free-agent market during the off-season, the Dominican Martinez and Puerto Rican Beltran qualified (and happened to be Hispanic). Then again, Minaya himself had spoken during the winter about building the visibility of the franchise in Latin America. And it seemed that a way to accomplish this objective was not just to land Pedro and Beltran, but to also make a concerted effort to surround them with

Hispanic role players. That goal resulted in signings such as Venezuelan icon Andres Galarraga to a minor-league contract, though the first baseman's declining skills prompted his retirement late in spring training.

Regardless, it was noteworthy that two years after Roberto Alomar had lobbied for the Mets to hire a liaison to Hispanic players because of a perceived lack of sensitivity, the Mets had made a dramatic turn. They had hired the game's only Hispanic general manager, a highly qualified deputy in the Puerto Rican Tony Bernazard, New York's first African-American manager in Randolph, and a major-league coaching staff that included three minorities, two born in Latin America. They also had one of only two Spanish-speaking head trainers in baseball, at least by their own count, the other being Baltimore Orioles trainer Richie Bancells, who is of Cuban descent and described himself as three-quarters fluent.

How remarkable was the turnaround? Two years after Alomar departed, his father, Sandy Alomar Sr., was now the team's bench coach.

"It's beyond me; it's amazing, in an area where communication matters so much, not to have a Hispanic trainer, or a person who is bilingual," Minaya said. "It's not only about speaking Spanish. It's being able to understand the culture, too. You can speak the language but not understand the culture."

Said Alomar Sr.: "By us coming from the same type of environment, we have a way of knowing what's going on with them. It's much easier for us to understand when there's something wrong with them than for the American guy that doesn't know the barrier or the culture."

The rapidity of the Mets' transformation, coupled with the profile of the players involved in the winter retooling—Leiter, Franco, Mike Stanton, and Vance Wilson, *out*; Pedro, Beltran, Heredia, Cairo, and Galarraga, *in*—may have given a false impression of the Mets' diversity relative to other clubs, even if veterans had noted that the amount of Spanish spoken in the clubhouse seemed atypically high. An analysis of Major League Baseball forty-man rosters at the beginning of spring training showed the Mets ranked tenth of thirty teams in the percentage of players born in Latin America (27.5 percent)— though it's worth noting that the team Minaya formerly led, the Montreal Expos-turned-Washington Nationals, tied with the Los Angeles Dodgers for highest percentage at 37.5.

Of the 1,187 players on forty-man rosters when Major League Baseball completed its 2005 spring-training media guide, 830 were born in the fifty states, 141 in the Dominican Republic, 78 in Venezuela, 39 in Puerto Rico, 21 in Mexico, 20 in Canada, 13 in Japan, 10 in Cuba, 8 in South Korea, 7 in Panama, 6 in Australia, and 14 elsewhere. The percentage of foreign-born players had trended upward for a decade, from 19 percent of Opening Day roster spots in 1997 to 27 percent in 2004.

"The game is becoming so diverse," Minaya said. "I was told by [Atlanta Braves general manager] John Schuerholz, 'Your players have to have trust in you as a front office.' To me, the 'trust work' becomes important. I feel as proud to be able to speak to the Spanish player as to be able to speak with an African-American player, or to be able to speak with a kid from Atlanta, Georgia, or the Midwest. To me, that's very important as a general manager, to be able to communicate with all the people in your organization."

Minaya maintained he had no agenda.

"I am proud to say I'm a New Yorker," he said. "It just so happens that I'm a Hispanic New Yorker, but I'm a New Yorker. If you are a true New Yorker, you look at people's credentials. You don't look at their heritage or race."

The Mets weren't subtle about promoting their newfound diversity, to the point of controversy. One spring-training radio advertisement, featuring Colombian-born comedian John Leguizamo, who grew up in Jackson Heights, Queens, particularly created a stir. In the ad, Leguizamo leaves a series of messages on Minaya's voice mail requesting tickets for games at Shea Stadium. He lauds the general manager for signing Pedro and Beltran, then proclaims: "Latins in the *hoooooouse!*"

On Richard Neer's show on the team's flagship radio station, WFAN, callers chastised the Mets for poor taste, though *Daily News* media critic Bob Raissman disagreed. "It shows a complete dismissal of Major League Baseball's demographics," Raissman said about the complaints.

To support his viewpoint, Raissman contacted Tim Brosnan, Major League Baseball's executive vice president for business, who noted at least twenty of thirty teams would have Spanish-language radio broadcasts for the 2005 season.

"The Mets are smart to market to the Hispanic community," Brosnan said. "The players are the product. If players are going to appeal to a certain demographic, who are proud of their heritage and connect with these players, then it's sound business for any club to target these fans."

WFAN must have agreed. The station launched a new program, *Latin Beat*, with hosts Roberto Clemente Jr. and Tanyette Colon, which sought to target the Hispanic community. The Mets signed up Banco Popular as the team's official bank. (The institution's ads during Mets broadcasts had a comically gringo-like pronunciation of "popular.") In September, the *Daily News* produced a seventy-two-page special section as a tribute to the Hispanic impact on baseball. The newspaper advocated the retiring of Roberto Clemente's No. 21 across baseball, like MLB had done with African-American pioneer Jackie Robinson's No. 42.

Randolph finally got to fill out a lineup card for the first time when the Mets held a pair of intrasquad games the two days before Grapefruit League action started. The manager had jotted down a lineup for the first time in late January, on a blotter on the desk in his home office, after the Delgado sweepstakes became resolved. His initial order had few surprises, but plenty of speed. Reyes led off for the "A" team, followed by Matsui, Beltran, Piazza, Floyd, Wright, Mientkiewicz, and Victor Diaz. If Cameron fully recovered from wrist surgery in time for Opening Day, Randolph expected Cameron would slide ahead of Mientkiewicz, and that Diaz would be bumped to Triple-A Norfolk.

Reyes had stolen twenty bases in winter ball, and his eagerness to demonstrate his health to Mets brass was obvious. Prospects Bobby Keppel and Matt Lindstrom both picked him off in the first intrasquad game. Reyes's second lead was so big the manager chuckled.

"Well, that's just energy," Randolph concluded. "Early energy. When you let a colt out of the stable, they want to run."

Beltran spent more than thirty minutes with Reyes in the clubhouse after the transgressions, offering base-running tips while telling the twenty-one-year-old shortstop he looked too eager. Reyes intently listened to Beltran, who entered 2005 with the highest success rate on steals of anyone with at least 100 tries in major-league history (89.2 percent).

Beltran noted upon arriving that he would be quiet, and sure enough, he had an understated presence, nothing like Pedro's high-octane demeanor. But Beltran did have the quirkiest contribution of the spring: a gadget known as an "enhanced ocular device," which agent Scott Boras had required the Mets to provide as part of Beltran's $119 million contract. Despite the device's fancy name, it boiled down to this—a pitching machine that fires tennis balls at the batter at speeds up to 155 mph. Written on each ball several times is a number, in red or black ink. Players try to decipher the number and its color, and the spin on the ball, as it whizzes by while they are in a batting stance.

Mike Victorn of Chicago-based Conditioned Ocular Enhancement stayed with the Mets at Shea Stadium all year, operating the device. In the past, Dave Roberts and former major-leaguer Wendell Magee, who used the contraption elsewhere, had the most success identifying the color, number, and rotation of the fired balls, getting it correct 80 percent of the time, according to Victorn. Similarly, Roberto Alomar once claimed he was better able to see the ball coming at him in the field because of using the device.

Upon finally seeing the contraption with the elaborate name, Mets brass had to chuckle slightly, thinking they had paid a six-figure sum for a glorified tennis-ball feeder. But if it kept Beltran comfortable and confident, so be it.

"When it's coming at you at eighty or ninety miles an hour you recognize it, but not at one hundred and fifty," Beltran said. "But after seeing it at one hundred and fifty, when it slows down again, it seems like the ball is coming in at forty miles an hour. It helped me lay off a lot of bad pitches in the dirt."

The New Mets' official unveiling occurred with the Grapefruit League opener, which was televised by ESPN because it also marked the debut of the Washington Nationals, Minaya's former squad, which had relocated from Montreal.

Nationals general manager Jim Bowden embraced Randolph—whom he had once nearly hired as manager of the Cincinnati Reds—behind home plate during batting practice and told the rookie skipper, "I'm going to give you your first loss." Then, standing on the mound at Space Coast Stadium in Viera, Florida, Glavine turned his back to home plate and surveyed the players behind him before making the first pitch of the spring. He couldn't help but feel positive as he saw Beltran standing in center, Reyes at shortstop, and Matsui at second—a far cry from the Cedeño-Rey Sanchez-Alomar up-the-middle defense that had greeted him two years earlier when he arrived as a free agent.

The Nationals won their first-ever game, 5–3, but the Mets could celebrate, too. Matsui and Reyes, who did not play together once during the 2004 Grapefruit League schedule because of alternating injuries, turned a double play in their first inning of work. As an instant reminder of the importance of a defensive first baseman, after catching converts Jason Phillips and Piazza and the immobile heavyweight Vaughn manned the position in recent years, Mientkiewicz picked Matsui's short-hop throw at first base to complete the inning-ending double play.

Glavine's old spring-training neighbors had nearly all departed, Geritol Row now occupied by Pedro, Victor Zambrano, Kris Benson, and Mike Matthews. Two years after Glavine was the newbie, with eyes fixed on his every move, the southpaw was now second only to Steve Trachsel in seniority on the pitching staff and very much under the radar.

"I'm holding up my end of the bargain," Glavine joked about the plummeting average age of Geritol Row, given the new occupants. "My circle got blown to pieces. It's making me make new friends. I'm working on it. My wife tells me I need to work on my social skills."

Pedro's debut came two days later, on March 4 in Jupiter, Florida. It began in the batter's box with a groundout to first base—not on the mound—the result of a four-run first inning against St. Louis Cardinals starter Mark Mulder. Then Pedro's eagerly awaited unveiling began in earnest, as the former Red Sox ace delivered a sixty-pitch performance in a 7–5 Mets win. Pedro allowed two runs, one earned, and three hits in three innings while striking out three and walking one. More importantly, he had zip on his fastball and used the opportunity to work out kinks with Piazza.

"The uniform is just the uniform," said Pedro, maintaining he was unfazed by switching employers. "To me it is no different. The colors might look different, but the uniform is just the uniform. Same size, everything."

"It's not an easy process," Piazza said about building a rapport with Pedro. "He's very spontaneous out there. If he sees a guy take a swing or react to a certain pitch, he may go away from what he was thinking when we were talking before the game. It's up to me to kind of feel what he wants to do and make it smooth. I don't want him shaking his head nine times an inning."

After Cardinals shortstop David Eckstein greeted Pedro with a single under Reyes's glove, Pedro repeatedly threw to Mientkiewicz at first base, trying to hold Eckstein to a reasonable lead. Pedro struck out the ex-Met Cedeño, who waved at a low-and-away fastball. Then Albert Pujols tattooed a full-count fastball off the right-field wall to place two runners in scoring position. A passed ball charged to Piazza allowed Eckstein to score. Scott Rolen's groundout to Matsui at second base plated Pujols.

Piazza said the passed ball was a miscommunication over signs, Pedro delivering a different pitch than he expected, nothing alarming for a spring-training opener. As for Pedro's repeated throws to Mientkiewicz during his three-inning outing, the ace alluded to Piazza's difficulty throwing out runners, though Piazza nailed Reggie Sanders on a stolen-base attempt to end the fourth after Roberto Hernandez had replaced Pedro.

"I really emphasized holding the runners," Pedro said. "I want to help Mike and actually make a habit of it, because he's going to be behind the plate, behind me, and I'm going to have to help him if I want to have good games and good results."

Piazza never expressed any resentment at the candor, which he understandably could have taken as a slight.

Pedro, who pitched seven scoreless innings in the World Series win against the Cardinals, said that the performance felt like yesterday. Unlike Beltran, who professed feeling nerves during his Mets debut, Pedro said he found it easy to remain composed.

"Only when I feel like there's something wrong in my family I get nervous," Pedro said. "Not many things make me nervous. I feel lucky when I'm out there."

Sixty pitches are more than most starters throw in their first spring-training outing—Mulder threw forty-four—but no one with the organization thought it was a major deal. Pedro, despite reports of shoulder weakness with the Red Sox, resumed throwing three weeks after the World Series, a shorter-than-normal respite because of Boston's postseason success.

"We're not going to get crazy about pitch counts here," Randolph said. "We're going to let him get his work in. If we didn't feel like he was feeling real strong, then we wouldn't have let him pitch that much. As the season goes on, we'll make some adjustments. We don't worry about that because he's in great shape. You look at him work and see what he does on the side; you know that he has a lot left in the tank. He's not going to break. He'll be fine."

Rain washed away Pedro's next start, but it proved an eventful week regardless. Darryl Strawberry slipped on a Mets uniform for the first time since leaving the team after the 1990 season and served as a weeklong guest instructor. Cameron ended the speculation he would demand a trade. And Beltran had a rocky day in the sun in Fort Lauderdale.

Minaya placed his hands on Cameron's shoulders on March 8 and summoned him into the home dugout at Tradition Field in Port St. Lucie for a private conversation. And when Cameron returned to his locker, Floyd, his closest friend on the team and his lockermate, couldn't resist.

"Hey, did you get traded?" Floyd needled him.

"You've got to stop that," Cameron insisted.

By nightfall, Cameron put an end to the trade speculation. He instructed agent Mike Nicotera to request that the Mets pull him off the trading block. The Mets never really wanted to part with Cameron anyway and only discussed deals—most seriously with the Oakland A's and Houston Astros—because of concern about how Cameron would mentally handle the shift to right field from centerfield.

"I always thought it was important that Mike wanted to be on board," Minaya said. "And I feel comfortable today that Mike wants to be on board and play that position."

Said Nicotera: "He's now told them, 'If you're trying because of me, you don't have to try anymore.' We informed them that he wants to stay there. He's had enough time to digest the change and get a feel about the team. He wants to stay in New York."

Minaya heaped praise on visiting instructor Strawberry for helping Cameron to arrive at the decision to remain, though that turned out to be more a public-relations reach than reality. Strawberry and Cameron spoke at length the day the '86 Met hero arrived, but Cameron indicated Strawberry was merely one of several people who had played a role.

"Like I told Cam, 'You're an athlete. You can play wherever you've got to go,'" Strawberry said. "Whatever it's going to be to sacrifice for this ball club, that's what players need to do. Sometimes you need to sacrifice to win, and I think they're starting to really understand that, and I think they're going to grab that and hopefully run with it. I just try to tell guys like that, 'You don't want to miss out on the opportunity to play in New York and win in New York.' It's a great opportunity. It's a window that you have, and it's an opening that's sitting in front of you. I don't see why he can't win a Gold Glove in right field if he's done it in center."

The day after Nicotera asked the Mets to stop shopping Cameron, Minaya again approached Cameron in full view of reporters, this time patting him on the head. No extended conversation in the dugout ensued, just smiles.

"Omar, please don't do that anymore when these guys are standing around," Cameron kidded the GM, referring to the media.

Cameron's situation resolved, matters turned more lighthearted, like Beltran arriving in the clubhouse with a crew cut. The explanation: His wife Jessica didn't exactly cut his hair like a professional barber, so he decided to shave it off, creating quite a stir.

"He got a haircut, too," the reliever Bell quipped, motioning toward the South Korean reliever Koo's interpreter, who wasn't receiving the same attention.

It rained that day, but Pedro still drew a crowd. The ace threw a simulated game on a covered mound in order to stay on the proper five-day schedule for Opening Day in Cincinnati. Pitching coach Rick Peterson and Pedro had decided against the alternative: pushing him back to start against the Baltimore Orioles in Fort Lauderdale.

Kris Benson, at one point standing outside in a cold, frigid rain, watched Pedro's entire workout. While acknowledging an inferior résumé, Benson noted he had a similar pitching style to Pedro's. And he wanted to learn what the ace does in 0–1 and 1–1 counts. Benson said batters had too high an average against him in those situations in 2004. "He's thinking, 'Expand the zone,'" Benson concluded about Pedro's approach in those counts.

In small-market Pittsburgh, Benson was the veteran on a young pitching staff, and he reveled in the resources he now had in his fellow pitchers, veterans like Pedro and Glavine.

Benson's wife Anna, an aspiring actress with a passion for the risqué, reveled in being in New York, too. She made spring-training headlines during a segment on Howard Stern's radio show. Anna amended a remark she had made during a previous appearance—that she would sleep with the entire team if her husband ever cheated on her. She revised it to proclaim that she would seek retribution with "just the hot ones," which prompted Stern to start rattling off a list of players to see who made the cut. Stern first named Koo, mangling his first name. Anna confessed to not even knowing who he was.

"Good stuff," Kris said. "I think Stern likes her."

Meanwhile, two days after Beltran had ratted out his wife for a bad haircut, he offered his own confession. "I'm not perfect. I can say that," he said.

Beltran had lost two fly balls in the sun in the Baltimore Orioles' six-run fourth inning at Fort Lauderdale Stadium, and the Mets had lost, 8–2. Orioles centerfielder David Newhan lost Piazza's shot in the sun the following half-inning, too, offering somewhat of an acquittal. Still, almost comically, the pro-Mets portion of the crowd booed Beltran when he led off the fifth, the half-inning after his misplays. He received the same treatment as he returned to the dugout after he grounded out. One person joked that the Mets were premature in sending the center-field prospect Lydon to minor-league camp earlier in the day.

"Sit 'em down, Willie," a fan shouted, presumably joking about Beltran to Randolph. The manager, in fact, inserted Kerry Robinson for the home fifth. Of course, Beltran's day was done as pre-scripted.

"You have to let the fans have fun," Beltran said. "They come here to have fun and see the ball game. When you don't make a play, they're going to let you know you should have caught that ball."

Regardless, the Mets mostly had a successful, upbeat spring, even if Pedro's health became a concern. On March 25, Pedro took an X-ray rather than the mound, with a teammate maintaining Pedro "couldn't even stand up straight" at one point.

Pedro, who had limited the Los Angeles Dodgers to one run and two hits in five innings in his previous start, faulted a team-wide off-day the day after that outing. He compensated by cramming a two-day workload into the next day, including an hour of running, medicine-ball work, and leg lifts. By the time Pedro threw a side session in the bullpen two days before his scheduled start against the Florida Marlins, his back had started to bark. Mets brass quickly tried to differentiate the trouble from Trachsel's back injury, initially downplayed but later diagnosed as a herniated disc, requiring back surgery that would keep Trachsel sidelined into August.

When Pedro finally returned to the mound for a bullpen session, an audience that included Spike Lee was watching him. On a concourse at Tradition Field that had a view of his session, fans shouted things like, "Hey, Pedro, how about twenty wins?"

"I can't do it without a little help," Pedro replied.

"One at a time," someone shouted.

"Exactly," Pedro said.

Pedro wouldn't throw another Grapefruit League inning, his final outing of the spring coming in a simulated game in a mostly empty stadium, except for minor-leaguers who had come over from the other side of the facility to examine the way he works. Instructor Gary Carter surveyed the vacant stands and shouted to Pedro, "You can really draw the crowds, man."

Pedro, shaking off the back stiffness that had nagged him for a week, then breezed through five innings against minor-leaguers and pronounced himself ready for the season opener in Cincinnati against Paul Wilson. The ace threw eighty-three pitches, limiting a lineup that included Jeff Keppinger, Brian Daubach, Prentice Redman, and Duncan to one run and three hits, while striking out eight and walking two. He ranged from 89 to 93 mph with his fastball.

"I'm right where I want to be," Pedro said. "I hope I wake up tomorrow on the right side of the bed."

Pedro didn't answer directly about whether he felt any back stiffness, but Peterson—who studies body language—detected no cause for alarm.

"He felt tremendous," Peterson said. "As you watched that game, and you watched the effort level and intensity of every pitch, you don't have to ask somebody how they're feeling. If you watch somebody walk across the room and they're limping, you don't have to ask them how their leg feels. Conversely, the other way. It's obvious."

Pedro pitched only eleven Grapefruit League innings, but expressed no concern about the limited competition.

"Would you feel like I have to prove anything?" he asked.

He also downplayed the significance of his eighth straight Opening Day start, even if it marked the regular-season launch of The New Mets. "It gets boring. There's too much 'yada, yada' about the first game of the season," Pedro said. "After all, they're all important and they're all one game. I would love to win a game, but it's not a guaranteed win. I'm going to try to bust my tail off to get a win. I'll pray to God I'm healthy and keep my team in the fight."

The Mets had loose ends to tie up. With Trachsel out following back surgery, the Mets traded Phillips, a backup catcher, to the Dodgers for pitcher Kazuhisa Ishii. Galarraga retired, leaving Tradition Field in tears, and one homer shy of No. 400 for his career. Benson had issues with a pectoral muscle that would sideline him into the season. And Cameron had to fly to New York for an MRI after feeling abnormal pain in his surgically repaired left wrist. Despite initial optimism about a quick return, Diaz would serve as the starting right fielder into May.

The Mets broke camp after a 12–4 win against the Marlins, taking a detour to Washington, D.C., for an exhibition game against the Nationals at RFK Stadium before heading to Cincinnati. They departed having topped the Grapefruit League in steals with thirty-five, while playing disciplined baseball. Their 16–11–2 slate was wiped clean, but still was important to instill confidence in a team that finished a combined sixty games under .500, and eighty-six games behind the Braves, over the previous three seasons.

Among the positives: Reyes remained healthy, going 8-for-8 in steals and recording a Grapefruit League–best five triples. Matsui looked like a second baseman, even if he wasn't tested with hard slides on double plays. Mientkiewicz played as advertised, anchoring a young infield with his Gold Glove at first base. Beltran proved a quiet leader, grabbing players like Reyes for tutorials.

"It went very fast," Randolph said about his first spring at the helm. "It was kind of like a whirlwind."

Said Minaya: "I like our team. I think we have good balance. We have a good bench. We have speed. We've got defense. Good starting pitcher. But I'm one of those, my job is not to be fully, completely happy. My job is always to find ways to improve this team. I always say the only time I'm really happy is when we win the World Series. That's just me."

On the final day the Mets spent in Florida, Conti—Pedro's white daddy—saw one final good omen. Pedro stood in the rain outside the team's clubhouse in Port St. Lucie as the Mets prepared to depart. Lifting his arms, Pedro started belting out, "God Bless America." That was a stellar sign, Conti noted to reporters. A loose, happy Pedro means a Cy Young–caliber Pedro.

# CLOSE, THEN A CIGAR

WILLIE RANDOLPH ENTERED the interview room at Great American Ball Park, settled into a chair, and immediately lit up the place.

"So I wanted to be a manager, huh?" the first-year skipper deadpanned, eliciting laughter from the assembled media.

With the Ohio River serving as the backdrop for Opening Day of a new era, The New Mets, as Carlos Beltran had dubbed them, had suffered a gut-wrenching defeat reminiscent of none other than the old Mets. In the process they had wasted Pedro Martinez's record-setting performance and Beltran's three hits and three RBI in their Mets debuts.

His 103-pitch outing complete, Pedro remained in the dugout for the seventh inning, as Beltran's single to left field scored Jose Reyes for a 4–3 lead that put the ace in position to earn the win against the Cincinnati Reds. The Mets' lead swelled to three runs before the inning ended, as Mike Piazza doubled off the wall in right-centerfield to chase ex-Met David Weathers, and Cliff Floyd followed with a two-run home run against left-hander Kent Mercker. When David Wright lined out to end the inning, Pedro shook hands with head trainer Ray Ramirez and pointed to the sky.

"He struck out the world. It seemed like he struck everybody out," closer Braden Looper said. "I feel bad for the guy, for him more than anything."

After Pedro allowed Adam Dunn's first-inning home run—a three-run shot on a 3–1 cut fastball that caught too much of the plate and sparked the unoriginal chant of *Who's your daddy?* from the Reds faithful—Beltran answered. He belted a two-run home run in the third inning on a 2–0 fastball from Paul Wilson to tie the score at 3. Pedro fanned all but two of the next fourteen batters he faced after Dunn's blast. His twelve strikeouts in the game were the most ever in a Mets debut, surpassing the nine by Don Cardwell on April 11, 1967, against the Pittsburgh Pirates. Pedro joined Nolan Ryan, Randy Johnson, and Roger Clemens as the only players in major-league history to have at least 100 double-digit strikeout performances in their careers. Randolph saw defiance in Pedro's body language.

If only the script ended better.

The Mets took a 6–4 lead into the ninth inning that Monday afternoon, after relievers Manny Aybar and Dae-Sung Koo surrendered a run bridging the two innings between Pedro and Looper. It was little secret the bullpen figured to be an Achilles' heel. It was the reason general manager Omar Minaya pursued Detroit Tigers setup man Ugueth Urbina and Tampa Bay Devil Rays closer Danys Baez during spring training. Looper surrendered a leadoff single to Austin Kearns, followed by a 434-foot home run to Dunn on a 2–1 sinker the closer did not get down quite enough, which tied the score and provided Dunn the opportunity to answer a second curtain call.

"How ironic that the one guy in that Mets bullpen who you had some solid faith in going into the season is the guy who gives up the lead?" radio play-by-play man Gary Cohen asked during the WFAN broadcast. After all, Cohen noted, Looper allowed only five home runs in eighty-three and one-third innings during the 2004 season.

Dunn's second home run provided only half of the Mets' agony. Looper then thought he jammed Joe Randa. Instead, as Cohen called it:

*Here's the 3–2 to Randa. . . . And a high fly ball into left field. . . . Going back Floyd. . . . Near the wall. And . . . IT'S OUTTA HERE! The Reds win the game. . . . Joe Randa hits one over the scoreboard fence in left field. The Reds get back-to-back ninth-inning home runs from Adam Dunn and Joe Randa, and they're all mobbing Randa at home plate. The Reds, with three runs in the bottom of the ninth inning, and Cincinnati wins it 7–6. A vastly disappointing Opening Day loss for the New York Mets. They took a 6–4 lead into the ninth, but Looper never got an out.*

"He must have just dug his hands in and got the ball up," Looper said about Randa.

Randolph clearly must have recognized he was no longer in the Bronx. With the Yankees, manager Joe Torre and Randolph had the luxury of the game's greatest closer, plus quality setup men throughout the franchise's dynasty—relievers such as Jeff Nelson, Ramiro Mendoza, Mike Stanton, and Tom Gordon.

"There's not many Mariano Riveras around, that's for sure," Randolph said. "Braden's a fine reliever and he's going to be my number-one guy."

Afterward, Pedro found Looper, patted the closer on the back, and told him, "Hey, tomorrow's another day." Still, it would never again be the ace's first-ever Mets start, or Randolph's managerial debut.

"It's not really frustrating," Pedro said. "It's too early to be frustrated at this point. I've been through everything. I know the game is not over until it's over. I'm not disappointed at all. I'm very happy I was able to settle down and give my team the opportunity to win."

Pedro reflected back on all the positives in Port St. Lucie, Florida, during the previous two months.

"I feel great. I feel happy," he said. "I feel like the team is going to be a lot better than people expected us to be. I think we're solid and we are for real. I saw it the whole spring training, consistently getting ahead, scoring runs. Now that I'm seeing it in the real game, I think it's going to stay with us. How well we hold it, how well our defense is going to play—I don't know yet. It's too early to tell. But I know that the team, at least offensively and defensively today, played great."

As the clubhouse door was about to open for the media ten minutes after Randa's shot cleared the wall, Minaya made a run for the stadium's exit, his suitcase in tow as he blew by reporters. Like Pedro, Minaya wasn't bailing on the Mets—not by any means—even if the scene looked humorously awkward. Minaya merely had a flight to catch. The general manager figured he would take advantage of ESPN analyst and former Reds star Joe Morgan's police escort, just departing for the airport.

"If I can tag along, why not?" Minaya said.

Randolph offered encouragement, patting his players on the back and telling them, "We'll get 'em Wednesday."

Despite having waited so long to become a manager, Randolph felt an almost alarming sense of calm throughout the game. Then, after relieving any tension with his opening one-liner in the interview room afterward, he also seemed at ease while dissecting the painful defeat and sharing his emotions.

"Maybe I'm not human," Randolph said. "I felt great all day. I've spent a lot of days in a dugout. Maybe that's what it is."

No one knew the extent to which Randolph's patience would be tested that first week as the Mets struggled to record their first win of 2005. Regardless, the manager remained unflappable and upbeat.

Piazza certainly did not expect much of a wait for victory number one. Down the block from the team's hotel in Cincinnati on Tuesday, Piazza visited a cigar shop on the off-day for the Mets after the opener. Piazza had spoken with Randolph about the manager's affinity for cigars. So the slugger decided to buy an El Rey del Mundo for Randolph to smoke after his first career managerial win.

When Piazza arrived at the ballpark the following day, the cigar was placed on the desk in the visiting manager's office at Great American Ball Park.

"I've been known to enjoy one myself occasionally," Piazza said.

Then, Piazza 'fessed up and amended the remark.

"*Nightly*," he said with a laugh.

Proclaimed a delighted Randolph: "I'm going to use it tonight, for sure. I'm going to enjoy this one."

Two days after Looper's blown save in the opener, however, Randolph received a rules tutorial, not career win number one. And a cigar that even noted aficionado Jack McKeon, the Florida Marlins manager, could appreciate remained unlighted. The Reds chased Tom Glavine in the fourth inning and won, 9–5, to drop the Mets to 0–2.

Glavine nearly escaped both of the bases-loaded jams that bookended his 95-pitch outing. The culprit in the Mets' estimation: Chuck Meriwether. The plate umpire had not been impressed with two critical, two-out, two-strike pitches that would have meant no damage if ruled strikes. The two pitches immediately following those offerings resulted in four Cincinnati runs.

After delivering an 0–2 fastball to Randa in the first inning, with the Reds scoreless, Glavine even took a step toward the dugout, convinced he had strike three.

"I think we all did . . . including Joe," the southpaw said, referring to Randa.

Meriwether disagreed, and Randa drove the next pitch to left field for a two-run single.

In the fourth inning, after solo home runs by first baseman Doug Mientkiewicz and Wright tied the score at 2, Glavine faced a bases-loaded, two-out situation with Ken Griffey Jr. at the plate. The southpaw again got ahead, 0–2. Glavine's next offering, an 88 mph fastball away, hit Piazza's glove. Meriwether indicated a ball. Griffey belted the next pitch to right field for a two-run single. Glavine departed with the bases reloaded after Sean Casey and Kearns followed with singles. His line: three and two-thirds innings, nine hits, five earned runs, three walks, two strikeouts. All nine hits were singles.

"They hurt, but what are you going to do?" Glavine said about Meriwether's calls. "You have to make the best pitch you can. If you don't get the benefit of the call, you have to make another pitch."

Randa launched a grand slam against reliever Mike DeJean in the eighth inning to stake the Reds to a six-run lead, which made Randolph's gaffe to start that half-inning more humorous than relevant. The first-time manager, whose career was spent mostly in the American League, which rarely required double-switches, misunderstood the rule when he inserted DeJean and infielder Chris Woodward. According to crew chief Tim McClelland, Randolph failed to signal the double-switch before DeJean entered the game and started throwing warm-up pitches. That meant DeJean, not Woodward, was due to bat second in the ninth inning. Cincinnati manager Dave Miley had raised the umpires' awareness of the transgression.

Mientkiewicz, another American League transplant, could not figure out what Randolph had done incorrectly and quipped that he was going to buy a rule book.

"I thought I understood the game, and I don't," Mientkiewicz said. "I'm from the AL, so call me stupid."

Still, things figured to look up for the Mets the following day in the series finale before they departed for Atlanta. After all, the only teams in the organization's history to open 0–3 were the 1962, '63, and '64 editions—the first three in the franchise's history, which finished a combined 144–340 under Casey Stengel. There was no way that The New Mets, with all the positive energy after an extreme winter makeover, could flirt with those futile starts.

At least that logic *sounded* good.

The Mets headed for Atlanta still winless, a 6–1 loss by Kazuhisa Ishii capping the Reds' sweep.

Ishii—who had walked the second-highest number of batters in baseball over the previous three seasons after arriving from Japan in 2002—walked Ryan Freel and Felipe Lopez to begin his Mets debut, the latter on four pitches. The left-hander recovered after a visit from pitching coach Rick Peterson. Ishii induced a ground ball by Casey. But countryman Kazuo Matsui, who had moved from shortstop to second base after a disappointing rookie season, had trouble with the in-between hop. The baseball scooted between Matsui's legs and into the outfield. The miscue allowed Freel to score. Lopez, who would score on a sacrifice fly, advanced to third base. The Reds held a 2–0 lead without a hit.

Ishii overthrew to Freel and Lopez, citing an adrenaline rush associated with his Mets debut, but expressed pride in the rest of his performance. Until he threw his hundredth and final pitch, he surrendered only one hit—a solo home run to Wily Mo Peña.

Yet the Mets managed only one hit in six and one-third innings against Cincinnati right-hander Aaron Harang, who flashed a mid-90s fastball to complement the curveball that served as his primary pitch when he worked under Peterson's tutelage with the Oakland A's.

With the Reds leading 3–0 in the seventh inning, Ishii hit Randa on the left foot, and then with two out, walked Jason LaRue. Randolph spoke with Ishii at the mound, but let him remain to face pinch hitter D'Angelo Jimenez. On Ishii's final pitch, Jimenez delivered a two-run double. DeJean, who surrendered the grand slam to Randa in the second game, then allowed a single to Freel, resulting in the sixth run, fifth earned, charged to Ishii.

"We'll get that W. We'll get it. I feel real confident we'll get it," Randolph kept repeating afterward with slight variations. "You'll notice I don't get excited about a few games either way. Sometimes when you start the season like this, it's not the end of the world, and you feel like you get a lesson from it."

Said Mientkiewicz: "There's not one guy in this room who expected this."

On www.nyfuturestars.com, one of the more popular Web sites following the team, which includes a fan message board, here-we-go-again fears had already surfaced. Someone using the handle NCMetfan started a thread titled "A

Brief Note to All the Ledge Jumpers . . ." Click on the thread and you received the advice: "You'll fall a lot faster if you all hold hands." (Scientifically, that's not correct, by the way. Physics 101: Heavier objects don't fall faster.)

Regardless, the panic—at least among the fan base—could not be mistaken.

To add to early concerns, the Atlanta Braves had rarely been hospitable, which new arrivals such as Pedro and Beltran quickly observed.

The Braves opened their home schedule with a tribute to their thirteen straight division titles on the largest video-capable scoreboard at any sports venue in the world, which boasted a high-definition, 5,600-square-foot screen that cost $10 million. Comedian Jeff Foxworthy, an Atlanta resident, narrated as Mets players, draped over the dugout railing, watched intently. Then Atlanta beat Victor Zambrano and the Mets, 3–1, dropping The New Mets to 0–4. The skid matched the 1964 start and crept closer to the franchise-worst marks of '62 (0–9) and '63 (0–8).

"No gloom and doom for me," Randolph insisted after the loss. "No drastic changes."

Zambrano had joined the Mets in Atlanta the previous season, after the club acquired him and reliever Bartolome Fortunato from the Tampa Bay Devil Rays for top pitching prospect Scott Kazmir, a flame-throwing left-hander, and minor-league pitcher Jose Diaz, in what instantly became an unpopular trade among fans. The Mets had stood six games behind the first-place Braves entering a three-game series when the Mets pulled off two deals in a five-minute span on July 30, 2004, a day before the non-waiver trading deadline. The other swap brought Kris Benson and second baseman Jeff Keppinger from the Pirates for third baseman Ty Wigginton, and prospects Matt Peterson and Justin Huber, with Huber winding up with the Kansas City Royals. (The Braves won all three games that weekend, though Zambrano did not pitch.)

Mets brass had been spooked by Kazmir despite the southpaw's upper-90s fastball. For one thing, even before Kazmir was drafted fifteenth overall in 2002, the organization was concerned that there was an elevated risk a ligament in his left elbow could eventually blow. Fear also existed about Kazmir's off-the-field behavior—for a much more serious reason than wrecking Huber's car, which had been widely reported in the media. Team officials suspected marijuana use, at least early in Kazmir's minor-league career, and thought he would be ill-suited for the fast pace and temptations of New York.

In the end, the crime was not in trading Kazmir, who made the Devil Rays rotation out of spring training. It was in the misevaluation of Zambrano, who had been signed in 1996 by Mets superscout Bill Livesey when he was Devil Rays director of player personnel. Livesey was at Tropicana Field watching Tampa Bay several times in the days leading up to the deal.

Mets staff had Zambrano pegged as a top-of-the-rotation starter after a little mechanical reworking. Peterson had uttered the infamous line on an internal conference call—that he could fix Zambrano in ten minutes—which was later leaked to the media. But Zambrano never emerged as a pitcher of that caliber. He actually pitched in only three games for the Mets in 2004 because of— *would you believe?*—elbow troubles.

Jim Duquette eventually criticized the Devil Rays to Scott Lauber, the Double-A team's beat writer, in the Binghamton *Press & Sun-Bulletin*, claiming Tampa Bay misrepresented the extent of Zambrano's elbow injury. Duquette was general manager at the time of the Zambrano and Benson trades.

"What was unfortunate to me was the information we got from Tampa Bay," Duquette said. "Quite frankly, they weren't up-front. There has to be an openness and a candidness between doctors, and they weren't straightforward with us. That's been my issue all along."

Had the Mets waited until the winter, Kazmir likely would have fetched a bona fide ace such as Tim Hudson or Mark Mulder from Oakland. Billy Beane, the A's general manager, sent Hudson to the Braves less than five months after the Zambrano trade for Juan Cruz, Dan Meyer, and Charles Thomas. He sent Mulder to the St. Louis Cardinals two days after that for Dan Haren, Kiko Calero, and Daric Barton.

Now, pitching in Atlanta with the Mets still searching for their first win, Zambrano mimicked Ishii's performance of the previous afternoon in Cincinnati. He nailed Marcus Giles in the back with a pitch and walked Andruw Jones in the first inning. Both Braves scored as the Mets allowed at least two first-inning runs for the fourth straight game. Only Floyd's dazzling play in deep left-centerfield prevented the Braves from scoring at least two more runs in the first inning. The oft-gimpy Floyd, whose legs had not felt this good in five years, raced to the track, reached up, and snared Raul Mondesi's line drive to end the inning and strand two Braves on base.

The Mets had not led since Looper blew the Opening Day save, though a controversial out call when Reyes clearly swiped second base in the first inning had them convinced they should have been up a run early against the Braves. Two pitches after Reyes was ruled out, Matsui singled.

After going RBI-less in Cincinnati, Piazza chiseled the Mets' deficit to 2–1 in the fourth inning with his first home run. The shot off ex-Met John Thomson tied the slugger with Tony Perez and Orlando Cepeda for fifty-second on the all-time list, with 379 career home runs. Zambrano, prone to wildness, flirted with danger but kept the Mets in the game. He loaded the bases in the fifth inning on a single and two walks, but then struck out Mondesi swinging on a diving, full-count changeup to escape the threat. Like Floyd's catch, though, while it stopped the bleeding, it didn't translate into momentum, and the Mets had suffered their fourth straight loss.

Although their rotation was deep after the addition of Pedro and the re-signing of Benson during the winter, the Mets nonetheless had to next rely upon a call-up from the minor leagues to try to stop the bleeding.

The strained right pectoral muscle Benson suffered during spring training had not responded when he tried to throw in the bullpen at RFK Stadium in frigid Washington, D.C., on the eve of Opening Day. In his place, the Mets turned to Aaron Heilman to try to prevent an 0–5 start. That is, they turned to Heilman once reports that Jose Santiago was slated to make the start were cleared up.

Back in Cincinnati during the middle game of the series, the Madison Square Garden Network crew thought they spotted Santiago seated in the stands in the first row behind the Mets' dugout. They placed him on camera and had roving reporter Matt Loughlin do a segment during the bottom of the fourth inning that "outed" the pitcher, who wasn't supposed to be at the ballpark if he wasn't on the active roster.

Santiago, who had been in big-league camp for the latter half of spring training, was a logical choice to take the start. Major League Baseball rules prevented Heilman, or anyone else on the forty-man roster, from being promoted from the minors during the first ten days of the season without someone simultaneously being placed on the disabled list. Benson had already landed on the DL when outfielder Victor Diaz was added to the roster for Opening Day.

"The Mets will need a starter Saturday in Atlanta. They're not saying anything. The Mets are keeping it kind of quiet as to who it will be," Loughlin said at the beginning of his report. "But we've had an indication it's going to be Jose Santiago. And one of the big signs is that Jose is sitting right above me here watching the game, enjoying all the action. . . ."

"Just a little to the right," Loughlin continued, directing a camera away from himself, toward a pair of Hispanic men in the front row behind the dugout.

"There's Jose. Now, the Mets aren't saying he's here because he's going to start on Saturday, but baseball rules say you can't call up someone who has been optioned to the minors—*there's Jose on the right*—unless an opening occurs because of a disabled-list situation. So, the Mets have no one to put on the disabled list; they can't call up some of the guys they optioned out; Jose is not on the forty-man roster. So they'll put him on the forty-man roster sometime before his start on Saturday, and he will go against the Braves."

At that point, the alleged Santiago's phone rang and he answered.

"Maybe somebody's calling him and saying, 'Hey, you're on TV, you've been caught,'" Loughlin said. "But, anyway, it looks like it's going to be Jose Santiago on Saturday."

"He's saying, 'I'm not supposed to be here,'" commentator Fran Healy chimed in from the TV booth upstairs.

"You know what?" Loughlin said. "Don't take a seat in the first row."

"Matty, you're right on top of this," play-by-play announcer Ted Robinson said. "I can tell you, one of the beautiful things about baseball is you come to the park every day and you'll see something you haven't seen. I've never seen that before, all these years. To have a guy sit in the first row behind the dugout who is probably going to pitch a game for you."

The *Post* picked up on the MSG report.

"Looks like Jose Santiago is set to start Saturday in place of Kris Benson (strained right pectoral)," the paper reported the following day. "Even though the Mets said no decision had been made, the minor-league reliever was seated behind the Mets dugout for last night's game. That's kind of a giveaway."

The only problem? It wasn't Santiago, who actually had shaggy hair unlike the man on television, and who looked about ten years younger. Santiago, in fact, was on a bus with his Triple-A Norfolk teammates en route to Scranton/

Wilkes-Barre at the time. It turned out the man on camera was an acquaintance of Pedro's, who helped with the ace's strength and conditioning.

Oops.

When Saturday arrived, the Mets placed Mike Cameron on the disabled list and promoted Heilman. Cameron's left wrist simply had not recovered quickly enough from the December 17 surgery that repaired some damaged cartilage, though the Mets had included him on the Opening Day active roster, hoping he would be healthy.

Heilman, the club's 2001 first-round pick out of Notre Dame, had been a bust in chances the two previous seasons, going a combined 3–10 with a 6.36 ERA while walking fifty-four batters in ninety-three and one-third innings and being particularly susceptible to yielding home runs (seventeen). But there were signs a breakout loomed. Midway through spring training, Mets pitching consultant Al Jackson thought he noticed similarities between Heilman and former Dodgers great Don Drysdale. Even if it sounded crazy to compare Heilman with a Hall of Famer, Jackson shared his belief with Guy Conti, the bullpen coach. Conti obtained old footage of Drysdale through a contact with the Dodgers and put both pitchers up on a split-screen display. Sure enough, the pitchers had similar mechanics—both of their palms pointed up at one point during their deliveries. They also had similar builds, in the 6-foot-5, 220-pound range. Former manager Bobby Valentine had once compared Heilman and Drysdale, too, after watching Heilman in a spring-training intrasquad game.

When the coaches presented Heilman with the Drysdale footage and inquired whether he might feel comfortable throwing at Drysdale's three-quarters arm angle, Heilman noted that's how he had thrown at Notre Dame, where he went 15–0 his senior year in fifteen starts. Only under the Mets' tutelage had Heilman's arm angle drifted fully overhand.

Returning to that college delivery, Heilman had opened eyes during the second half of spring training, including tossing three scoreless innings during the final week against the Marlins.

The return to his college form didn't help against the Braves, however, and the Mets lost, 6–3. Brian Jordan hit a mammoth grand slam over the center-field wall off Heilman in the second inning.

"I got my arm up a little bit and the pitches started flattening out," Heilman said.

With the Mets 0–5—and very much in danger of arriving in New York winless, considering Pedro had to face Braves ace John Smoltz in the six-game trip's finale—the newspapers started feeling the license to take shots. The New Mets were becoming a punching bag, just like the old Mets.

In the *Post*, Mark Hale wrote: "If these Mets really want to be ambitious, the 1962 club started 0–9. Here's to the dream."

"Somewhere, Art Howe must be laughing," David Lennon wrote in *Newsday*, referring to Randolph's predecessor, whom the Mets still owed $4.7 million. "Whatever Howe's shortcomings, the Mets were no worse during his tenure than they are right now, and he's home counting his millions while Willie Randolph keeps coming up empty in his search for answers."

"Aaron Heilman tried changing the mechanics of his delivery," Peter Abraham wrote in *The Journal News* of Westchester. "Perhaps it's time he tried changing professions, because pitching doesn't seem to be working out too well for him. The first-round flop gave up hits in bunches last night as the Mets remained the only winless team in baseball."

I wrote:

> *Aaron Heilman took the mound for the Mets last night, trying to stop the bleeding. The Mets might as well have sent out the front-office executive who drafted him in the first round in 2001. . . .*
>
> *Heilman remains one of the primary symbols of the Mets' failures since the 2000 World Series appearance. He's polite, quiet, and intellectual, an avid reader. He has management information systems and philosophy degrees from Notre Dame, and a crossword puzzle always nearby. He also was the best available arm to promote in the system for last night's start, which underscores how barren the highest level of the minors has become. Triple-A Norfolk's starting lineup for a doubleheader game yesterday included only one prospect, centerfielder Angel Pagan. Otherwise, the Tides serve as a holding pen for other organizations' castoffs.*
>
> *Jose Santiago, who would have taken the start instead of Heilman had Mike Cameron not landed on the disabled list, was knocked out in the third inning of Norfolk's other doubleheader game after surrendering four runs and eight hits.*

When Heilman became one of the team's most valuable relievers months later, Jack Bowen reminded me of that "front-office executive who drafted him" line. Bowen, by now a National League East scout for the Pirates, formerly had been the amateur scouting director for the Mets.

Others prematurely labeled Heilman a bust, too, even within the organization. The Mets aggressively shopped Heilman during spring training and found no trading partners offering anything of value.

At 0–5, things had become comically bad for the Mets. Under the headline MET SCOUT CRASHES POTTY, the *Daily News* mentioned that nice-guy scout Howie Freiling had been kicked out of Tropicana Field in Tampa Bay by Devil Rays owner Vince Naimoli the same day as Heilman's outing in Atlanta. Freiling's transgression? He got caught using the owner's private bathroom adjacent to the press box, which set off the excitable Naimoli. Freiling was threatened with a lifetime ban from the ballpark, though that never happened. Naimoli thankfully completed the sale of the Devil Rays after the season, and a group headed by former Wall Street securities executive Stuart Sternberg took over controlling interest.

Before the final game of the trip, 1ST DAY OF A NEW SEASON! was written on a grease board in the visitors' clubhouse at Turner Field. Someone later added in blue marker: WILLIE NEEDS A BALL.

Then, finally, Pedro and Beltran ended the futility and ensured the introduction of The New Mets at Shea Stadium would not turn ugly. As the Mets flirted with the futility of their early 1960s counterparts, and with Smoltz back as a starter and looking in Cy Young form after three-plus seasons as one of the game's most dominant closers, Pedro willed the Mets to victory. In fact, Pedro refused to surrender the baseball until he handed the memento to Randolph after his 101st pitch coaxed Chipper Jones into a game-ending flyout to Beltran in centerfield. The ace delivered a complete-game two-hitter as the Mets snapped their season-opening skid with a 6–1 victory.

"I understood the situation we were in," Pedro said. "They needed a big performance from me."

Said Smoltz: "He still has intimidation, whether hitters want to admit that or not."

The Mets had not led for forty-three innings, since Looper blew the save in Cincinnati on Opening Day in Pedro's Mets debut. And their prospects did not look promising entering the eighth inning. Smoltz had already struck out fifteen batters, matching a career high, and the most by a Braves pitcher in the forty seasons since the franchise relocated to Atlanta. Before the game, Mientkiewicz half-seriously predicted to teammates that Pedro–Smoltz might be a preview of Game 1 of the National League Championship Series.

For a while, the Mets seemed destined to return to New York winless. Jose Reyes was thrown out while retreating to third base on Miguel Cairo's third-inning double, after coach Manny Acta put up a late stop sign. The Mets also stranded runners in scoring position in the first, fifth, and seventh innings. In the middle threat, they placed two runners aboard with no out, but Pedro failed on a sacrifice-bunt attempt, and Reyes and Cairo struck out, the latter on three pitches.

"That's the best I think I've ever seen Smoltzie," Braves manager Bobby Cox said.

Having to face an intimidating and determined Smoltz, who was stung after getting knocked out in the second inning on Opening Day against the Marlins, and who was grieving over the unexpected death of his grandmother three days earlier, Mientkiewicz had prepared remarks for any Brave who arrived at first base complaining about the misfortune of facing Pedro.

"If they get to first telling me how nasty Pedro is, I'd just tell them, 'Cry me a friggin' river,'" Mientkiewicz said.

"I feel like the old John Smoltz," Smoltz said as he bit his lip and fought back tears after an emotional week.

Beltran had already lugged his lumber back to the dugout twice, the victim of nasty split-finger fastballs from Smoltz. But with the Mets five outs from a winless road trip, Beltran stepped into the batter's box and told himself, "Just wait for a pitch you can drive." Beltran then received a down-and-in curveball and deposited Smoltz's 113th and final pitch into the right-field stands for a two-run home run and a 2–1 Mets lead.

Smoltz was shocked that Beltran took him deep. He had not planned to give Beltran a quality pitch to hit.

"It never even crossed my mind. I mean, if I walked him, who cares?" Smoltz said. "It's a tough way to come out of the game."

Said Beltran: "I just wanted to put the ball in play. Smoltz was pitching a great ball game. He was locating balls, outside corner, inside corner, throwing splits. He drove me crazy. When I stroked that ball, I was the happiest man. . . . Only God knows how much we needed it."

Pedro described the sensation as a five-foot monkey being yanked from the team's back.

The pressure off, and relieved by Smoltz's departure, the Mets pounded Atlanta's relievers. Floyd and Wright also homered in what became a five-run inning. Mientkiewicz belted a shot off the top of the wall in right-centerfield, narrowly missing a fourth home run of the frame.

After surrendering a run-scoring double to Johnny Estrada in the fourth inning, Pedro didn't allow another batter to reach base, retiring the final sixteen Braves he faced. It was the same dominance Pedro flashed in Cincinnati, when he struck out twelve of the next fourteen Reds batters after Dunn's first-inning home run and did not surrender another hit during his outing. Pedro matched David Cone for nineteenth on the all-time strikeout list at 2,668 when he caught Andruw Jones looking in the fourth inning. He then struck out six more Braves to finish the game with nine.

Mientkiewicz, who had witnessed Pedro's dominance in Boston when they were Red Sox teammates during the second half of the 2004 season, knew something special might occur way back in the first inning, when he had noticed the ace's velocity.

"When he's throwing 93, 94 mph in the first inning, he's got an agenda," Mientkiewicz said.

Said Randolph: "I'm not a crazy pitch-count guy, but Pedro said, 'I'm not coming out.'"

Mientkiewicz said the victory had the feel of a two- or three-game winning streak because of the uplift it provided. Floyd admitted dreading the prospect of facing Mets fans winless had the road-trip finale not ended happily.

"One-hundred percent, yeah. It would have been horrible," Floyd said. "But still, in my mind, regardless of if we went home oh-and-six, I still felt like we played good ball."

"If we would have come back oh-and-six, you wouldn't have seen anything different from me," Randolph insisted. "I believe in my team. I feel good about them. I think they're going to get the kinks out. I think they're going to start to reveal themselves."

Before the start, teammates didn't tell Pedro how desperately they needed him to step up, but he knew.

"They didn't have to," Pedro said. "I was totally aware of that. . . . I'm taking a big satisfaction out of handing my team the first win of the year."

Once the team's chartered plane landed in New York and Randolph arrived at his Franklin Lakes, New Jersey, home that night, he could finally puff away on the cigar Piazza had purchased five days earlier. Actually, Randolph enjoyed the El Rey del Mundo on the deck, because his wife Gretchen did not want smoke in the house.

"It almost had bugs in it by the time he was able to smoke it," Piazza quipped. "He had to get a humidor for it because it was getting dry."

Randolph had waited far longer to manage. He had an enormous cheering section at Shea Stadium the following day, including his parents up from Holly Hill, South Carolina, for a glorious home opener against the Houston Astros.

"I'm just so happy. I'm proud of him because he's always been a hardworking person," Minnie Randolph told Loughlin during an in-game interview. (Yes, it really was Randolph's mother.) "I'm just happy you work hard and you accomplish. I thought it was really amazing to grow up in New York, play for two famous teams, and then be able to manage the team. I knew he would manage the Yankees or the Mets. I'm just so happy. I've seen that dreams do come true. As I say, it's a blessing. It's wonderful. I feel like a millionaire myself sitting here."

Loughlin—a diligent reporter, who was always in the clubhouse asking questions and keeping abreast of developments with the team—asked Willie Sr. if he ever thought this day would come.

"Yes, I did think it would come one of these days because, you know, Willie doesn't give up on things," said the elder Randolph, who served as a construction worker building Shea Stadium in the early 1960s. "He likes to keep on fighting for it. And I think he would have gotten a manager's job if it wasn't here. I didn't know he would get it here, but he would get it someplace."

Of course, it would not be New York without a little controversy added to the mix. Up in Boston the same day, the Red Sox were receiving their championship rings at Fenway Park in a forty-five-minute ceremony their fans had waited eighty-six years to witness. Virtually every Beantown athletic hero was there—Bill Russell, Bobby Orr, Johnny Pesky, Carl Yastrzemski, and even Tedy

Bruschi, who had suffered a mild stroke two months earlier, ten days after the New England Patriots beat the Pittsburgh Steelers, 24–21, in Super Bowl XXXIX. Even 2004 Red Sox Derek Lowe and Dave Roberts, now with National League West clubs, attended the event. But Pedro wasn't there, which somehow turned into a soap opera. Chris Russo of "Mike & the Mad Dog" drive-time fame railed on sports-talk radio station WFAN about how the ace ought to have been at Fenway Park for the ceremony rather than at Shea Stadium to celebrate the home opener with his new supporters at the dawn of a new era in Flushing.

"Pedro's been a Met for two weeks. This is about baseball history," Russo said on the air, unmoved even the following day. "For the sake of baseball history, Pedro had to be at Fenway. He had to be there."

The resounding welcome Pedro received during pregame introductions strongly suggested the ace was where he belonged.

"For me, in such a short period, I was really shocked to get such a warm reception," Pedro said. "And I really appreciated it. I'm going to take it in my heart and do what I have to do for them and hopefully keep them happy."

Said Randolph: "It was Opening Day, and I think you'd want to be with the team Opening Day. He didn't bring that up, but he wanted to be here, because he's a Met."

Pedro got his ring three weeks later when Red Sox chairman Tom Werner made a private presentation in a back room of the home clubhouse at Shea Stadium. Not that Pedro intended to wear the ring.

"My fingers are long and ugly," he said.

Pedro knew his lengthy but supple fingers actually were a blessing because they helped create movement on his pitches.

Mientkiewicz got his ring that day, too, though he joked his was probably cubic zirconia, considering his public dispute with the Red Sox after he held onto the ball from the final out of the World Series. Werner assured Mientkiewicz the ring, in fact, included seventy-four diamonds weighing 1.89 carats.

More importantly, the Mets beat Houston, 8–4, in the home opener during an eventful day that included a fourteen-minute Pedro/Cablevision delay, and a second consecutive eighth-inning rally of five runs that overcame a one-run deficit. Reyes beat out an ill-advised double-play attempt by reliever Russ Springer, allowing Diaz to score the tying run from third base. Reyes then stole second base and Matsui drove him in for the go-ahead run.

"When I hit that ball I said, 'Man, I have to beat it. I have to beat it to first base.' So I ran as fast as I can," Reyes said. "I put a little bit extra there."

As Smoltz did Sunday, Andy Pettitte dazzled before a sellout crowd of 53,663 on what surely was a nostalgic as well as momentous day for Randolph. The manager and wife Gretchen had served as babysitters for Pettitte's son, Josh, while Randolph and Pettitte were with the Yankees, and the families lived nearby. Randolph chuckled, recalling how enraged Yankees owner George Steinbrenner got in 2002, when Josh, then seven years old, was photographed wearing a Mets hat in the dugout at Legends Field in Tampa, Florida, during spring training, even though that was the name of the boy's Little League team.

"George is like, 'Get that kid out of here. What are you always doing around here with a Met hat on? Get 'em out of here.' Andy was really upset about that, really hot," Randolph said. "Josh went away crying. The poor kid didn't even know what was going on."

Pettitte, who had undergone season-ending elbow surgery in August 2004, two weeks after gutting out a pain-filled but effective outing at Shea Stadium against the Mets, took a 1–0 lead into the sixth inning this time, when his fielders failed him. Floyd and Wright singled, and Mientkiewicz sacrificed both ahead. Right fielder Jason Lane then misjudged Diaz's fly ball, and the Mets tied the score. Cairo, pinch-hitting, followed with a run-scoring blooper over shortstop for the lead. Ex-Met Dan Wheeler entered and struck out Reyes, but Matsui delivered a stellar drag-bunt single that scored Diaz, who had led a double steal.

That provided Glavine a 3–1 lead. But things never came easy for the southpaw; at least, they hadn't since he'd become a Met.

A half-inning earlier, when Glavine had taken the mound for the top of the sixth inning, the black sign behind the centerfield wall—which flips to advertisements between innings—became stuck on an advertisement featuring Cablevision's high-definition TV service that read SEEING HD IS BELIEVING! The ad included a picture of Pedro delivering a pitch. Initially, Astros batter Morgan Ensberg had stepped out of the batter's box, stalling for a bit as he waited for the vertical panels to flip to black. (Batters get the optimal view of the pitches when the panels are at this all-black setting.) After fourteen minutes and a computer reboot, the panels still wouldn't flip. The malfunction was remedied only after workers, perched on the top scoreboard, manually flipped over the final flaps. Glavine twice returned to the dugout during the delay.

During the stoppage, which included failed attempts to drape black tarp over the sign, Pedro—amused when he finally noticed it was his face plastered on the ad—danced against the dugout railing as the crowd went crazy, chanting his name.

"I was just having fun with the moment," Pedro said. "I felt bad for Tommy, having to wait that long that inning."

Said Piazza: "I don't understand how you don't have a manual override. It's like The *Three Stooges*. . . . It looked like *Master and Commander*, trying to put the sails down."

On TV, Robinson playfully alluded to his remark in Cincinnati, when Santiago was supposedly spotted behind the dugout.

"Well, remember our famous phrase?" he said during the MSG telecast. "The best thing about baseball is you come to a ballpark and you're always going to see something you've never seen before. This qualifies. I don't think I'm aware of this kind of delay before in a game."

"I've never seen it," Healy said. "Ralph?"

"I don't think I have," said Ralph Kiner, who had been in the broadcast booth since the team's inception. "Of course, at one time they didn't have a batter's eye at ballparks."

Healy, never shy about plugging sponsors, added, "They can always go to the concession stands. There's good food at Shea."

Aybar and Koo blew the lead, depriving Glavine of earning the victory. At least it wasn't like two years earlier, when Glavine debuted and the Mets suffered a 15–2 loss to the Chicago Cubs. That was the most lopsided opener in the majors in fifty-two years, and the Cubs' largest Opening Day output since 1899.

This time, Glavine even benefited from a generous call from plate umpire Mark Wegner, a far cry from his fate in Cincinnati. Wegner called a third strike against Jeff Bagwell on a low-and-way-way-inside fastball, which stranded three Astros in the fifth inning and kept the Mets' deficit at 1–0. Astros manager Phil Garner had to separate Bagwell from Wegner.

"I think it's one of those, if you look at the replay in slow motion, it's a little bit different than if you look at it at fast speed," Glavine offered, hinting he knew he had received a gift.

"Fast speed?" I asked the soft-tossing southpaw.

"Well, *my* fast speed," he replied.

Said Bagwell: "Just like any of those arguments, it's a difference of opinion. He said it got part of the plate. And I know it didn't."

Still, Reyes had to run wild to turn the game around. With runners on first and third base and one out, and the Mets trailing, 4–3, in the eighth inning, bench coach Sandy Alomar Sr. turned to Woodward in the dugout and said: "If he could just hit a ball back to the pitcher, they're not going to turn it." Sure enough, it happened that way, with Reyes beating the relay throw and Diaz scoring the first of the inning's five runs.

Said Mientkiewicz: "He can beat a team by himself a lot of ways."

Looper pitched a 1–2–3 ninth inning, but didn't get the save because the Mets held a four-run lead. The closer, who blew his only save opportunity when he couldn't close out Pedro's Opening Day performance, maintained he wasn't eagerly awaiting a chance to remedy the previous week's letdown.

"I don't care if we had won the first ten and I had blown that game," Looper said. "I would have felt the same way. To me the most painful thing is when a starting pitcher goes out there and really pitches. He battled that first day. He didn't pitch nearly as well as he did Sunday [in Atlanta]. He got us in a situation to win. As a closer, it's your job to get that game home, and I didn't do it. I felt bad for him. He should be sitting here two-and-oh right now."

Looper had received some boos during the pregame introductions, but joked, "I thought they were saying, *Looooooop.*"

As for Pedro, he always seemed to find himself in the middle of events like the stuck advertisement in centerfield, even if he was just a bystander. Nearly two months later, during the first inning of a June 2 game against the Arizona Diamondbacks, just after Luis Gonzalez fouled off a 2–2 pitch, the infield sprinklers went off, causing Piazza and plate umpire Hunter Wendelstedt to scurry into foul territory. Rather than race to drier surroundings, Pedro reveled in the moisture, just as he had on the final day of spring training when he stood in the rain and sang "God Bless America." Pedro had also raced through the sprinklers with children at Tradition Field in Port St. Lucie, Florida, while taping a public-service advertisement for the Boys & Girls Clubs of America.

"Water is a blessing, so I got wet," Pedro said.

Randolph shook his head and grinned as Pedro ducked his noggin into a sprinkler. The manager also smirked thinking about how Steinbrenner might have reacted had the sprinklers gone off during a game in the Bronx.

"I got a bigger kick out of watching Jeff Wilpon scrambling to find someone to shut it off," Randolph said. "George would have fired the whole staff."

Now, nothing could cool off the Mets, who went on to sweep the Astros, eventually rattling off six straight wins to jump over .500 despite the sorry start.

The fans even got the chance to celebrate two homecomings. The six-game home stand against the Astros and Marlins marked the returns of pitchers John Franco and Al Leiter, who received different receptions.

Franco, a Staten Island resident who saved 273 games as a Met, arrived at Shea Stadium for his former employer's home opener only to find his old parking space occupied by dumpsters. He hugged Jeff Wilpon and Minaya during batting practice. Franco then received a video tribute after the first inning and generally was greeted with cheers.

On the mound, it was a different story. The forty-four-year-old left-hander departed to chants of *Fran-co, Fran-co* after he surrendered a critical two-run single to Floyd, the only batter he was asked to face during the Astros' 8–4 loss.

"Sometimes you have to go on your way," Franco said. "There's no animosity, no hatred, nothing like that. The Wilpons were great, the whole organization was great."

Leiter, now a Marlin, took his family to Central Park before the series opener between the Mets and Florida, but kept quiet once he arrived at the ballpark. He had a far more hostile reception than Franco, getting booed when the Mets played a video tribute during that series opener.

The animosity toward Leiter was partly related to the Mets' ill-fated pursuit of Carlos Delgado to play first base. David Sloane, Delgado's agent, had revealed during spring training that Leiter had negatively recruited against the Mets. Leiter had also ducked a Grapefruit League start against the Mets because he would have been too "geeked up." In its place, Leiter could not get three outs in the first inning of a game against minor-leaguers.

Delgado did not exactly receive a warm reception, either, during an 0-for-3 performance in the opener. Caught by first base during the seventh-inning stretch, he did stand, facing the flag on the scoreboard, for the rendition of "God Bless America." His reluctance to do so while with the Toronto Blue Jays, as a protest against U.S. government policies, had created a stir in the past.

"I'm not talking about 'God Bless America,'" Delgado said afterward.

"I don't know what they were booing at," Leiter said about his own reception. "One guy in the bullpen said, 'Al, we love you and I think you're great, but I'm still going to boo you.' You have fans that root for the marks and logos of their teams. You root for the fabric and I understand that. That's probably what it is."

When Leiter pitched the following day, he did quiet the crowd to an extent. He abandoned his standard pattern of relying on cut fastballs and out-pitched Pedro, limiting the Mets to one run and three hits in seven innings. It was the longest outing Leiter would have during an abbreviated tenure with the Marlins that lasted only into mid-July. The Mets nonetheless earned their sixth straight win to improve to 6–5 when Ramon Castro, a defensive replacement for Piazza a half-inning earlier, delivered a ninth-inning single against Marlins closer Guillermo Mota. This scored Diaz with the winning run in a 4–3 victory, which overcame another blown save by Looper—this one before a sellout crowd in Pedro's first home start.

"This whole week the fans have been on their toes, especially the way we've been playing," Pedro said. "It's nice to see that Shea Stadium was today 55,000 people just wanting to see me—that it wasn't just at Yankee Stadium. Seeing those people come over here is a good sign for the team, for management, and I hope I can continue to do that. I hope I can continue to be a ticket every time I come out for those fans. Now the Latin population is coming in, and you're starting to see some Dominican flags and stuff like that. Everything is probably going to change."

During the six-game winning streak, the Mets surged back to respectability despite facing capable starters Smoltz, Pettitte, Roger Clemens, Brandon Backe, and Josh Beckett before Leiter. The only blemish came in the series finale against the Marlins, when the Mets fell a game short of the best home start in franchise history, set in 1985. A.J. Burnett's complete-game four-hitter handed the Mets a 5–2 loss.

"We faced, what, six Cy Young candidates in the first eleven or twelve games?" Mientkiewicz said. "To split, six-and-six, that's not bad. You run into Clemens, Pettitte, Burnett, Beckett, Smoltz, guys like that—that's as good as it gets in the big leagues. Considering we won most of those, I'd say we're doing all right. We're doing better than all right."

# COME TO DADDY

THE SILVER CHEVY VAN CARRYING PEDRO MARTINEZ left the ace's Westchester home at 3:20 P.M. for the drive down the New York State Thruway and Major Deegan Expressway, and onward to Yankee Stadium. But before Yankees fans could serenade him with chants of *Who's your daddy?*, another question arose: *Where's Pedro?*

With a disabled truck stalling traffic, Pedro's driver told him, "I'm going to take another shortcut."

"Hey, it's five o'clock; are you sure?" Pedro replied.

Still not overly concerned, the ace told head trainer Ray Ramirez by telephone: "I'm on my way over. Get the Jacuzzi ready."

But soon afterward, as he spoke with Jay Horwitz, the team's vice president for media relations who had already arrived at the ballpark, Pedro had a bad feeling.

"Oh my God, we took the wrong exit," the ace said as he embarked on an unexpected tour of the South Bronx.

Said Pedro: "When I saw that little turnaround, NO EXIT, I'm like, 'We're lost, aren't we?' . . . 'Well, we're going to take this . . . , this . . .' I'm like, 'Oh my God, Jay, I'm lost.' It was scary."

Pedro finally arrived at Yankee Stadium at 6:08 P.M., exactly one hour before the first pitch, after flagging down police officers who escorted the van. Horwitz pulled up just behind him. He had jumped into the backseat of another officer's car to try to locate Pedro on the Major Deegan.

"That was really impressive," Pedro said, about the police officers' willingness to help. "I thought, these guys are going to have an attitude—'Oh no, we're not supposed to do that.'

"No, they turned those lights on. *Weeee, Weeee, Weeee, Weeee,*" he continued, mimicking a siren. "There I was, Yankee Stadium."

The Mets, including Pedro eventually, arrived in the Bronx on June 24 a quintessential .500 team. After their six-game winning streak erased an 0–5 start, the Mets spent the next three-plus months within three games of breakeven for all but one day.

Those early months flew by for manager Willie Randolph, despite several noteworthy occurrences.

Five days after his matchup with the Florida Marlins' Al Leiter during the season's opening home stand, Pedro dominated in a rematch in Miami. Leiter was rocked for eight runs in three innings, and the Mets won, 10–1.

Carlos Beltran tweaked his right quadriceps muscle in Washington, D.C., on May 1, though he contributed a two-run double in the ninth inning that day anyway in a 6–1 win against the Nationals. Beltran played three more weeks before seriously aggravating the quadriceps while rounding second base on Mike Piazza's first-inning single, playing against the Yankees at Shea Stadium. The injury should have forced Beltran to the disabled list, but he had no interest in landing there. Instead, he missed only eight starts and wasn't the same upon his return because of reduced mobility.

Beltran had a .302 average and team-leading 28 RBI when he left the game against the Yankees in Flushing. By the time the second Yankees series opened in the Bronx a month later, his average had dropped 38 points, and he remained stuck on one stolen base. His average would bottom out at .258 the following week.

Despite his injury, Beltran always managed to step up for Pedro during those early months. The day after he originally suffered the quadriceps injury in Washington, D.C., after a two-hour rain delay at the start of a May 2 game against the Philadelphia Phillies, Beltran broke a 1–1 tie with a three-run home run on Terry Adams's full-count offering. The blast, estimated at 460 feet, struck the scoreboard in right field at Shea Stadium more than halfway up the Mets' lineup, just to the right of the bulbs forming "30 LF," which denoted Cliff Floyd's cleanup spot in the batting order. Pedro had departed at the end of the previous half-inning for pinch hitter Marlon Anderson, but was on the winning side of the ledger after Beltran's blast.

"Every time he pitches, it seems that I have a good day. And I was happy to help him," Beltran said while donning a Pedro-issued WHO'S YOUR DADDY? T-shirt. "I hope he can pitch every other day, but unfortunately, that's not going to happen. I want to do well no matter who takes the mound. . . . But that's just the way it's going right now."

During Pedro's next start, in Milwaukee, Beltran continued his uncanny production supporting the ace. He belted a pair of two-run home runs for his thirteenth career multi-homer game as the Mets beat the Brewers, 7–5.

Nine of Beltran's ten first-half home runs came in games started by the ace.

That same day in Milwaukee, a "conspiracy theory" ended. At least that was how Randolph had begun referring to the subject of supposed personal catchers, to mock the media's fascination with the topic. After slamming two home runs a night earlier against the Brewers, Piazza was in the starting lineup to catch Pedro. His presence snapped a string of three straight games in which Ramon Castro had been the ace's batterymate.

Piazza had not caught Pedro since the first matchup with Leiter, when the ace had tossed three wild pitches that Piazza hadn't been nimble enough to control. Of course, the furor over Piazza not catching Pedro for that three-start stretch ignored a few pertinent facts: The thirty-six-year-old catcher *was* in the original lineup for the first of those games, the Pedro–Leiter rematch in Florida. He was scratched after telling Randolph he felt banged up. In the second instance, Piazza was nicked at the base of the left thumb by a bounced Roberto Hernandez pitch in the eighth inning the day before. And the Mets had an afternoon game the next day anyway, which Piazza would not otherwise have started had he caught Pedro. Piazza was also fatigued and unenthusiastic about starting the May 2 home game; this was the night after starting the ESPN-televised eight o'clock game in Washington, D.C., during which Beltran originally injured his quadriceps muscle.

"I know it would have been a nice story to keep that going," Randolph said about Castro catching Pedro. "I told you guys before—I'm going to play whoever I think is right for that day. Mike Piazza is one of my big boys. If we get into a situation one day where he has to play, I'm not sitting him down because of that personal-catcher thing going on. I told you that from day one."

Highlights and lowlights often occurred in tandem to keep the Mets near the .500 mark during the first half. The day Beltran pulled up lame against the Yankees, South Korean reliever Dae-Sung Koo made himself a short-lived folk hero in a 7–1 Mets laugher.

Mr. Koo, as he preferred to be called (which tickled his teammates), smashed a double off Randy Johnson's 91 mph fastball. The unexpected shot off the Big Unit cleared centerfielder Bernie Williams's head and two-hopped the wall. Koo then scored from second base on Jose Reyes's sacrifice bunt, sliding headfirst into an uncovered home plate. Incredibly, and inexplicably, Koo had a weighted ball in the pocket of the warm-up jacket he wore while running the bases. The run resulted in raucous laughter on the bench, as well as throughout the stadium. What made Koo's performance that much more remarkable was that less than a week earlier against the Cincinnati Reds' Todd Coffey, in Koo's first at-bat in what he estimated was twenty years, an uncomfortable Koo never took the bat off his shoulder and stood as far away from the plate as the batter's box allowed.

Koo would not make it through the entire season as the Mets struggled to find competent left-handed relief. But he did have his share of comedic behind-the-scenes moments during his stint with the club. One day, Koo scrunched himself up and hid in the back of his locker behind some clothes in the visitors' clubhouse in Colorado. He swiped an obscene amount of Skittles from the candy rack in Washington, D.C., which ended up mentioned in at least one newspaper. In Florida he dominated his teammates at poker, which he claimed not to have played before, while raising on odd hands not in his favor.

"He set us up," said Piazza, referring to Koo's double and dash from second base. "I think he was kind of playing possum on us. We were all just kind of dumbfounded. *Who is that guy?* Not only that, but to get a hit off Randy Johnson in his second major-league at-bat? You got me. I guess you see something new every day."

Pedro had been slated to start the opener of the first series against the Yankees the day before Koo's dramatics. But the ace, experiencing right-hip discomfort, received a cortisone shot earlier in the week and was pushed back to the finale, a rubber game the Mets lost, 5–3. Pedro did his part. He limited the Yankees to one run in seven innings despite the hip beginning to nag in the fourth inning. Once Pedro departed—and after principal owner Fred Wilpon, in a rare sighting, tossed peanuts and Cracker Jack to spectators from his stadium perch during the seventh-inning stretch—third baseman David Wright and Reyes committed errors on consecutive eighth-inning plays. A two-run lead became a deficit.

At least Pedro's hip was serviceable. Back in Miami later that week, soothing *bachata* music blared in the visitors' clubhouse before the game, demonstrating that Randolph *did* have some bend in his mandate from the spring when he had declared that headphones must be worn. Then, the tropical, 86-degree weather, which reminded Pedro of his native Dominican Republic, kept the cranky hip loose. Pedro tossed eight scoreless innings in a 1–0 win. He struck out Juan Encarnacion looking on an arcing curveball, and then Mike Lowell swinging on a cut fastball, to strand Carlos Delgado on third base in the seventh inning, and make Floyd's RBI double stand up.

"I didn't tell anybody, but there were times in the past couple weeks when I questioned myself and wondered if I was still strong enough to do this. But I was able to do a lot of work down here," Pedro told Lee Jenkins of the *New York Times*, alluding to the hip troubles, after the media had mostly wandered away from the ace's locker following the game. "This is my type of weather."

Pedro topped that performance two outings later. He nearly no-hit the Houston Astros on June 7, improving his record to 7–1 by limiting Houston to two hits while striking out twelve in a complete-game effort. The bid for Pedro's—and the organization's—first no-hitter ended on Chris Burke's first major-league home run, on a 1–1 curveball with one out in the seventh inning. Still, Pedro was dominating the National League, leading in strikeouts (104), opponent batting average (.151), strikeouts per nine innings (10.6), and fewest walks per nine innings (1.3). The 3–1 victory allowed the Mets to move four games over .500 for the first time since July 31, 2002. It was their lone day at that plateau before the All-Star break.

Pedro, meanwhile, swore he had no idea he was working on a no-hitter—at least not until Burke homered and he lost the bid.

"I didn't really realize it until I heard the fans continue to clap after he rounded second," Pedro said. "I never look at the scoreboard. I'm normally looking everywhere else, but not the scoreboard."

Pedro remained a bundle of energy the next day. When he arrived at Shea Stadium and spotted Danny Graves in a Mets uniform, which the recently released

Cincinnati Reds closer wore while pitching a simulated game against Castro, Pedro shouted: "Papaya Head! Another crazy guy in the locker room."

For Pedro, *Papaya Head* was an affectionate term most often reserved for Floyd, but in this instance extended to Graves.

Graves arrived with frosted hair, five piercings, and an overwhelming number of tattoos, which he had stopped counting because they now ran together. If he weren't a baseball player, he believed he would be a rock star or an actor, which partly explained his close friendship with entertainer Nick Lachey, Jessica Simpson's husband, though that couple would split after the season.

"Not that I need attention, but I love being in the middle of it," Graves said. "I love being in the middle of all the practical jokes. Whatever it is, I want to be a part of it."

Well, not one thing.

Graves was born in South Asia, his father Jim an American serviceman, his mother Thao a Vietnamese woman working at the U.S. Embassy. At the age of fourteen months, he fled the country with his family, just before the fall of Saigon. So when a Reds fan insulted his Vietnamese heritage on May 22 by using the derogatory term, *gook*—which Graves equated with similar terms, saying "Just like the N-word"—the closer replied with a hand gesture. He found himself unemployed the next day.

"I regret doing it," Graves said. "I even planned an apology for it the next day. And I didn't have time to do that. I was already released. The guy verbally insulted my family. I know you're going to get that as a professional athlete, but it really hit home."

Graves had picked up the win on Opening Day against the Mets, when he tossed a scoreless ninth inning, then benefited from home runs by Austin Kearns and Joe Randa against Braden Looper. He then earned his first save in the series finale against the Mets by getting the pinch-hitting Piazza to fly out to right field. But Graves joined the Mets at a time when he was pitching poorly. After a forty-one-save season in 2004, he had a 6.52 ERA and ten saves in twelve chances when the Reds dumped him in late May.

His arrival created awkwardness for a far different reason. Graves wasn't immediately activated when he joined the club, but he was assigned a locker in the clubhouse and worked out in uniform before games, which went on for nearly a week. With the Mets already carrying seven relievers, Mike DeJean and

Manny Aybar were both in jeopardy of being shipped out. They felt the pressure, too.

Aybar had seven children, DeJean noted, no matter what the media guide said about his having only two. DeJean felt badly that Aybar was in danger of a demotion, because Aybar and his family would find it difficult living on a minor-league salary. Not that DeJean felt secure. Obtained from the Baltimore Orioles during the 2004 season for outfielder Karim Garcia, the Mets had hesitantly re-signed DeJean at the December deadline.

It was Jim Duquette who had made the trade to obtain DeJean while general manager, and who had advocated re-signing him over the winter. And Duquette no longer was the head honcho. DeJean never felt that the new front-office staff had ever embraced him being there.

The stress showed. Both pitching for the first time in five days on June 10, DeJean allowed two runs and four hits in one inning against the Los Angeles Angels of Anaheim. Aybar fared worse, allowing five runs on two hits and three walks in an inning.

"You pitch like you have the weight of the world on your shoulders," said DeJean, being completely candid, but also revealing an insecurity that translated into disaster on the mound. "It's a very, very tough situation to go in and try to get guys out when, number one, you have four days off, and number two, you are worrying about your job or somebody else's job. It's very, very draining."

Aybar was designated for assignment the following day to make room for Graves.

It's likely that no one in the stands noticed Aybar's absence. That day the buzz was all about Marlon Anderson, who hit an exhilarating inside-the-park home run against the Angels, with the Mets two out from defeat, to force extra innings. The Mets won, 5–3, in the tenth inning after Floyd's three-run home run rallied them from another deficit. Anderson, who took three stitches as a result of a collision with Angels catcher Jose Molina at the plate, had sent reliever Francisco Rodriguez's 3–1 offering into the right-centerfield gap. Centerfielder Steve Finley slid as he converged with right fielder Vladimir Guerrero. The ball bounced off Finley's thigh and ricocheted along the track to the corner.

It was an eventful 6–6 home stand against the Arizona Diamondbacks, San Francisco Giants, Astros, and Angels.

Against Arizona, Mike Cameron leaped at the wall in right-centerfield to snare Luis Gonzalez's shot. The only problem? It was never necessary for Cameron to jump for the ball, which landed much lower than he had anticipated. Although he did make the catch, he still drew ribbing from his teammates for the awkward-looking grab. The next day, to further mock the catch, someone even fashioned a white-tape outline of Cameron at the exact spot on the outfield wall. The artwork, which included a ball drawn below Cameron's glove, was removed after batting practice.

"I don't like it, and I don't think it's funny," snapped Cameron, whose pride in his fielding clearly prevented him from seeing the humor in the situation.

That night Cameron made a legitimate circus catch, grabbing Jose Cruz Jr.'s fly ball by reaching out while on the ground, after falling in the sixth inning. Pedro, who had been soaked in the first inning when the sprinklers accidentally went off, bowed to Cameron twice on the mound. The ace also pointed with his fingers at the right fielder with his signature gunslinger pose.

As for the white-tape-outline incident, Cameron changed his tune when he found out who had ordered the prank, which was carried out by Shea Stadium personnel. The culprit: Jeff Wilpon, the chief operating officer. Asked if his newfound humorous outlook on the incident resulted from learning who had masterminded it, Cameron initially said, "No." Then he amended the remark. "Maybe," he conceded.

DeJean didn't make it through the ensuing road trip to Oakland and Seattle. He was released June 20 to make room for Koo, who, it turned out, had bruised his left shoulder on the headfirst dive into the plate against the Yankees. In DeJean's final Mets appearance, he allowed four runs in two-thirds of an inning against the Mariners in the capper of a 1–5 West Coast swing.

Not that Graves ended up positively contributing on the mound. Unlike Koo, Graves at least made it to the end of the season. Like Koo, Graves contributed a comedic moment; actually, his friend Lachey did. While Lachey was appearing as a fill-in host for Regis Philbin on *Live with Regis and Kelly*, Kelly Ripa asked him if he planned to attend any sporting events while in New York. Lachey mentioned the Mets. When Ripa volunteered that she was friendly with Randolph, Lachey good-naturedly replied: "Why don't you tell your really good friend to give my really good friend more playing time?"

Pedro contributed much of the behind-the-scenes levity, always welcomed by his teammates. Outfielder Jeromy Burnitz had donated a bright orange suit to assistant trainer Mike Herbst when he was traded to the Los Angeles Dodgers in July 2003 for Victor Diaz. Pedro located it in a closet in a back room of the home clubhouse at Shea Stadium. The ace adopted it as the Mets' rally suit and wore it in the locker room for humor. The reintroduction of the brightly colored suit, which included a jacket several sizes too big for Pedro, coincided with the Mets winning back-to-back games against the Reds leading into the first Yankees series. (For the record, Burnitz thought it was fashionable.)

"Am I exciting or what?" Pedro asked before entering Randolph's office to show off the ensemble to the skipper.

His well-received goofiness aside, Pedro acted with class—behavior diametrically opposed to the dire off-season predictions that had stemmed from his diva reputation. When Pedro heard Don Burke, the beat writer from the Newark *Star-Ledger*, had a daughter graduating from college, he engaged him in a conversation about higher education, in particular the quality and cost of Massachusetts schools. Then, moments later, after the veteran reporter had initiated a conversation with a teammate of Pedro's elsewhere in the cramped clubhouse at Wrigley Field, Pedro tapped Burke on the shoulder and—unsolicited—handed him a baseball with a personalized message for his daughter, offering congratulations.

The one thing the engaging Pedro unfailingly hated talking about was the Yankees—at least, as the subject related to him. During that same series against the Chicago Cubs at Wrigley Field, as the buildup began for the Flushing installment of the Subway Series, Pedro declined to address the topic in any detail. He even invoked the name of bullpen catcher Dave Racaniello to make the point that he thought the meeting was no big deal, no matter what the media and fans thought. Pedro originally was not lined up to face the Yankees. But Tom Glavine leapfrogged him in the pitching order to maintain his preferred every-five-days work schedule and give Pedro an extra day of rest.

"I thought I ran away from all that crap that you guys write about. I thought when I left the Red Sox, it's over with," Pedro said playfully. "A game is a game and that's it. Tom Glavine against the Yankees. Racaniello against the Yankees. It's the same."

Pedro had even more distaste for discussing the second series against the Yankees—the one in the Bronx where he was supposed to oppose Mike Mussina—which began with him showing up only an hour before game time because of the van driver's snafu.

It was after a Yankees–Red Sox game at Fenway Park on September 24, 2004—after Pedro wilted in the eighth inning and Boston lost, 6–4—that he offered the now-immortal phrase: "What can I say? I just tip my hat and call the Yankees my daddy."

It did not matter that weeks later the Red Sox overcame historic odds, rallying from a three-games-to-none deficit to oust the Yankees in a best-of-seven American League Championship Series. *Who's your daddy?* chants followed Pedro no matter where he traveled from the moment he first uttered those words.

"I just had to go out there and compete and let you guys do the job," Pedro later explained about his reluctance to discuss his impending visit to Yankee Stadium. "To write twenty pages, you guys are going to put stuff that wasn't even crossing my mind. It was pressure I didn't need. As much as you guys think it's fun, guess what? The stadium was going to be sold out regardless."

Horwitz did not even want anyone approaching Pedro during the preceding series in Philadelphia—not that it stopped people from trying. Speaking in Spanish in the clubhouse, Pedro shouted to teammate Roberto Hernandez that he could not understand why people were consumed with Pedro versus the Yankees. It's not Beltran versus the Yankees, he reasoned. Nor was it Piazza versus the Yankees, though Pedro obviously had no awareness of the Piazza-versus-Roger Clemens buildups in recent years.

Of course, Pedro was wearing a gray, Spanish-language-version WHO'S YOUR DADDY? T-shirt at the time he was speaking with Hernandez, so he wasn't too distraught over the chants. The conversation did not last long anyway. Pedro was peeking at a College World Series game between Arizona State and Miami at the time. He switched to marveling that the ASU pitcher was wearing his No. 45.

The trip to the Bronx was far more welcome for Randolph, who played thirteen seasons in pinstripes and coached there another ten years. He was now returning as a manager for the first time. As the series approached, Randolph recalled throwing peanuts at Roy White—his future teammate—during the summer months of his youth, after getting free tickets for the left-field bleachers through a Con Edison program. He also opened up about his frustration with the Yankees brain trust and his belief that he never was earmarked to be Joe Torre's successor as manager, despite serving as his bench coach in 2004 and third-base coach beforehand. In true Mets form, Randolph even questioned why Clemens threw that bat shard in the direction of Piazza during the World Series in 2000.

"I still don't understand that explanation," Randolph said, referring to Clemens's claim that he was so emotional he didn't realize what he was doing.

Randolph, criticized for never managing in the minors, revealed that the Yankees once offered him the job as Triple-A Columbus skipper, which he declined. It was a "real bad offer," he said, that would have cost him $500,000 annual World Series checks.

"You might get lost in the shuffle, but take that shot," Randolph said, portraying the attitude of Yankees officials.

Said Randolph: "My mama didn't raise no fool. I'm like, 'I'll stick it out.'"

Randolph relished his return to Yankee Stadium in a visiting uniform. He recalled his average was .400 in the Bronx as an opponent, which a call to the Elias Sports Bureau verified as dead-on accurate.

Outside, by the dugout in Philadelphia that same day, Duquette was musing about how the Mets–Yankees rivalry was not as much of a grudge match for the front-office executives as for the fans, George Steinbrenner and Horwitz aside. The Yankees had the Red Sox to worry about. The Mets, two games under .500 and in last place in the National League East when the second series arrived, had their entire division to overtake.

Duquette and Yankees general manager Brian Cashman actually had an excellent rapport.

"We always had a good relationship and would kid each other," Duquette said. "We had similar personalities. I always used to try to put pressure on him by saying that they were always the favored ones—'We're just the underdog. Let us win a game.'"

During Duquette's lone winter as Mets general manager, he and Cashman were the featured speakers at Ed Randall's Bat for the Cure charity fund-raiser to combat prostate cancer. There the duo remembered a conversation they once had about Duquette's in-season trade of closer Armando Benitez to Cashman after Benitez had several high-profile meltdowns on the mound. The Mets received Jason Anderson, Ryan Bicondoa, and Anderson Garcia in the deal—no great bounty.

"You were smarter than me," Cashman told Duquette. "You traded him to me."

"No, you were smarter than me," Duquette replied. "It took you two weeks to figure out what it took us two years [to realize]."

True enough; Cashman had flipped Benitez to the Mariners for reliever Jeff Nelson less than three weeks after acquiring him. In nine shaky games as a Yankee, Benitez allowed eight hits and six walks in nine and one-third innings.

Early in the 2005 season, Mets fans were gloating as the Yankees struggled out of the gate with an 11–19 record. But Floyd always chuckled when he saw the tabloid headlines or heard of the talk-radio chatter decrying the end of the Yankees' dominance. Floyd on more than one occasion in the Mets clubhouse noted how, when all was said and done, the Yankees would be back atop their American League East perch. Sure enough, the Yankees had moved over .500 by the time the Mets visited the Bronx, even if they entered the series coming off a pair of ugly losses to the Tampa Bay Devil Rays.

The Yankees still dominated the media attention in the city, even if it required events such as Johnson shoving a CBS cameraman to bump the Mets' impending introduction of Beltran from coveted placement on the tabloid covers.

Another example of the Yankees' uncanny ability to steal the spotlight had occurred on April 26. The two teams rarely played host to opponents on the same day, with Major League Baseball generally scheduling one team for an out-of-town game and the other at home. But here they were, on this early season day—the Mets entertaining the Braves, and the Yankees playing host to the Angels.

A classic Pedro–John Smoltz matchup had actually driven a handful of the city's premier columnists to attend the Shea Stadium game. Well, for a few innings at least. When word filtered to Flushing that Alex Rodriguez had hit three home runs in the Bronx, the *Daily News*'s Mike Lupica, the *New York Times*'s Jack Curry, and Newark *Star-Ledger*'s Dan Graziano all abandoned Flushing to chronicle A-Rod's feat.

Of course, New York hadn't always been quite so Yankees-dominated.

"A lot of people forget it was a National League town," Duquette said. "We still think that there's a National League slant to it. It's hard when you're going

*Carlos Beltran,* right, *at a spring-training press conference, signed a seven-year, $119 million contract with the Mets, then signed autographs in Port St. Lucie, Florida,* below. *The import received his share of jeers in Flushing, however, as he struggled during his inaugural season as a Met.* PHOTOS COURTESY OF GARY I. ROTHSTEIN.

*Pedro Martinez always was good for zany antics to keep the mood light. Here the ace borrows the head from a batting-practice dummy and balances it on his own noggin.* PHOTO COURTESY OF HOWARD SIMMONS/DAILY NEWS.

*When the infield sprinklers unexpectedly went off during the first inning of the Mets' June 2 game against the Diamondbacks at Shea Stadium, Pedro Martinez didn't seem to mind. The ace got soaked, then earned the win by limiting Arizona to one run and five hits in eight innings.* PHOTO COURTESY OF HOWARD SIMMONS/DAILY NEWS.

*Pedro Martinez points to the sky to celebrate his success in Flushing.*

PHOTO COURTESY OF HOWARD
SIMMONS/DAILY NEWS.

*Pedro Martinez kept head trainer Ray Ramirez (left) busy. The ace battled through hip, back, and foot injuries while logging 217 innings in 2005.*

PHOTO COURTESY OF GARY I.
ROTHSTEIN.

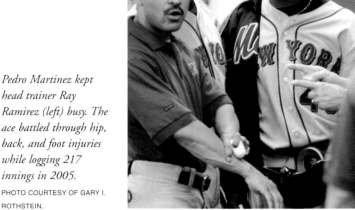

*A newly married Mike Piazza reported to spring training with a beard, but first-year manager Willie Randolph's new list of standards quickly resulted in a shave.* PHOTO COURTESY OF GARY I. ROTHSTEIN.

*Mets GM Omar Minaya (left) created a stir with his winter signings of Pedro Martinez and Carlos Beltran, but his Atlanta counterpart, John Schuerholz, traded for Tim Hudson and the Braves earned their 14th straight division title.* PHOTO COURTESY OF GARY I. ROTHSTEIN.

*Cliff Floyd (30) greets teammate Chris Woodward at home plate after Woodward's two-run homer staked the Mets to a 2-0 lead en route to a 10-6 win against the Cincinnati Reds on May 18. Floyd heard chants of "MVP, MVP" at Shea Stadium during the season.*

PHOTO COURTESY OF SUZIE O'ROURKE.

*Mike Cameron smiled during spring training, but he wasn't comfortable with the shift to right field to accommodate Carlos Beltran.*

PHOTO COURTESY OF SUZIE O'ROURKE.

*Carlos Beltran (left) and Mike Cameron had a horrific collision August 11 while diving for David Ross's sinking line drive at San Diego's PETCO Park. Cameron suffered multiple facial fractures, spent six days in the intensive-care unit at Scripps Clinic in La Jolla, California, and did not return during the 2005 season.* PHOTO COURTESY OF LENNY IGNELZI/ASSOCIATED PRESS.

*First-year manager Willie Randolph loved to be involved with his team by throwing batting practice. He also relished maintaining an even keel, which served the streaky Mets well as they battled for him into late September.* PHOTO COURTESY OF GARY I. ROTHSTEIN.

*Shortstop Jose Reyes (left) and left fielder Cliff Floyd had experienced a litany of injuries through-out their careers. But both stayed healthy in 2005, missing only a combined thirteen games.*
PHOTO COURTESY OF GARY I. ROTHSTEIN.

*Third baseman David Wright had a banner first full season in the big leagues. The twenty-two-year-old emerging star batted .306 with 27 homers and 102 RBI.* PHOTO COURTESY OF SUZIE O'ROURKE.

The Mets were so high on Kazuo Matsui they moved Jose Reyes from shortstop to sign him out of Japan. In 2005, it was Matsui who was banished to second base, then into manager Willie Randolph's doghouse because of a lack of production and injuries. PHOTO COURTESY OF GARY I. ROTHSTEIN.

Omar Minaya's infatuation with Red Sox slugger Manny Ramirez was no secret. But Mets brass got a little queasy when this in-house ad concept inadvertently got circulated and was obtained by the Daily News in November 2005. Ramirez had not been traded by Boston.

through the success the Yankees have had to remember back to the late '80s when the Mets really owned the town."

When he stopped by the Mets' January promotional caravan in Manhattan, a month after signing, Pedro had announced that he did not plan for New York to be Yankees-consumed for much longer. And after his harrowing traffic experience, he had his chance to help foster a change in his first appearance at Yankee Stadium since pitching in relief in Game 7 of the American League Championship Series, when the Red Sox had completed their improbable comeback.

Leadoff batter Derek Jeter greeted Pedro with a home run to open the bottom of the first inning, eliciting a predictable response in the Bronx. But Pedro got Robinson Cano to pop out on the next pitch and allowed only one more run, on an RBI single by A-Rod in the third inning. Pedro's outing ended when Beltran made a stellar grab to complete the eighth inning and preserve the Mets' 5–2 lead, the back of the centerfielder's head slamming into the wall as he caught Hideki Matsui's shot. Beltran's hat popped off as he made contact and he slumped to the ground. Pedro kept his right fist raised in celebration after the catch and waited for Beltran to trot in from his position before entering the dugout. Given that Pedro was on the mound, Beltran also homered. After an anxious ninth inning that included Tino Martinez's two-run home run against Looper, the Mets completed a 6–4 series-opening win.

"Coming to Yankee Stadium, I guess people have taken it—including you guys, members of the media—more personally than anything else," Pedro said. "I guess I attract a little bit more fans. I attract a lot of attention from you guys. And I don't understand why. I've done my job, I've failed. I'm not afraid to do either one. And I'm gonna be just me."

The Mets had the upper hand the next day, with the Yankees forced to again start rookie left-hander Sean Henn, who was pressed into duty because of Kevin Brown's back ailment. Floyd greeted Henn with a two-run home run in the first inning, then another two-run shot in the fifth inning to give the All-Star-worthy Floyd twenty long balls for the season and three in two games in the Bronx.

"Hitting after him, I'm getting an inferiority complex," said Piazza, who had started to be de-emphasized in the lineup.

Glavine, who had not won since June 4, limited the Yankees to two runs in six innings to earn the victory. Wright, who created a buzz before the game by showing up with a buzz cut, also homered as the Mets routed the Yankees, 10–3.

"We kind of lost being the best-looking corner guys in the big leagues when you did that," first baseman Doug Mientkiewicz kidded Wright.

Said Wright several weeks later: "I told you from day one, I can't wait for my hair to grow back. I didn't think it would take this long."

Incredibly, the Mets and Yankees had identical 37–37 records entering the finale, where the Mets could win the season series for the second straight year and somehow finish a four-stop trip at 6–6 after the 1–5 start in Oakland and Seattle.

The final day started loosely, with Pedro leading the way. He broke up Randolph's pregame news conference—literally—with laughter. Pedro, scheduled to use the same room for a Sunday chapel service with teammates, mimicked the Mets manager's commercial with Yankees skipper Joe Torre for Subway restaurants that had been widely aired in New York.

"I've got a question! Are you going to finish it?" Pedro asked from the back of the room, referring to the interview session, not the sandwich that had been the butt of the joke in the commercial.

"I ate it already," Randolph replied.

The manager ended his news conference and then high-fived his ace as he left the interview room/sanctuary.

"That's pretty good, Pedro," Randolph said while exiting. "I like that. Next commercial, me and you."

The Mets came close to the sweep before suffering a heartbreaking 5–4 defeat as Looper had a streak of fourteen straight converted save opportunities snapped.

Nursing a one-run lead, Looper first lost pinch hitter Tino Martinez. The closer fell behind Martinez, who had belted the two-run home run against him Friday, 3–1. Martinez eventually fouled off two full-count pitches before Looper missed with a sinker.

"You can't walk the leadoff hitter," Looper said. "There's no excuse for that. . . . It's just like any other one-run game you come in; you just try to start with strike one and go from there. Unfortunately, I fell behind. He fouled off some tough pitches. He's been in this game a long time, and he's a very accomplished hitter. The last pitch—I yanked it, basically, and wasn't close to the zone. You have to try to make a pitch there, and I didn't make a pitch."

A-Rod doubled over the third-base bag for his fourth hit of the game and ninth of the series, pushing Martinez as the tying run to third base. Looper then intentionally walked Matsui to load the bases and bring up Jason Giambi, who had been 0-for-3. Looper, against whom lefties were hitting .310, tried burying a 1–1 split-finger fastball in the dirt, hoping to get a swing and miss. Giambi, instead, lined a base hit to the right-centerfield gap, all the way to the wall. Martinez scored. A-Rod scored. And the Yankees salvaged the finale of the series, rallying to beat the Mets.

Looper, a stand-up guy, offered an explanation at his locker after failing to record an out, but no excuses.

"At that point the margin for error is so small, I was trying to do everything I could. I just left it up a little bit. All he has to do is get the bat on the ball, and he did," Looper said. "Basically I cost us the game today. We should have won the game. When you have a one-run lead going to the ninth inning with your closer on the mound, you've got to win the game."

Looper's teammates defended him.

"The only people who don't blow any games are those guys who are not in that position," said Hernandez, who worked out of a bases-loaded jam in the eighth inning by getting Ruben Sierra on a flyout. "He saved fourteen in a row before that. It's not an easy job. Unfortunately, [Dodgers closer Eric] Gagne did that ridiculous streak. There aren't many Gagnes. Early in the year, Mr. Mariano [Rivera] over there had trouble. So what, are they going to release him, too? C'mon, you're human. You go through bumps in the road. I know I've been through many of them. You just have to get up off the canvas and come back and start another streak. Unfortunately for us, it's such a high-profile game because it's the Subway Series. Sometimes you try to make perfect pitches. Even I tried to make perfect pitches. You realize it's just a game."

Said Floyd: "Loop, we're going to ride him until the wheels fall off. We need him. He knows that."

The Mets obviously needed Pedro, too, so his health, particularly his balky hip, bore watching. By all accounts, Pedro had an All-Star first half. He just had no interest in attending the Midsummer Classic in Detroit.

Pedro was due to pitch the first-half finale in Pittsburgh against Kip Wells on July 10. His normal between-starts bullpen session would be two days later, the day of the All-Star Game, but Pedro said his side work is performed at less than 100 percent, at a level he would not want to compete at with World Series home-field advantage at stake. Pedro had been selected to play in six other All-Star

Games, but had pitched in only three, the last one in 1999 while with the Red Sox, when the game was played at Fenway Park in Boston. In '98, Pedro recalled, he did not pitch because David Wells was named the starting pitcher by Cleveland Indians manager Mike Hargrove. Pedro gladly would have deferred to Roger Clemens, for whom he had immense respect, but not for Wells.

The decision to skip the All-Star Game was made in Washington, D.C., during the series preceding the Mets' arrival in Pittsburgh.

Pedro professed it was better to decline his All-Star invitation than to attend without pitching. He consulted with general manager Omar Minaya and Jeff Wilpon, but maintained that the decision was left to him.

"If I couldn't pitch, it makes no sense for me to occupy that place," said Pedro, who was replaced by Phillies closer Billy Wagner.

Said Minaya: "When it's all said and done, it's about his health."

As Pedro prepared to leave the clubhouse in Washington after the Mets won the series finale, 3–2, to capture three of four games and cool off the wild-card-leading Nationals, the ace halted in his tracks. The television in the visitors' clubhouse was tuned to ESPN's *Around the Horn*, and as Pedro walked by, the segment happened to be about how it was Pedro's duty to represent the Mets and the National League in the All-Star Game. Pedro silently listened to the multiple columnists, including the *Boston Globe*'s Jackie MacMullan, bash him for not attending. After quietly digesting their diatribes, Pedro reiterated that it was essential to have Wagner actually *able* to pitch and assist the National League, rather than going himself purely for ceremonial purposes. Since the 2003 season, the opening games of the World Series had been awarded to the league that won the All-Star Game.

"Home-field advantage was huge for us last year," Pedro said, referring to the Red Sox playing host to Games 1 and 2 of the World Series against the St. Louis Cardinals en route to a sweep.

The Mets were upbeat when they arrived in Pittsburgh, which was evident in the clubhouse before the series opener, even if the room would turn morgue-silent later that night. When Floyd walked in wearing a dark sweater vest, Wright was all over him, ragging his schoolboy look. Chris Woodward chimed in, too.

"How'd you do on your exam?" Woodward asked.

The guffaws continued outside during batting practice, where the Mets always looked forward to seeing a woman who closely resembled Horwitz, the team's PR man. Mike Herbst, the assistant trainer, once had even had Horwitz and the woman pose for a photo, which he made into T-shirts that were widely distributed among the players. Howie Freiling, the quiet, mild-mannered scout who had been accused of "crashing the potty" in Tampa Bay, was there, too, and could chuckle about his new notoriety as he spoke with assistant general manager John Ricco.

But bad things always seemed to coincide with the Mets' visits to Pittsburgh. The previous September, after Art Howe decided to stay on as lame-duck manager—and with the Allegheny River that flows behind the right-field stands fourteen feet above normal and overflowing its banks, flooding the players' parking lot—the Mets blew a seven-run lead at PNC Park, only to survive for an 8–7 win in ten innings on Mike Cameron's sacrifice fly.

This time, Ricco's U.S. Airways flight from New York, which should have lasted just more than an hour, became an all-day travel ordeal. An air show in the region delayed the plane's landing, eventually leading to low fuel levels and a diverted landing in Akron, Ohio. A wing-flap problem then prevented it from taking off and completing the trip. Ricco eventually bused ninety minutes to Pittsburgh.

Then there was the series opener that night.

The Mets, bidding to move two games over .500 for the first time in nearly a month, took a 5–1 lead into the ninth inning. But after Aaron Heilman departed with two out in the ninth inning following a walk that loaded the bases, Looper could not close it out, despite having Tike Redman behind in the count, 0–2. Looper threw eleven straight fastballs to Redman, figuring the pinch hitter would be behind the offerings since he was coming off the bench. Of course, Redman saw so many of the same pitch, he got his timing down well enough to send the final pitch up the middle for a two-run single, cutting Pittsburgh's deficit to two runs. Floyd then misplayed Matt Lawton's otherwise game-ending flyout. The left fielder lost the baseball for an instant in the lights, then took a circuitous route, slid, and had the ball scoot behind him as the Pirates tied the score.

"I was doing what I thought I had to do to help us win," Floyd said. "It was a bad decision only because I didn't catch the ball. I feel the worst out of anybody about it."

The Mets lost, 6–5, in the tenth inning, when Humberto Cota plated Rob Mackowiak.

Mackowiak had no business reaching base to be in position to score the winning run. On Mackowiak's one-out squibber to second base, Miguel Cairo initially intended to flip the ball to Jose Offerman at first base. But Cairo glanced at Mackowiak heading down the first-base line, thought he needed to hurry, and instead fired an overhand throw past Offerman. When Cairo's throw hit a camera, Mackowiak was awarded second.

"You're done when you do that," Cairo said about glancing at Mackowiak. "I've got to make that play. There's no excuse. Just flip it."

Said a surly Offerman, who froze on the off-line throw, which he was helpless to reach: "I was ready for any throw that he makes. The fuckin' ball was too far from me. That's the only thing I can say."

The Mets displayed terrible baseball fundamentals during the final days of the first half, which Randolph suggested may have been the result of mental fatigue. Castro committed the week's latest base-running faux pas after helping the Mets push their lead to four runs in a two-run ninth inning. He stopped as he approached third base on pinch hitter Brian Daubach's double off the right-field wall, thinking coach Manny Acta was holding him up, even though Castro had started the play on second. Acta actually was holding *Cairo*, who began on first.

"My mistake," Castro said.

That capped a woeful week on the bases for the Mets. Beltran did not run out a pop-up and was the victim of a double play six days earlier when Delgado, the Marlins' first baseman, spotted the lack of hustle and intentionally let the baseball drop. In Washington, D.C., the Mets ran themselves out of an inning when, on a throw to the plate, the ball bounced off the runner (Wright), and Castro, who had just singled, was caught having rounded first base too far. Anderson was doubled off second base on a lineout to right field to end that inning. The next day, Piazza and Floyd were involved in a bizarre, inning-ending 9–2–4–2 double play that scored Beltran.

"We deserve what we got," Randolph said after the Mets lost to the Pirates in the opener. "It was just a tough loss. Just a tough loss. The series before that doesn't matter much. It's a game we should have won."

Randolph indicated Castro was due more playing time, with Piazza scheduled for increased rest to avoid overtaxing his thirty-six-year-old body. Castro merited the increased workload. Despite his difficulty on the bases, Castro nonetheless had his first Mets homer and produced a two-hit, two-RBI game for the second time in two starts on the trip in the Pittsburgh opener. Randolph proved he was serious about increasing Castro's playing time, too. In the series finale in Washington, Piazza had produced three hits and two RBI to beat the Nationals and was quite surprised he was not in the lineup in Pittsburgh. He would sit out two of three games in the series, even though a three-day All-Star break was coming up immediately afterward.

"Am I not in the lineup? Really?" Piazza asked when told by reporters before he checked the lineup card the day of the series opener. "That's cool. Is there a day game tomorrow?"

Told it was a night game, Piazza speculated that Randolph wanted to pair Victor Zambrano with Castro. Piazza caught all fifteen of Zambrano's previous starts. He also suggested the lack of an All-Star break for him might have contributed, since fans had voted him and Beltran to the game.

"He's the mad scientist. There's no rhyme, nor reason," Piazza good-naturedly said about Randolph.

The next day, Saturday in Pittsburgh, the Mets lost again, 11–4, courtesy of meltdowns by Graves and fellow reliever Heath Bell. Contributing to the ugliness, Floyd got spit on. He even left the sunflower seeds on his left elbow until he could show it to a security guard to prove it.

The incident happened in the seventh inning, when Floyd went to the left-field wall to pursue Jack Wilson's grand slam. The fan, wearing a backward Pirates hat, initially leaned over the wall and pointed at and taunted Floyd. When Floyd turned his back and was returning to his position, he was hit. He eventually identified the perpetrator to stadium personnel—at least, the one he *thought* was the perpetrator based on the verbal exchange.

"Of course, the coward did it when I turned my back, so I assume it was him," Floyd said. "I feel bad if I got the wrong guy, but I just assumed it was him. He was the one in my face."

Asked about what the fan said during the R-rated exchange, Floyd said with a laugh, "You can't print that," though he indicated it had no racial overtones.

Asked what he replied, Floyd said, "Aw, you can't print that."

Said Floyd: "I wasn't going to say anything, and then I was like, 'You know what? It's one thing if you curse me out and everything, I can deal with that. When you spit on me, I've got problems with you.'"

Floyd complimented security personnel, who swiftly ejected the fan.

"I was going to wipe it off, and I know he was going to ask me where it's at," Floyd said about the stadium guard who checked with him. "I was like, 'I might as well just keep the shit on my arm.' It was disgusting, looking at the sunflower-seed spit on my arm. He actually spit on me.

"For six innings here, it's great. You might have one guy here saying something, and rightfully so. They're fans, they can say whatever they want. But once the seventh inning comes, the beer sets in and whatever the hell else they're drinking, and it's bananas. . . . You have some idiots sometimes that want to get out of line and have too much alcohol and don't know when to stop. It's like [it's] their first beer."

Thankfully, Pedro won the final day before the break, limiting the Pirates to one run in seven innings in a 6–1 victory, to put the Mets at 44–44 entering the All-Star break. Of course, Beltran opened the scoring with a two-run home run in the first inning, his tenth homer of the season, and ninth in a Pedro-pitched game.

Beltran readily acknowledged he'd had an undesirable first half. Voted an All-Star, Beltran headed to Detroit having batted .266, with 44 RBI and four steals, in 316 at-bats.

"I'm looking forward to playing better baseball than I did in the first half," Beltran said.

Beltran, a strong second-half player, had history on his side. Entering 2005, he had a lifetime .272 first-half average and .298 second-half average. He now had health on his side, too. The quadriceps injury that had sidelined him for eight starts and hampered him for weeks afterward had seemingly healed. Beltran hit .317 with four doubles, a home run, and six RBI over his final ten games of the half.

"We need him to have a monster second half. That's the bottom line. And I'm pretty confident he'll do that," Randolph said. "I think he'll be a lot more comfortable in this environment and know how to handle the everyday stuff that goes on. He's starting to feel healthier."

Said Beltran: "I depend on my legs more than anything else. I couldn't do a lot of things. Now that I feel 100 percent, I'm looking forward to playing my game the way I want to, getting on base, stealing bases, and trying to help the team any way I can."

Pedro posted his tenth win in the first-half finale, putting him on pace for his third twenty-win season. He lowered his ERA to 2.72, fifth in the National

League. His 138 strikeouts also led the league. He raised his career strikeout total to 2,791—twelve behind the immortal Cy Young, for sixteenth on the all-time list.

"I'm feeling stronger, and I'm feeling healthy going into the second half," said Pedro, who intended to stay in New York over the three-day break. "So far I'm thanking God for that, not missing any starts."

Randolph suggested the Mets could be six or seven games over .500 with more crisp play during the first half, but he would not dwell on missed opportunities.

"If you ask me," Randolph said, "I think we should be in first place."

# "BELTRAN SUCKS"

THE FIRST CLEAR EVIDENCE THE RECEPTION would be hostile could be found outside Minute Maid Park.

At a sports bar known as The B.U.S., teeming with Houston Astros fans across Texas Avenue from the stadium, manager Joey Fink was peddling BELTRAN $UCK$ T-shirts at $15 a pop. Down the block, bartender Scott Dillworth and manager Rick Costello from Home Plate Bar & Grill were also hawking the merchandise.

Together they sold nearly a thousand shirts, though one cynic suggested they could have done even better by setting up operations in Flushing.

"If they're going to do good things with that money, I'll help them make more shirts," a seemingly unfazed Carlos Beltran professed.

Beltran had arrived in Houston via a trade on June 24, 2004, which cost the Astros closer Octavio Dotel. He proceeded to lead the organization to within a game of the World Series by smashing eight home runs against the Atlanta Braves and St. Louis Cardinals. Two of the home runs came in a winner-take-all Game 5 of the division series against the Braves, as clutch as those shots come. Yet somehow, Beltran came to be viewed as a greedy traitor when he departed as a free agent after the season, his postseason production having cemented a $119 million offer from the Mets.

What obligation did Beltran have to sign with the Astros? After all, he had been involuntarily traded to Houston by Kansas City Royals GM Allard Baird.

Still, in the *Houston Chronicle*, columnist Richard Justice prepped fans for Beltran's July 28 arrival for a four-game series between the Mets and Astros. Justice wrote:

*Did he lie? Sure, he did. He said he was about more than money. He wasn't. He said he wanted a place where he could be comfortable, where he could grow and win. He said money was one consideration, but not the consideration. In the end, it was about nothing except greenbacks. He hired an agent, Scott Boras, who believes money is pretty much the only thing that matters. Beltran might be realizing too late that he should have considered things other than money. He apparently wanted to play for the New York Yankees. He wanted to be in a clubhouse with Derek Jeter and Alex Rodriguez because their star power would have allowed him to fly under the radar screen. The Yankees weren't interested, and Beltran was forced to settle for the Mets.*

Though it fell on deaf ears, Beltran reiterated his position on the afternoon of the series opener: Money was not the determining factor in choosing the Mets over the Astros, who made a franchise-record $105 million offer. After playing in small-market Kansas City for six years, where the threat of being dealt escalated with each additional dollar he earned, Beltran maintained he wanted his first free-agent deal to include a blanket no-trade clause for the length of the contract. That way, Beltran reasoned, he would never have to worry about being uprooted against his will.

Beltran professed some uncertainty about what his reception would be like, though he speculated jeers would probably be forthcoming.

"I don't expect to get a standing ovation. I don't expect that at all," Beltran said. "No matter who you are, no matter what you did, no matter what you accomplished, what happened last year is in the past. I don't play anymore for the Houston Astros, so I'm guessing I'm going to be booed."

Beltran had no idea how venomous the jeers would be. Every time he came to the plate or touched the baseball in the field, fans lustily booed him; when they let up ever so slightly on the fourth day, he suggested it might have been out of boredom. The *Chronicle* reported that thirteen people were ejected during the opening game for transgressions that included excessive profanity. The newspaper found one fan who brought a fishing pole with a twenty-dollar bill attached and a sign that read HOW TO CATCH A BELTRAN (MONEY NOT TO SCALE).

"They must be pissed off, I guess," manager Willie Randolph said. "He must have really hurt their feelings. He hurt 'em bad, I guess. That's as bad as I've heard."

The fans were aggressive and persistent. When beat writers Lee Jenkins of the *New York Times* and Peter Abraham from the *Journal News* in Westchester described the intense reaction to Beltran's presence in less-than-flattering terms, a grassroots effort emerged to try to get the reporters' bosses to censure them. No such luck. The talented Jenkins, slated to be promoted, left the beat shortly afterward and took over as a sports feature writer. Abraham's wit continued uninterrupted in his newspaper, though he switched to the Yankees after the season.

As Beltran addressed reporters outside the visitors' clubhouse before the series opener, Jenkins, Abraham, and the rest of the New York media had their attention elsewhere and only caught the tail end of the centerfielder's pregame Q&A session.

For one thing, the trading deadline loomed in three days. And the Dallas-based ESPN radio affiliate was supposedly reporting the imminent trade of second baseman Alfonso Soriano to the Mets, with Mike Cameron and outfield prospect Lastings Milledge, the organization's 2003 first-round pick, headed to the Texas Rangers. The rumor proved to be unfounded, however, and amusing to Mets officials, who claimed to have not even spoken with their Rangers counterparts that day, though there *had* been recent dialogue. Of more pertinence was the hubbub created over Tom Verducci's midweek piece in *Sports Illustrated*, which reported Boston Red Sox slugger Manny Ramirez had requested a trade for at least the third time in four years. This time, it was because of displeasure with his lack of off-the-field privacy, presumably caused by living in Red Sox Nation.

Sox teammates dismissed the trade talk with a commonly uttered remark: *That's just Manny being Manny.*

No doubt, Ramirez had his quirks. A week before the trading deadline, he left his outfield position for a bathroom break inside the Green Monster while Red Sox pitching coach Dave Wallace visited Wade Miller on the mound. Ramirez returned to left field with a grin at the last instant as Miller was poised to deliver the next pitch. (If only the Green Monster had a urinal.) Within days of that incident, Ramirez balked at starting, despite the Red Sox lacking out-fielders once teammate Trot Nixon suffered a strained oblique muscle. Ramirez had been promised a day off before Nixon's injury.

Red Sox manager Terry Francona professed no knowledge of Ramirez's trade request while speaking with the team's beat writers during a series against the Tampa Bay Devil Rays in St. Petersburg, Florida.

"When was this—when he was pissing in the scoreboard?" Francona asked, according to *Boston Herald* baseball columnist Tony Massarotti. "I'm at a loss on that one. You guys can have fun with that one because I know it'll have some legs for a couple of days. So go ahead and knock yourselves out."

It most certainly did have legs—and validity. As the weekend approached, Red Sox CEO Larry Lucchino acknowledged Ramirez had shared his desire to depart with front-office brass. The Boston executive added that while comply-ing with Ramirez's trade request would be difficult because of the $64 million still owed to him through 2008, the organization would entertain offers. Mets and Red Sox officials had spoken intensely about Ramirez in December during the winter meetings, before the Mets had zeroed in on Pedro Martinez. And as the Mets prepared to open their series with the Astros, talks figured to reheat in the seventy-two hours before Sunday's 4 P.M. EDT non-waiver trading deadline.

In the meantime, a former Red Sox player's status as the Mets' first baseman drew the most immediate interest among New York reporters at Minute Maid Park. Mientkiewicz, who arrived in Houston with a .225 average, appeared to have lost his job, even if Randolph had made no formal declaration. The left-handed-hitting Mientkiewicz had sat only two games, both against southpaws, since returning July 16 from a stint on the disabled list to mend a right ham-string strain. But Randolph had inserted Marlon Anderson in the lineup at first base against right-hander Ezequiel Astacio that night. That didn't bode well for Mientkiewicz, considering the Mets were scheduled to face left-handers Wandy Rodriguez and Andy Pettitte the next two days.

"I don't make the lineup," Mientkiewicz responded when approached.

"Given the pitching matchups coming up, the lefties, do you read any-thing into it?" I asked.

"I don't make the lineup," Mientkiewicz repeated.

"Do you interpret it at all?" I asked.

Mientkiewicz only responded by exhaling, so Mark Hale from the *Post* asked: "Do you think you have Willie's confidence?"

"I don't make the lineup," Mientkiewicz said.

"What would the question have to be to get a different response?" Hale asked.

"I don't know if you're going to get one," the generally loose-lipped Mientkiewicz said.

"Let me ask this," I proposed. "You played against every right-hander since coming back. How do you think you did in that period of time?"

"Better," Mientkiewicz said, before taking a long pause. "But saying better, I should hope so, because I was pretty much awful," he added.

The previous year, Mientkiewicz had won a World Series championship with Boston. But he had played only sporadically down the stretch, as Francona used Kevin Millar more often at first base. Knowledge of that experience prompted Steve Popper from the *Record* of Bergen, New Jersey, to ask Mientkiewicz regarding the current situation: "Did you learn anything last year about how to go through it?"

"How to cope with being shitty?" Mientkiewicz replied. "I don't know if you cope with it. . . . You just know in your heart you can play this game."

Things had quickly soured for Mientkiewicz as a Met. At the end of spring training, when reliever Matt Ginter got traded to the Detroit Tigers, Mientkiewicz's bag mistakenly got shipped instead of Ginter's belongings. When he arrived in New York, Mientkiewicz's neighbors pestered him because his cats, one a miniature cheetah, apparently weren't legal as house pets in the state, though they were permissible in his home state of Florida.

A few hours after Mientkiewicz's exchange with reporters, when Pedro and Astacio faced off, Mientkiewicz was no longer quite so cranky. At numerous ballparks, including Shea Stadium, a "Kiss Cam" is featured once during the game between half-innings on the video board, during which fans are encouraged to give a peck to their significant others when they appear on camera. There's often a kicker at the end. This time, stadium personnel flashed infielder Chris Woodward and Mientkiewicz on the board at the end of the segment. Mientkiewicz played along in the dugout and reached to hug Woodward, who hastily retreated.

Anderson went 0-for-4 in Mientkiewicz's place. Woodward started at first base the next day, followed by Jose Offerman in the third game as Mientkiewicz remained on the bench.

With a 3–2 win in the series opener before the second-largest crowd of the season at Minute Maid Park, the Astros caught the Washington Nationals for the wild-card lead. The Mets, at 52–50, trailed both teams by three games and dropped into last place in the National League East, failing to capitalize on Pedro's solid start. It had been another miserable beginning to a road trip for the Mets, who arrived having lost two of three games to the downtrodden Colorado Rockies. The Mets had mustered only six runs in hitter-friendly, high-altitude Coors Field in their two defeats. Randolph had sensed they were swinging for the fences, deviating from a solid approach at the plate.

After Pedro's 117-pitch performance, a season high to that point, he described himself as exhausted and flat. He cited the Mets' hectic travel that week, which included three different time zones—Eastern (New York), Mountain (Denver), and Central (Houston). The ace, who had improved to 12–3 with a win against the Los Angeles Dodgers in his previous start, had a problem with his right foot, which he used when pushing off the mound. Mientkiewicz, wearing a microphone for Fox's nationally televised game between the Mets and Dodgers, had unintentionally outed Pedro's injury. The first baseman noted how he had to be more vigilant in getting to the bag because Pedro was having trouble covering due to the previously undisclosed injury.

Still, Pedro went eight innings against the Astros and left with the score tied at 2. In his final inning, he rescued Mike Cameron by stranding Craig Biggio at second base after the right fielder's one-out error. Cameron had dropped Biggio's fly ball while transferring it from the glove to his throwing hand. The Mets lost in the ninth inning as generally sturdy Roberto Hernandez, who emerged as closer Braden Looper's setup man, left a fastball over the plate, and Brad Ausmus doubled to right-centerfield to plate Orlando Palmeiro with the winning run.

Despite the team's loss, Pedro passed Cy Young for sixteenth on the all-time strikeout list by getting Morgan Ensberg looking in the fourth inning. The ace was in awe of the feat, and of the Hall of Famers whom he had started to pass in the record books on a routine basis at this stage of his career. Pedro recalled how during the previous August with the Red Sox, he had topped Sandy Koufax for fourth on the all-time list of ten-strikeout games with his ninety-eighth. That touched Pedro. He arrived at Dodgertown as a teenager and remembers feeling numb while sitting in his chair listening to Koufax during a clinic.

"When they mentioned Sandy Koufax, I was like, *Wow, Sandy,*" Pedro said. "I just thank God so much for having the opportunity to be mentioned with those names."

Pedro was similarly awestruck at the thought of the strikeout list and passing Cy Young—the namesake of the award annually given to each league's best pitcher, which Pedro had won three times.

"Cy Young," he said. "*Cy Young.* I just hope one of these days I'm mentioned with Roger Clemens or Nolan Ryan."

Pedro finished 2005 with 2,861 career strikeouts, fourteenth on the all-time list, though well behind Ryan's record 5,714 and Clemens's second-ranked 4,502.

To the delight of the hostile crowd, Beltran went 0-for-4 in his return to Minute Maid Park, reaching on an error, then grounding out to third base, flying out to centerfield, and grounding out to first base.

"I wasn't surprised," Beltran said about the extent of the jeers. "I was expecting what happened today. They just booed me. What can I do? What's in the past is in the past. I have to move on. It didn't hurt me. I tried to block it. You're going to hear everything they say because you can't block it. This happens every place. Being honest, I don't care. They can boo me, whatever they want."

During the game, Mets radio play-by-play announcer Gary Cohen thought he had spotted Beltran wearing earplugs to try to block the noise and asked his WPIX television counterparts to zoom in to get a look. Before Cohen received an answer, a colleague mentioned the possibility over the air. Pulled aside after his postgame interview with reporters and told of the suspicion, Beltran shook his head in disappointment and insisted he was not wearing them. It might not have been such a bad thing. When Bobby Bonilla got all the flak for wearing earplugs as a Met in 1992, it was to drown out the *home* crowd's booing.

Then again, the Baltimore Orioles' Rafael Palmeiro wore earplugs in Toronto a month after the Mets–Astros series, after Palmeiro's vehement, finger-waving spring-training denial of steroid use in testimony before a congressional committee, followed by a positive test. The earplugs only generated more unwanted attention. Palmeiro didn't play again during the 2005 season.

On Friday, the second day of the Mets–Astros series, there was news of a Mets acquisition. Team brass had quietly signed Wil Cordero to a minor-league contract. Cordero, thirty-three years old, had hit .118 in fifty-one at-bats before being released by the Nationals.

"*That's* our savior?" Hernandez joked, given that Soriano's name, and then Ramirez's, had been swirling around as possible acquisitions.

Cordero never made it to the big-league club.

Beltran had a minimal impact in the second game, going 1-for-3 with a walk and run scored. When Kris Benson surrendered home runs to Biggio, Lance Berkman, and Ensberg, the Astros beat the Mets, 5–2, behind six solid innings from Wandy Rodriguez. The Mets had trouble with rookie pitchers all season. To that point, Atlanta's Kyle Davies, Arizona's Brad Halsey, Oakland's Joe Blanton, Colorado's Jeff Francis, and Rodriguez had beaten them. Pittsburgh's Zach Duke would later join that list.

The Mets continued to sputter in the third game. Southpaws Tom Glavine and Pettitte took a scoreless duel into the seventh inning, when Glavine surrendered a first-pitch home run to Jason Lane, who guessed curveball, Glavine's third-best pitch. The Mets could not touch Pettitte and dropped to .500 with a 2–0 loss, five games behind Houston in the wild-card standings. Beltran went 0-for-4. He dropped to 1-for-11 in the series and 3-for-24 through six games of the road trip.

"I feel good. I feel healthy," Beltran said. "Nothing seems to go my way. Sometimes you don't have an explanation."

Randolph wished Beltran had used the jeers as fuel, motivation for a big weekend. That's how Randolph approached similarly hostile environments during his eighteen seasons as a major-league second baseman. Randolph went 9-for-15 with five walks against the Yankees, his longtime former employer, in five games in the Bronx as a Milwaukee Brewer in 1991.

"I loved when people booed me and got on my case," Randolph said. "Send 'em home mad. That's the way I like to look at it. Send 'em home mad."

Randolph had come to realize that Beltran's personality was more stoic than demonstrative, his emotions guarded rather than worn on the sleeve of his No. 15 Mets jersey. Not that it meant the Mets' seven-year union with Beltran would be a bust. Bernie Williams, New York's other centerfielder, was similarly reserved, Randolph noted. Williams thrived as a Yankee, earning five All-Star selections, four Gold Gloves, and four World Series titles.

"He's had the same type of demeanor for a long time," Randolph said about Beltran. "If it works for him, that's fine. I'd be totally different, but that's just me. I just want production. I don't really care how a guy handles himself. Would I like to see something different? Yeah. I like to see all my guys get after it."

The big news was being made back in Flushing, where team brass was discussing a blockbuster deal that would bring Ramirez—plus Devil Rays closer Danys Baez and infielder Julio Lugo—to the Mets. The trade would ship Cameron and pitcher Aaron Heilman from the Mets and outfielder Aubrey Huff from the Devil Rays to Boston, while delivering elite prospects from the Mets and Red Sox to Tampa Bay. The Mets had been engaged in separate talks with the organizations, but general manager Omar Minaya realized Red Sox GM Theo Epstein was requesting the same players as the Devil Rays. Epstein came clean that he intended to flip the Mets' prospects to Tampa Bay for Huff, and the talks merged.

With those talks raging, the delicate topic of the ethnic composition of the Mets quietly resurfaced among some players, after remaining mostly dormant inside the clubhouse since spring training. In the weeks preceding the road trip, Puerto Rican relievers Juan Padilla and Jose Santiago had been promoted, replacing native Californians Royce Ring and Heath Bell in the bullpen. Coupled with Ramirez and Lugo hailing from the Dominican Republic and Baez a defector from Cuba, a handful of players were drawing the conclusion that maybe Minaya really *did* want an overwhelmingly Hispanic clubhouse. One player suggested the ultimate composition of the team would be up-and-coming third baseman David Wright and twenty-four Hispanic players.

Minaya had always refuted the assertion that he was assembling a Hispanic clubhouse, and during spring training, he'd even gone so far as to say the *Los Mets* label bordered on racism.

In the end, the roster makeup proved to be about talent, just as Minaya had maintained. Bell would use the minor-league stint to dust off a split-finger fastball he had thrown early in his minor-league career, which gave him a viable third pitch. He would eventually call the demotion to Triple-A Norfolk invaluable. Padilla became one of the Mets' best relievers, finishing the season with a 3–1 record, 1.49 ERA, and a save.

At the time, with the trade rumblings swirling, Cameron wasn't handling the situation particularly well emotionally. In spring training, Cameron had pulled the plug on Minaya's trade talks regarding him because of the distraction it was creating, plus his genuine desire to stay a Met—even if it had to be in right field to accommodate Beltran. Now he was helpless to halt the dialogue.

"Don't even come over here with that," he instructed reporters in the clubhouse who were looking for a comment about his situation. "I didn't get any sleep last night. I'm serious. I can't even handle it anymore."

"We make each other go," said left fielder Cliff Floyd, Cameron's best friend on the team. "I just told him, 'These situations happen.' He understands that. He's not going to 'trip.'"

Cameron's difficulty coping was understandable. And Floyd was particularly in tune with Cameron's emotions, both because of their close relationship and his own history of being traded. Three years earlier, Minaya—then Montreal Expos general manager—acquired and dealt Floyd in a nineteen-day span. The latter trade—to the Red Sox for South Korean pitchers Sun-Woo Kim and Seung Song—occurred even though Expos manager Frank Robinson had assured Floyd earlier in the day that he was staying put. Floyd's girlfriend Maryanne had just decorated their new apartment in Montreal, down to the pillows and sheets. A Mercedes had just arrived from a dealership, too.

Needless to say, they lived in a hotel in Boston after the second trade.

"Oh, man. You don't understand," Floyd recalled about Maryanne's reaction when he broke the news they weren't staying in Montreal. "You have no clue. She did everything. She unpacked. She got groceries. She was cooking. I got home, I was like, 'Well, you can't be mad at me. Be mad at whoever else you want to be mad at, but we got traded again.' She just sulked. If I had two kids, she would have had a nervous breakdown. Luckily she wasn't pregnant and she was able to do a lot of it pretty easy. But it was stressful. It was stressful as hell. I mean, she was struggling."

The couple had their first child the following year, daughter Bria Shae, after Floyd signed a four-year, $26 million contract with the Mets.

With Ramirez, a major stumbling block figured to be the $64 million still owed to him over three and a half seasons, though in the end it wasn't an impediment. The money issue certainly had not stopped Pedro from gleefully endorsing the acquisition of his former Red Sox teammate, who hailed from Washington Heights at the northern edge of Manhattan.

"I think it would be a great fit," said Pedro, who went so far as to volunteer to act as a liaison between Ramirez and Mets beat writers to avoid a repeat of any difficulties with the Boston press.

During the first four months of the season, there were some weeks when Pedro and Ramirez spoke three times, with the slugger calling Pedro to share a joke and then passing his cell phone around the Red Sox clubhouse to David Ortiz and Pedro's other former teammates. Other weeks, Pedro and Ramirez did not speak at all. Pedro chuckled while revealing that Ramirez's voice-mail message was the slugger coughing. He noted how Ramirez's wife Juliana had been uncomfortable in Boston and was a driving force behind his dissatisfaction there.

Pedro also expressed amusement at chatter on Boston sports radio station WEEI, which suggested that the ace was the one planting the bug in Ramirez's ear to push for a trade.

"I'm the one dragging him over here? Shocker!" Pedro declared.

The early driving force behind the spirited discussions between Mets and Red Sox officials had been Lucchino, the Red Sox CEO, who had been incensed by Ramirez's behavior.

In addition to the antics leading up to the trading deadline, Ramirez had once offended Red Sox Nation by calling in sick (with a throat infection) to a series against the Yankees. Even though he was under the weather, he still managed to meet Yankees infielder Enrique Wilson at the Ritz-Carlton in Boston, where the slugger had a condominium and the Yankees were staying. The initial reports of the Saturday-night rendezvous in August 2003 had misidentified Randolph, then the Yankees' third-base coach, as Ramirez's social partner and claimed the setting was the hotel bar. Randolph had replied at the time: "We're not that tight." Two months after that incident, after Ramirez had also declared he would like to finish his career as a Yankee—blasphemy in Beantown—Red Sox executives had placed him on irrevocable waivers, inviting any team to take over the five years and daunting $104 million that remained on his contract at the end of the '03 season. Not one had interest.

Lucchino's current willingness to part with Ramirez had created a division within the Red Sox hierarchy. Other front-office personnel were against trading Ramirez, at least during the season, realizing that this move would initiate a need to revamp the team. American League rivals, including the Yankees, were ecstatic at the prospect of the feared one-two punch of Ortiz and Ramirez being separated. Opponents would then be able to pitch around Ortiz. Pedro believed Ortiz might be the toughest out in baseball with the game on the line and Ramirez behind him, and that Ortiz was the deserving recipient of the 2005 American League MVP Award that ultimately went to Alex Rodriguez. Cameron and Huff might have substituted two bats for Ramirez's one, but neither had the intimidation factor Ramirez instilled.

Randolph, presented with the prospect of managing Ramirez, indicated he expected no trouble keeping him in line should the trade occur. He had expressed the same confidence during the winter amid all the chatter about how a first-year manager would possibly be able to handle Pedro's antics, which now seemed a non-issue.

"If Manny were playing with me, that'd be fine," Randolph said. "Just like Pedro is fine."

Said Pedro: "He's a little cuckoo when he's playing in the outfield and the things he's going to do. That's Manny. A very different person. But Manny is a great, great person—a great human being. Manny is just different."

Ramirez entered the trading-deadline weekend atop the American League in home runs (28) and RBI (92), the perfect power infusion to any lineup. In the four full seasons he had played in Boston, he had averaged hitting .321 with 39 home runs and 117 RBI per year. And while his erratic fielding often forced the Red Sox to go with late-game replacements, his bat more than made up for any lapses with the glove. Ramirez's best run-producing season in Boston came in 2004 when he helped the Red Sox win their first championship in eighty-six years, after the dramatic comeback from three games down in the American League Championship Series, to oust the Evil Empire, the moniker Lucchino applied to the Yankees. Ramirez batted .308 with 43 home runs and 130 RBI during the '04 regular season. He was named World Series MVP after he hit .412 against the Cardinals.

"I hope he loosens up," Pedro said. "New York is his hometown. Just respect his family."

Ramirez was booed during each plate appearance that Friday night at Fenway Park in what was an 0-for-3 performance. He wasn't available to the media after the game and did not start Saturday or Sunday.

The Mets planned to use Lugo at second base, where Kazuo Matsui had faltered. Matsui had been on the disabled list since suffering a bruised knee in Oakland on June 16, on Jason Kendall's game-ending takeout slide. He had finally appeared in a rehab game with the Gulf Coast League Mets, but Randolph offered no indication he would play much upon returning, given his .234 average at the time. Asked about Matsui's timetable, the manager even suggested there was no urgency coming back. Regardless of Lugo's addition, Miguel Cairo had pretty much leapfrogged Matsui on the depth chart anyway.

Baez would shore up the back end of the bullpen, likely supplanting Looper as closer. It would give the Mets a serviceable relief triumvirate with Hernandez. Looper had converted twenty-two of twenty-six save chances to that point, but three of the blown saves had translated to devastating defeats—on Opening Day, to cost Pedro a win in his Mets debut against the Cincinnati Reds; at Yankee Stadium, with the Mets in position to sweep; and in Pittsburgh, when he combined with Heilman to blow a four-run lead with two out in the ninth inning.

"Hey guys, if you're talking, you have a chance to get something done," Minaya said on a conference call with reporters, speaking generally about the organization's prospects for making a trade. "I will tell you that my staff, we are working together here, and we plan to stay on the phones all the way through the end of the trading deadline. I'm open to anything, but I will tell you, what we acquire has to be better than what we have right now. Our club is a funny team. Our club can play very good at times and can go out and play like the first two games in Colorado. I think it's fair to say we've got to get more offense and we have to try to improve the pitching, meaning the bullpen in general."

Minaya added that the Mets, like other buyers, were hamstrung by the lack of "difference-makers" on the market. So many teams were within striking distance of a playoff spot and not inclined to dismantle. And the few sellers had not made many players available—at least without trying to gouge the suitor. With baseball attendance thriving and organizations financially healthy, general managers were not particularly desperate to unload contracts, as had been the case in the past.

The morning of the trading deadline, a review of the National League standings showed the Mets in last place in the East at .500, and still in buying mode. Everyone in the West was under .500, which meant virtually everyone remained in the race, with the exception of the Rockies at fourteen and a half games back. Only the Pittsburgh Pirates and Reds were double-digits behind the Astros in the wild-card race among Central teams. In the American League, only five teams had sub-.500 records—Tampa Bay, Kansas City, the Baltimore Orioles, the Detroit Tigers, and the Seattle Mariners.

At 7 A.M. that Sunday, Anderson was thinking about spiritual matters, not about potential trades. He took the slumping Beltran to the Compaq Center, the old home of the National Basketball Association's Houston Rockets, for church services. The facility had just received $75 million in renovations to transition from a sports venue to a house of worship. Anderson lives in nearby Sugarland, Texas. Two weeks earlier, his Lakewood Church congregation, led by televangelist Joel Osteen, had moved into the 16,000-seat former basketball arena, which the church had no trouble filling for its televised, nondenominational Christian services.

Osteen's 320-page book, *Your Best Life Now: 7 Steps to Living at Your Full Potential*, which had sold nearly three million copies, had been widely circulated in the Mets' clubhouse, in both English and Spanish versions. Chapters dealt with developing a healthy self-image, discovering the power of your thoughts and words, letting go of the past, finding strength through adversity, and choosing to be happy.

Anderson had emerged as one of the team's leaders from a spiritual perspective.

Late in spring training, he had presented Pedro with a T-shirt that had the slogan ¿QUIÉN ES TU PADRE? across the front. Translation: "Who's your daddy?" On the back it read: JESUS.

Given that Pedro had created a storm by calling the Yankees his daddy the previous season, leading to *Who's your daddy?* chants at Yankee Stadium and elsewhere, the T-shirts were seen as hilarious, as well as meaningful from a religious perspective. They spread throughout the clubhouse in both English and Spanish versions once a shipment arrived during the season. Anderson's friend and former University of South Alabama baseball teammate Hugh Lopes, founder of A More Excellent Way Ministries, had been using the saying, with the Jesus kicker, well before Pedro made the "Who's your daddy?" part famous on a national stage. Lopes had started printing the T-shirts to raise money for faith-based projects in Anderson and his native Mobile, Alabama.

The garment quickly outnumbered two fading favorites whose suppliers were no longer with the team. Reliever John Franco's orange NEW YORK CITY DEPARTMENT OF SANITATION T-shirts had been widely worn at one point. Second baseman Danny Garcia's SLUMP BUSTER T-shirts—which celebrated the not-so-wholesome ritual of sleeping with an overweight woman to snap out of struggles at the plate—had also made the rounds in some circles and had been particularly popular among the minor-leaguers.

Now, at the service, Anderson and Beltran heard an all-too-appropriate sermon, given the centerfielder's struggles amid the hostile reception in Houston: *Always expect good things to happen.*

"You may be going through some tough times," Osteen preached. "You think, 'Man, I'm so far off plan.' But you need to know that God can turn any situation around. You may have made some mistakes in the past, but today can be a time of new beginning. The great thing about God is, He'll take what the enemy meant for evil, and if we'll keep the right attitude and keep our trust in Him, He will use it in the end to our advantage. So there's always hope with our God. I always like to remind you this: God works where there's an attitude of faith. God has all the power in the world, but He's not going to do you any good if you're negative and discouraged and focused on your problems and complaining. You know what? That just negates God's power. So that's why I like to challenge you every day to be a believer and not a doubter. . . .

"He said, 'In life you're going to have difficulties. But be of good cheer, for I have overcome the world.' The modern-day Texas translation is: Don't lose your joy. Keep a smile on your face. Keep an attitude of faith no matter what comes your way. Some of you today, you're discouraged and you're too focused on what's wrong in your life. As I said earlier, focus on what's right in your life. You may have a long way to go, but you can look back and see how far God's already brought you."

The message seemed to perfectly suit Beltran's situation.

"It just worked out that way," Anderson said. "Believe me, he didn't change his sermon. That's the whole power. That's how God works. There's nobody getting together and putting everything together. I always tell people, 'He seems to give you the word that you need at the time that you need it.'

"Carlos is a good guy. He understands the game. He understands life. He understands what people there thought about him, the reason why. He knows what he believes in. He knows he's going to go out every day to do the job wherever he's at, whatever the circumstance. That's the kind of person he is."

For a team teetering at .500 and due to face Roy Oswalt in the finale, the Mets were loose that morning in the hours leading up to the trading deadline, Cameron excluded. One Met privately confessed, "We're done," referring to the postseason chances without an upgrade to the lineup, but the atmosphere was overwhelmingly light.

Catcher/prankster Ramon Castro grabbed a watermelon from the players' lounge. Beltran, an unlikely coconspirator given his reserved nature, drew a face on it using a marker. Castro then placed it in Floyd's locker, with the left fielder's hat on top. Minutes later, Floyd entered the clubhouse. Knowing Castro's reputation for playful mischief, though with no direct evidence he was the culprit, Floyd walked across the room and tossed the watermelon at Castro, causing it to splatter on the floor amid chuckles. A clubhouse attendant quickly cleaned up the mess.

"I can't believe he threw it," Wright said.

Said Floyd: "Well, I figured it's Castro if I had to take one guess."

During the game, which began less than two hours before the trading deadline, Floyd confessed to continually peeking at the clock. He wondered at what point Cameron would be removed, confirming that a deal had been struck. When the clock flipped from 2:59 to 3:00 at Minute Maid Park, the trading deadline in the Central Time Zone, the Mets were wrapping up an inning in the field. Cameron had not been pulled from the game, which meant he was happily staying a Met and his stressful weekend was over.

"You're all right now," Glavine told Cameron once he'd reached the dugout. "You can relax a little bit."

Cameron's mind had been racing all over the place with the prospect of being traded. He was thinking how he would need to collect his belongings on Monday's Red Sox off-day before joining his new teammates for a series at Fenway Park against the Royals.

"I was like, 'Damn, I've got to go get my clothes. Where am I going to be?' Just certain things that come to your mind," Cameron said. "You get traded in the middle of the season, you have to figure out what you're going to do. You know you can play. There's other things in your environment and your surroundings that could be a hindrance. I had to be realistic about it. There was a good possibility something could have happened. I had to put myself in a position where I wouldn't be totally surprised by it. I didn't really stress it too much. It was only like one day. Maybe that day it was like, 'This could possibly happen.'"

In the end, it was Tampa Bay general manager Chuck LaMar who seemed to save Cameron, but again screw the Mets. LaMar had swiped flame-throwing left-handed pitching prospect Scott Kazmir from the Mets for Victor Zambrano at the previous year's trading deadline. This time, Red Sox brass might have hastily pulled the trigger and handed Ramirez to the Mets (before fully realizing the consequences) had LaMar not stalled the negotiations, while trying to pillage both teams of all of their elite prospects—pitcher Yusmeiro Petit and Milledge from the Mets and shortstop Hanley Ramirez, pitcher Anibal Sanchez, and catcher Kelly Shoppach from the Red Sox.

LaMar got his comeuppance after the season, when he was fired once Stuart Sternberg took over as Tampa Bay's principal owner.

The Mets went without a July trade for the first time since 1997, when Steve Phillips succeeded Joe McIlvaine as general manager two weeks before the deadline. They did not even engage in any substantive discussions on Sunday. Other potential deals, such as for Pirates first baseman Daryle Ward, never got too serious during the final weekend.

"I knew he wasn't going to come," Pedro said about Ramirez. "It was too much we had to give away to get a Manny. I knew that it was going to be difficult, and the Red Sox would be stupid to actually do something like that in the middle of the season for a guy so popular in the clubhouse. David (Ortiz) was, like, really upset. David was already thinking differently if Manny wasn't there. But they knew what to do. Manny pretty much told them they were going to make a mistake. You could see David doesn't get pitched if Manny's not there. It would be the same way if you kept Manny and let David go. Manny wouldn't be pitched. Those two guys, if they don't hit, Boston is done. The other guys are not, like, big threats."

Floyd was relieved not to lose Cameron. From a team chemistry perspective, the Mets were fortunate, too. While Pedro and Castro's antics maintained a certain level of energy in the clubhouse, Cameron rivaled them as an emotional leader. Actually, as an everyday player he had even more ability to have an impact.

"When you lean on somebody as much as I lean on him, you need those dudes to push you," Floyd said. "It would have been devastating to me. I know it would have been devastating to a lot of other guys in here had he left. . . . Of course, having Manny around would have been outstanding. If we had him and kept Cam, and the commissioner changed the rule to the DH, it would be sweet."

A year after standout players—including Nomar Garciaparra, Orlando Cabrera, Paul Lo Duca, Steve Finley, and Benson—changed addresses at the trading deadline, the 2005 deadline proved all hype and little headline-grabbing action. More noteworthy was which players rumored to be dealt actually stayed put: Florida Marlins pitcher A.J. Burnett and third baseman Mike Lowell, Soriano, and Ramirez.

The late-July action:

◆ Outfielder Matt Lawton went from Pittsburgh to the Chicago Cubs for outfielder Jody Gerut.

◆ Atlanta obtained reliever Kyle Farnsworth from Detroit for pitchers Roman Colon and Zach Miner.

◆ Seattle sent outfielder Randy Winn to the San Francisco Giants for catcher Yorvit Torrealba and pitcher Jesse Foppert, and sent pitcher Ron Villone to Florida for pitchers Yorman Bazardo and Mike Flannery.

◆ The San Diego Padres obtained catcher Miguel Olivo from the Mariners for catcher Miguel Ojeda and pitcher Nate Mateo, and obtained Chan Ho Park from the Rangers for outfielder Phil Nevin.

◆ Colorado acquired outfielder Larry Bigbie from Baltimore for outfielder Eric Byrnes.

The Red Sox made a trade, too. They obtained outfielder Jose Cruz Jr. from the Arizona Diamondbacks for minor-league shortstop Kenny Perez and pitcher Kyle Bono.

"I think you see throughout baseball today, there were no big, major names being traded. I think it's just one of those years," Minaya said on a conference call with beat writers shortly after the deadline passed, during the latter innings of the Mets' series finale with the Astros. "We were looking for something that was going to make an impact on our club. There were some teams that asked for some players, mostly minor deals. We just felt at the time that it wasn't going to make a difference—at least, on our club—the players we were adding. To me, to make a trade and take on some minor guys and give up some of our prospects did not make sense."

Minaya advised Mets fans who were envisioning Ramirez and Soriano in Flushing to not be disappointed. The GM added that he did not believe the flirting with Texas regarding Soriano, and then, Boston regarding Ramirez, had distracted team brass from what might have been more fruitful negotiations elsewhere.

"I think our fans have seen we're out there as a front office working hard, and we are attempting to improve our club," Minaya said. "Although we may not be able to get some of the players we think can improve the club, we *are* making an attempt and an effort to be able to do that. And I think that's very important for our fan base. Look—from the front office and from ownership, we are dedicated to working as hard as we can to put the best product on the field for our fans and our players. The trading deadline is not going to stop that. We will continue to work hard at putting the best product possible on the field. We did it this winter. . . . And we will continue to do so."

Said Glavine: "We have enough people in here to win."

In Boston, Ramirez delivered an eighth-inning, pinch-hit single to drive in the go-ahead run fifty-four minutes after the deadline passed as the Red Sox beat the Minnesota Twins, 4–3. Before the game, Ramirez had interrupted Francona's meeting with reporters to announce: "I want to stay here. I'm going to stay here for 2005 and help this team win the World Series." Millar, his teammate, provided a mock translation into Spanish gibberish for comedic effect.

Minus a new big bat, the Mets did fine, too. They produced a season-high seventeen hits and avoided their first four-game series sweep at the hands of Houston in forty years by beating the Astros, 9–4. Cameron laced a double off the wall in left-centerfield thirty-six minutes after the deadline passed and scored the go-ahead run that inning on Castro's single. Beltran had a big finale, too. He had three hits and a walk. He also had a wide grin after a leadoff double in a four-run ninth inning that gave Looper a cushion.

"Listen, all year long I've been seeing a lot of weird things happen," Randolph said. "There's no irony in anything I see here. It's been a weird year here so far."

Said Cameron: "I'm definitely happy where I'm at."

The victory kept the Mets a manageable distance behind the Astros—four games—in the wild-card race. Had they lost, the deficit instead would have been six games.

"I was satisfied because we won," Beltran said. "It would have been tough if we got swept in Houston."

Afterward, Beltran took no shots at Astros fans, though he openly discussed attending the church service with Anderson.

"Sometimes you need to get away from your routine," he said.

Castro had emerged as a viable alternative to Mike Piazza behind the plate. He hit .313 with 3 home runs and 12 RBI in 32 July at-bats. He had not been challenged by would-be base stealers, either. In 54 games—24 started—to that point, opponents had tried only 14 steals, indicating their respect.

Even Mientkiewicz, benched for three games—and whose lack of production had been a major reason for Minaya's trade overtures to add a bat—went 3-for-5. Mientkiewicz had joked upon arriving in the clubhouse that morning and noticing himself in the lineup that he was returning from vacation.

The Mets got retribution for injustices, even if they didn't acknowledge satisfaction. Floyd, plunked by Oswalt with a pitch in Flushing, homered off the All-Star right-hander to open what became a two-run fourth inning that evened the score at 2. The Mets also showed fire, led by their sixty-one-year-old bench coach. Umpire Rob Drake ejected Sandy Alomar Sr. for jawing at the crew after Berkman was allowed to return to first base despite being tagged out. Berkman moved toward second base believing Ensberg had walked on a 2–2 pitch. Randolph said the umpires gave him some "double-talk" about time being called. The manager had watched a near-identical play involving Pittsburgh's Ward and the Braves on television the previous night, and Ward was ruled out. Alomar said Major League Baseball officials later acknowledged the crew had missed the call. He received a one-game suspension for leaving the dugout to chew out Drake anyway.

The Mets swiped four bases in the finale, moving ahead of Houston for the National League lead in steals. There was another positive byproduct of the game, too, even if it resulted from an underwhelming performance. Left-hander Kazuhisa Ishii lasted only four innings. It would be his final start for the Mets, who recalled Jae Seo from Triple-A Norfolk that week to assume the spot in the rotation. The Mets might have waited too long. Ishii's record at the time: 3–9 with a 5.04 ERA.

"I'm confident I'm able to play at the major-league level," Ishii said through interpreter Nozomu Matsumoto.

Seo had tossed seven scoreless, one-hit innings against the Phillies on May 4 in his last Mets outing, before heading to the minors to make room for Benson's return from the disabled list. Now back, he allowed only four hits while blanking the Cubs into the eighth inning in his return to the rotation during the ensuing home stand. He even out-pitched Greg Maddux, who had 313 career wins, in the 2–0 victory. Though Trachsel's return was looming, Seo would not let go of his spot in the rotation again during the season.

As for Beltran, he might have been out of Houston, but he wasn't quite free from jeers yet. He returned to New York, went 0-for-6 against the Milwaukee Brewers in the opener to a six-game home stand and got relentlessly booed by the Shea Stadium crowd, too. Still, Beltran had a superb home stand against the Brewers and Cubs. Throw out the dreadful opener, and Beltran hit .400 and scored eight runs in five games. Yet somehow the booing persisted to the end. During Pedro Bobblehead Day, an ESPN Sunday-night telecast a full week after the trading deadline, it seemed a tad harsh to boo Beltran when he grounded into a double play in the seventh inning. After all, Beltran had reached base and scored his previous three plate appearances, even astutely racing home from first base on Floyd's routine single fielded by centerfielder Jose Macias, a natural infielder.

"They were thinking I'd hit a home run every at-bat, like I did in the playoffs," Beltran speculated about the motivation behind the crowd reaction.

Meanwhile, who needed Ramirez or Soriano?

Since whiffing at the trading deadline, the Mets had been on a tear at the plate. After the season-high seventeen hits in the series finale against the Astros, the Mets topped that the next game, with eighteen against Milwaukee. They scored nine runs four times that week.

Sure, there were minor blips, like Pedro and Floyd missing the annual team picture due to tardy arrivals at Shea Stadium. But things seemed to be clicking. In the home-stand finale, Jose Reyes's hitting streak reached twenty games.

Beltran looked at ease as the Mets departed for the West Coast at 57–54 following a sweep of the Cubs. Familiar faces were there to greet him in San Diego, too. His agents—Boras and lieutenant Mike Fiore—were in attendance at PETCO Park. The duo hobnobbed with Mets chief operating officer Jeff Wilpon, Minaya, and special assistant Tony Bernazard, who had made the trip to rub elbows with the team's corporate sponsors. Former team icons including Lenny Dykstra had also arrived for that shindig.

Against the Padres, the Mets dropped the series opener, 8–3, and fell eleven games under .500 on the road. Their .396 winning percentage away from Shea Stadium only topped the Pirates (.393), Reds (.353), and Rockies (.250) in the National League.

Pedro surrendered five runs in five innings in his shortest outing as a Met to that point. He departed for pinch hitter Kazuo Matsui, who had finally returned from the disabled list after a nearly eight-week absence.

Reyes's hitting streak ended at twenty games. It matched Floyd's for the longest in the National League to that point, but fell four shy of the franchise record held by Piazza and Hubie Brooks.

Matsui replaced Mientkiewicz on the active roster. The first baseman had injured himself when he rolled into Brewers second baseman Rickie Weeks, breaking up a double play at Shea Stadium the previous week. His lower back felt like a bag of burning fluid was resting on it. Mientkiewicz, who had finally started to feel hot, going 8-for-12 that week, was adamant he would remain with the Mets rather than head to the team's rehab center at its complex in Port St. Lucie, Florida—an unpopular destination among the players.

"I told them that if they sent me down there, I'm not coming back," Mientkiewicz said. "The ice isn't any colder in Florida."

The series-opening loss in San Diego included Wright's circus, over-the-shoulder, bare-handed catch while retreating into left field on Brian Giles's flare.

"That's going to be one of the catches of the year," Pedro declared. "Just pure instinct. Just a young boy doing what he does best—react."

In Seattle on June 18, Wright had crashed into the third-base stands to catch Raul Ibañez's foul pop, bruising his right hip and left knee on a seat's armrest in the process.

Wright continued his highlight show the following day, this time with his bat. In a 9–1 Mets win in the second game of the series, the blossoming third baseman matched a career high with six RBI.

Beltran reached base and scored his first three plate appearances, each time courtesy of Wright. Beltran also recorded the first steal of home by a Met since Roger Cedeño at Yankee Stadium in 2002, though he wasn't aware he was credited with it. With Beltran on third, a stealing Wright pulled up short of second base to force the Padres to throw home or concede the run. The duo was taking advantage of Olivo's aggressiveness behind the plate. Beltran knew Olivo from their time together in the American League Central and was confident the strong-armed catcher would throw through to second base trying to nail Wright, so he broke for the plate without hesitation.

Afterward, an at-ease Beltran was funny and smiling at his locker.

"You've got to be a little bit crazy to do that," Beltran said about stealing home. "Olivo is one of those guys who love to throw people out. I was thinking, 'Man, if [Wright] goes, he's going to throw the ball to second.' I took a real good lead at third and took off for home as soon as he released the ball. Olivo was going to throw to second no matter what."

It was only Beltran's ninth steal of the season, but he finally felt good. The quadriceps injury he initially suffered in Washington on May 1, then exacerbated during the Yankees series three weeks later, no longer seemed to hinder him.

"My leg is a hundred percent. Thank God for that," Beltran said. "If I can get on base, I can do things like stealing bases, the little things. I feel good. I was seeing the ball good. I felt comfortable. It's time for me to get hot. I started the season doing good. I got hurt. I went through a really tough stretch. Now I'm healthy. I feel good. We're playing good. It's time for me to do well."

# BAD BREAKS

CARLOS BELTRAN PEPPERED ASSISTANT TRAINER Mike Herbst with the same question dozens of times.

"*Where am I?*"

"I had the same answer," Herbst recalled.

La-la land. Well, two hours from Los Angeles, anyway, at Mercy Hospital in San Diego.

Diving in right-centerfield for David Ross's sinking liner at the Padres' PETCO Park, Beltran smacked head-to-head with right fielder Mike Cameron, a scary jolt that left both players dazed and lying in a pool of blood.

Not until the next morning did Beltran fully grasp what had occurred—that the jarring blow he suffered in the seventh inning of the series finale against the Padres on August 11 had sent the outfielders to separate hospitals with concussions and facial fractures, and fears of much worse among the teammates who had sprinted to the scene. Of course, the replay ran nearly every five minutes on the ESPN-tuned television in Beltran's hospital room. Watching it at least two dozen times (by his estimation) during those first twenty-four hours helped refresh his memory.

"It didn't scare me watching it," Beltran said. "But it was ugly."

Yet even then Beltran had no recollection of a fifteen-minute phone conversation he'd had with his wife Jessica, which occurred shortly after the incident, nor of a postgame interview he had somehow conducted with reporters.

"Mike told me that I was able to walk off the field, take a shower, get dressed, talk to you guys," Beltran said three days later, after his head had cleared from a concussion. Unshaven since the incident, Beltran made these comments at Dodger Stadium, referring to a conversation with Herbst, who had stayed in a cot by Beltran's side that first night. "What I said to you guys I don't know. I hope I said something good," Beltran added.

Marty Noble, the longtime *Newsday* beat writer who had moved to MLB.com, informed Beltran he had promised each of the eight traveling writers a cut of his $119 million contract. Beltran smiled. He was lucid enough not to reach into his pocket.

Actually, inside the visitors' clubhouse at PETCO Park after the 2–1 loss to the Padres, Beltran said he felt like he had been hit by a train. Dizzy, his left shoulder wrapped, and dried blood near his left temple (where his sunglasses had dug into his face upon impact with Cameron), Beltran had eventually risen to his knees, grasping his left shoulder. He'd somehow managed to trudge off the field without assistance, head bowed, while the crowd applauded his resolve.

"I couldn't imagine being a paramedic going to the scene of a wreck. That's what that was, pretty much, a wreck," said teammate Marlon Anderson, who raced to the scene from first base.

Cameron had received the far worse end of the exchange. He momentarily blacked out after the front of his face smacked the left side of Beltran's. As a precaution, in case spinal damage had occurred, Cameron was carted off strapped to a board and wearing a neck brace more than ten minutes after the impact. Blood clogged his nose and mouth, which scared him because it made it difficult to breathe.

"The last thing I remember is lying on the ground and a kind of blurred vision of somebody standing over me," Cameron said. "Then they told me it was Marlon, because I just didn't know what was going on. I was just in a daze, and it was kind of crazy. I couldn't really breathe. I couldn't breathe because I had blood coming out of my nose and my mouth at the same time. I didn't know that my nose was broken. I couldn't really smell. I was coherent, but I was just out of it. . . . You see football hits like that all the time, but when you have no equipment on, no face masks—that can be pretty gruesome."

Cameron tried to remain calm as he went into shock and his vision blurred. He hummed during the roughly fifteen-minute ambulance ride to

Scripps Clinic in La Jolla, California, though he could not recall the tune. The following night he would undergo a lengthy procedure to repair a broken nose, fractures to both cheekbones, a broken orbital bone, and a burst vessel that had caused his right eye socket to fill with blood. Cameron described the MRI as resembling a cracked windshield that spread. He spent six days in the intensive-care unit with screws in his mouth and stitches in both lips. Titanium plates were inserted in both cheeks and above his right eye during surgery. The plates remain to this day.

Anderson, among the first on the scene on the sunny, 74-degree afternoon, had first checked on Beltran when he arrived in right-centerfield, asking "You okay?" Anderson quickly became more alarmed by Cameron's glassy eyes and the pool of blood.

"*Cam*, can you hear me?" Anderson asked.

"Yeah," Cameron mumbled back, though Anderson could tell he "wasn't really there."

When Ray Ramirez arrived after racing from the dugout, the head trainer signaled for more medical assistance, immediately realizing the severity of the injuries. Cameron blinked his eyes and shook his head, easing some fears of paralysis.

"Before that," Anderson said, "I was like, 'Just breathe. Can you hear me? Just breathe.' . . . You looked at Cam, just his eyes—you could tell he wasn't right."

Cameron's best friend, Cliff Floyd, watched the collision from left field and was among the most alarmed. Floyd prayed and made the sign of the cross. He had heard in the past that when a person's arms go up, as Cameron's had, it could be a reflexive action after being paralyzed. Fortunately, Cameron had lifted his arms only to shield his suddenly sensitive eyes from the bright sun.

Never much for blood, Floyd wasn't able to watch. It was the opposite reaction to the one he had experienced in the minutes before the trading deadline less than two weeks earlier. On that day, Floyd had constantly peeked at the clock, hoping 4 P.M. EDT would arrive with Cameron still in right field. During that July 28–31 visit to Houston, Floyd had merely been concerned with losing Cameron to the Boston Red Sox because of the proposed three-team trade. Now, he had a far more grave concern.

"It choked me up for a minute," Floyd said. "We were laughing, giggling one minute. The next minute my man was laying on the ground."

Mike Nicotera, Cameron's agent, was driving home from his New Jersey office and heard the call of the collision on the radio. He phoned senior vice president Jim Duquette, who was at PETCO Park, watching in horror with special assistant Tony Bernazard. Nicotera described Duquette's voice as sounding similar to someone reacting to seeing a ghost.

On the Fox Sports New York telecast of the game, announcers Ted Robinson, Fran Healy, and Ralph Kiner instantly realized the severity, too, as their call indicated.

*"Shallow right-center . . . Beltran . . ." Robinson began, calling the play like any other.*

*"Oh, geez," Healy said.*

*"Oh, what a terrible collision," Robinson said.*

*"Oh, boy," Healy said.*

*"Beltran and Cameron . . . The ball is free apparently . . . That's absolutely of little concern right now," Robinson said.*

*"Oh, man, that is nasty," Healy said. "That is as bad a collision as I have seen."*

*"Well, [George] Theodore of the Mets years ago had a horrible collision like this," Kiner said. "This could be very serious."*

*"These guys made contact head to head," Healy said. "Oh, boy."*

In the series opener against the Padres, third baseman David Wright had made a dazzling, over-the-shoulder, bare-handed catch. The grab was played and replayed on sportscasts throughout the country and was so sweet that injured first baseman Doug Mientkiewicz had already informed Wright he would be his date for the ESPYs, the annual highlight awards show on ESPN. Now, it was the footage of the gruesome, head-to-head collision between Beltran and Cameron that had replaced Wright's catch on telecasts. The *Daily News* and *Post* and even *Sports Illustrated* ran frame-by-frame shots of the collision, which had been captured by an Associated Press photographer. Many players suggested it was the most gruesome collision they had ever seen. Robinson asked the production truck to stop showing it after a couple of replays during the FSNY coverage.

"After the second graphic replay," Robinson recalled, "I blurted out, 'We don't need to see it again.' It was purely emotional and based largely on my experience calling a college football game in 2000, when a player was injured making a tackle, died on the field, was saved by the team doctors, left a quadriplegic, and died a year later. I couldn't shake those thoughts and only wanted to see Cameron move his limbs. To me, this was the Theismann-L.T. play from *Monday Night Football* all over again. TV is usually quite willing to exploit gruesome moments, and I didn't want to be a part of that. . . . I had many fans thank me in person for asking for restraint."

By that night, Cameron was speaking in his hospital room. He told Nicotera he tried to get up after the collision, but medical staff on the field would not let him. Typical Cameron, a two-time Gold Glove winner as a centerfielder, he also remained consumed with the near-catch.

"At the time I spoke to him he was probably less disturbed than I was," Nicotera said. "He was certainly, given the circumstances, in very good spirits. He was like, 'Nic, *I had that ball.*' He said it out of the blue. I said, 'I'm sure you did. I'm glad you're all right.' He was hard to understand. He has stitches in both of his lips. His nose is broken. He's got fractures in the cheekbones."

Nicotera told Cameron: "This may put a crimp in your modeling career, but you're going to be all right."

Floyd also spoke with Cameron that night and could exhale. After the conversation, Floyd joked that Cameron at least was smart enough to collide with Beltran in the correct state.

"He's in California. You know they have the best plastic surgeons here," Floyd quipped. "I know he's looking forward to getting his face right, because he's a pretty boy."

Cameron offered examples of his wit, too, a good sign considering the gravity of his injuries. His face was so swollen and numb as he rested in his hospital bed in the intensive-care unit, he told Floyd he looked like Will Smith's character Alex Hitchens in the movie *Hitch*—after the character known as "the Date Doctor" experienced an allergic reaction that caused his face to swell up. The lone difference, Cameron noted, was that his own ears weren't enlarged like Will Smith's were in the movie. Cameron described his face as two sizes bigger than normal. Ramirez, the trainer, took a photograph, presumably for the "before" picture in a before-and-after sequence.

Unable to eat solid food, Cameron dropped to under 190 pounds for the first time in five years. His muscular frame began to melt away. He experienced sensitivity to even moderate light for weeks to come. When Cameron finally watched his first game from the dugout at Shea Stadium three weeks later, he wore sunglasses, despite the fact it was a night game.

"My body was, like, numb, and I couldn't really talk," Cameron said. "But I had movement and everything. And all I remember, too, was that the sun was really, really annoying to me."

Nine days after the collision, when he did his first interview, Cameron was still experiencing headaches.

"Half of my face is numb," he said, before amending the remark. "*Everything* is numb. My right eye is filled with blood from one of the vessels in there that broke. The braces in my mouth are really tight, along with the screws in my mouth. I'm just trying to take care of myself, make progress. The worst has already happened, and it's only going to get better from here."

Beltran had broken the zygomatic arch, the barrier separating the eye socket from the maxillary sinus, which formed the shape of his left cheek. He had also suffered a concussion, plus a significant bruise on the bicep. When he was transferred to Scripps Clinic the day after the collision, the injured outfielders briefly spoke. Cameron told Beltran his nose was sore but managed a smile.

"He didn't look good," Beltran said.

Former great Lenny Dykstra—at both stadiums during the Mets' West Coast trip, and Duquette's good friend—recalled a similar incident that took place at Shea Stadium years ago. On June 5, 1987, he and Mookie Wilson collided face-to-face in deep left-centerfield, on Sid Bream's fly ball. This happened to be the same night that Dwight Gooden returned from drug rehabilitation with a 5–1 win against the Pittsburgh Pirates. Dykstra, the centerfielder, and Wilson, the left fielder, both had center-field mentalities, too. Dykstra said his own experience, which resulted in a blood-spewing cut on his nose, paled in comparison, although he found Wilson's head to be plenty hard. Wilson made the catch, and neither player was forced to leave the game.

Pedro Martinez recalled centerfielder Johnny Damon's collision with second baseman Damian Jackson in Game 5 of the 2003 American League Division Series, between the Red Sox and Oakland A's, on Jermaine Dye's shallow fly ball. That jolt left Damon unconscious for several minutes, and with headaches and vision problems that persisted into the following season. Jackson was now at PETCO Park as a Padre. In fact, he pinch-ran for Ross, who had stopped at third base during the incident because second baseman Kazuo Matsui had retrieved the baseball and returned it to the infield.

"This one was a little bit uglier than the other one," Pedro said, comparing the Beltran–Cameron and Jackson–Damon collisions. "The other one at least you didn't see any necks twisting around. You saw a lot of body other than the head."

Jackson just hoped for the best.

"At that point, when you see guys down, you forget about the game," he said. "We were all in our dugout saying a little prayer for them."

Pedro could think of only one other moment he had witnessed that came close to rivaling this collision. He recalled Rondell White's headfirst crash into the wall after catching Larry Walker's line drive on April 27, 1996, at Colorado while they were Montreal Expos teammates. That incident left White with a bruised spleen and kidney. It turned out White also had a fractured rib, which wasn't detected until he was seemingly ready to return from the disabled list sixty-eight games later.

"I've seen three that actually have really scared me," Pedro said. "It brings you a lot of bad thoughts."

Jackson scored the decisive run in the crushing 2–1 loss, on new Met-killer Joe Randa's two-out single to centerfield against Tom Glavine. Randa, obtained from the Cincinnati Reds on July 23 for two minor-league pitchers, had ravaged the Mets in April, too. He had delivered the Opening Day walk-off home run to spoil Pedro's debut. Randa then produced six RBI the following game, which the Reds won, 9–5. With this loss, the Mets dropped to 58–56, in fifth place in both the National League East and wild-card races.

"I hated to win that ball game the way we did," Padres starter and winner Woody Williams told the *San Diego Union-Tribune*.

Ray Ramirez spent the night of the collision in a cot alongside Cameron, as Herbst did with Beltran. When Cameron's wife JaBreka and eight-year-old son Dazmon arrived later from the family's home outside Atlanta, Georgia, the head trainer excused himself and accompanied Beltran for the two-hour drive to Los Angeles, where the team had bused. San Diego closer Trevor Hoffman visited Cameron at Scripps Clinic a few days later wearing his Padres jersey.

That made Cameron think of all the times he and other ballplayers had visited sick children in hospitals wearing their uniform tops to lift the kids' spirits. Padres outfielder Eric Young also came to cheer up Cameron.

So much had happened to Cameron leading up to that low point. He had undergone December 17 surgery to repair cartilage in his left wrist, which sidelined him until May 5. The Mets had improbably landed Beltran, pushing Cameron to right field despite his immense talents at his natural position. And general manager Omar Minaya had entertained trade offers for him into spring training, until Cameron had surveyed the clubhouse, with Floyd lockering next to him and talent staggered throughout the room, and decided to stay. Then Cameron nearly got dealt anyway in July, as the Mets engaged the Red Sox in trade discussions that were beyond his control.

From the day in February when he had arrived at spring training, Cameron had diplomatically coped with being displaced in centerfield by Beltran. Clearly, though, he had never let go of the position, which was truly his identity on the baseball field.

"We all know what I am," Cameron had said during an ultra-candid moment in an otherwise deferential interview in Port St. Lucie, Florida.

Sure enough, the Mets could take Cameron out of centerfield, but they would never be able to take the centerfielder out of Cameron. Not the aggressiveness. Not the range.

Not that Minaya, who was so enamored with having Cameron patrol right field, wanted to remove those traits.

So while Floyd, a left fielder, would have peeled behind Beltran had Ross's shot been to the other gap—that is, if Floyd could have covered enough ground to get there—Cameron did not have that instinct or inclination. Cameron dove headfirst, never seeing Beltran, not even immediately before the impact.

"He has the centerfield mentality," Beltran said. "We're both centerfielders. We just went for the ball. You don't think about it. You just go for the ball."

Said Cameron: "If I had to do it all over again, I'd probably do it again. It's just the way that we play. It's the way I've always played, and that's the way it is. I can't really change that. People have told me I need to stay off walls and stop diving, but that's the only way I know how to play."

Months later—as he was clearing out his locker at Shea Stadium at the end of the season, packing belongings that included a Pedro wig—Cameron conceded one thing: During the lowest moments after the crash, he briefly thought to himself how things might have been different had he not stopped Minaya from listening to trade offers during spring training. *What if he had in fact been else-where, patrolling centerfield?*

"A little bit after I got hurt, that's about it," Cameron said. "They always say everything happens for a reason. The worst things you overcome can only make you stronger. I guess I hadn't figured it out yet, why the good Lord decided to just let my face be broken. If I look back on it, all I can say is, I got a chance to really experience something a little different."

The Mets had remained on the periphery of the wild-card hunt, but it seemed likely that leaving two of their marquee teammates behind as they bused to Los Angeles was the jolt that would finally sink them.

At that point, suggesting the organization had been cursed with injuries and misfortune did not seem too far off-base. Sure, they had made ill-advised acquisitions in recent years, such as trading for overweight first baseman Mo Vaughn, whom team brass should have known would never fulfill his bloated contract because of the arthritic knee supporting his girth. But how could the crash—quite literally—of Glavine, who arrived from the Braves with 242 career wins, 11 straight division titles, and Hall of Fame credentials, be explained other than by suggesting the organization had bad karma?

Glavine signed with the Mets for three years and $35 million, plus an option for 2006 based on innings pitched. He proceeded to lose his two front teeth on August 10, 2004, on the way to Shea Stadium. En route from La-Guardia Airport, an SUV suddenly plowed into the passenger side of his taxi, right at the Grand Central Parkway overpass on 94th Street. Anyone who has ever been to a Mets home game knows how short that drive is, simply by the fact that planes appear full-sized by the time they whiz past the stadium. Glavine, who shattered the bones in his upper mouth, pitched in '05 with two temporary front teeth, which would sometimes drop out while he ate. The area was not stable enough to have posts inserted until after the season, more than a year after the accident. Glavine did not believe permanent fakes could be implanted until sometime in mid-2006.

At least in Glavine's case a moral existed: Always wear a seat belt. The Cameron–Beltran crash had no redemptive value. It only served to painfully add to the Mets' difficulties as they bobbed around the .500 mark.

In the meantime, Floyd had experienced his own injury in the series finale in San Diego, albeit of far less severity than the ones suffered by Cameron and Beltran. Padres reliever Akinori Otsuka plunked the left fielder on the inside of the left knee with a pitch in the eighth inning, shortly after the game resumed. Floyd dropped to the ground in agony and pounded the dirt. He believed Otsuka had done it on purpose, in lieu of an intentional walk. Padres manager Bruce Bochy apparently tried to call over to the Mets' side to apologize after the game, and to relay the fact that no intent was involved. Considering the collision had occurred just an inning earlier, this would have made any malice truly tasteless. Whoever answered in the visitors' clubhouse hung up right away. An X-ray was negative, but the discomfort was real. Floyd indicated he likely would have left the game had Beltran and Cameron not been severely injured. Reliever Roberto Hernandez had a line drive graze his right middle finger a half-inning later, too.

Yet somehow the Mets, who fed off manager Willie Randolph's ability to remain calm through the roller-coaster drops of the season, managed to hold things together, even through a rocky, emotional, and gut-wrenching matchup with the Los Angeles Dodgers.

Sore knee or not, Floyd's services were desperately needed in Los Angeles, minus the two outfielders, so he gutted through the series opener. Already, Gerald Williams, who had turned thirty-nine two days earlier, was slated to start in centerfield against the Dodgers, in place of Beltran. The Mets had also swiftly summoned Victor Diaz from Triple-A Norfolk to man right field for Cameron.

Diaz had joined the organization on July 14, 2003, shortly after principal owner Fred Wilpon fired Steve Phillips as general manager and named Duquette to the post, then on an interim basis. Duquette, charged with getting the team's $117 million payroll at least under the luxury-tax threshold, obtained Diaz—a stocky infielder and two-time minor-league batting champ—from the Dodgers, with young relievers Kole Strayhorn and Jose Diaz, for outfielder Jeromy Burnitz. Victor Diaz turned out to be the most legitimate return from Duquette's five money-saving trades, which also landed reliever Royce Ring, while shipping out Armando Benitez, Roberto Alomar, Graeme Lloyd, and Rey Sanchez. In fact, Duquette once joked that instead of receiving minor-league pitcher Shawn Sedlacek for Lloyd, he should have taken the alternative $20,000 that was being offered by the Kansas City Royals.

The twenty-three-year-old Diaz had been labeled Mini-Manny, at least by some members of the media, because of his physical resemblance to the Red Sox left fielder. He also bore a resemblance to Manny Ramirez because of his similar style at the plate and occasional lapses in the outfield. Diaz's quick start at the big-league level in '05 with Cameron injured—.292 with 3 home runs, 10 RBI, and 15 walks in April—had fans euphoric. But Randolph, wary of hyping young players, cautioned that Diaz was no Roberto Clemente—actually a subtly humorous observation, since Diaz had attended Roberto Clemente High School in Chicago. By the time Diaz was demoted on July 2 to ensure regular work, his average had dipped to .242, with a .129 average in June.

Diaz had just been introduced to the outfield in the spring of 2004, after committing a rash of errors playing second base and third base in the minor leagues. And right field remained very much a work in progress. But given the black hole at first base, with Mientkiewicz unproductive and now on the disabled list, Diaz had played twenty-six games at that position during his six-week stretch at Norfolk before returning to the Mets. The rustiness in the outfield was evident when he resumed playing at the big-league level against the Dodgers. Neglecting the position to concentrate on first base had affected his ability to judge balls and get quick first steps in the proper direction.

Fortunately for the Mets, Diaz's bat was just fine.

With Beltran at the team's posh hotel in Century City on the Avenue of the Stars at the recommendation of trainers, rather than at the ballpark, Diaz belted two home runs against his former organization in the series opener. The latter long ball, a titanic 438-foot shot, staked Victor Zambrano to a 6–3 lead in the sixth inning.

Diaz was no stranger to magical moments. After a September 2004 call-up when rosters expanded, he had delivered a three-run, game-tying home run with two out in the ninth inning against reliever LaTroy Hawkins to send the Chicago Cubs into a tailspin that cost them the National League wild-card berth.

This time, however, the Mets did not win a game that included Diaz's dramatics. As the clock read 2:20 at home on the East Coast on Saturday morning, ex-Yankees farmhand Dioner Navarro sent Braden Looper's full-count fastball over the right-field wall for his first major-league home run to hand the shorthanded Mets a 7–6 loss in ten innings. The Mets had coughed up a three-run lead when Zambrano walked the first two batters of the seventh inning and the Dodgers tied the score at 6 once Aaron Heilman succeeded him. Heilman—no Sandy Koufax, according to Randolph—surrendered two singles, sandwiched around a hit batter that forced in a run.

"Overall, a horrible day yesterday, and today we matched that," Floyd said. "We ain't going anywhere if we don't win games like this. . . . The thing with this whole process is, we have to figure out if we can play without these guys. If we win, it eliminates that figuring."

The Mets dropped to 58–57. They remained seven and a half games behind the National League East–leading Atlanta Braves, but fell five games behind the Houston Astros in the wild-card race. Don Burke from the Newark *Star-Ledger* aptly described the Mets as tethered to .500. In all, they were remarkably within a game of .500 on 86 of the 182 days during their season—including 26 straight days from June 24 through July 19.

"We'd love to have our big boys in there, but we're going to keep playing, man," Randolph vowed after the series-opening loss. "This team has always stepped up this year, so I feel in my heart that we'll be okay. We'll just pick each other up and do what we've got to do to win some more ball games."

Jae Seo, no stranger to big games or pressure, most certainly picked up the Mets the next day.

Seo, who played high school baseball with the Colorado Rockies' Byung-Hyun Kim and the Dodgers' Hee-Seop Choi, once pitched the South Korean national team to victory with enormous stakes. How big? Lose, and the entire squad had to fulfill its military-service obligation.

So the pressure of needing a solid performance to preserve his rotation spot, with Steve Trachsel's return from back surgery seemingly imminent, must have seemed insignificant. Likewise, the pressure arising from the team's desperate need of a win after the collision, which raised questions about the Mets' ability to remain competitive, must have felt minimal.

Sure enough, Seo ensured that only modest production at the plate would be needed. The right-hander extended his scoreless-innings streak to twenty and one-third innings before allowing a run as the Mets beat the Dodgers, 5–1. Seo's streak, which spanned a three-month demotion to Norfolk, fell three and two-thirds innings shy of the longest in the National League to that point in the season, which the Astros' ageless Roger Clemens and Florida Marlins sensation Dontrelle Willis had accomplished.

The Mets played a complete game, too, shaking off some sting from the ten-inning loss in the series opener. Ramon Castro and Williams, the latter still subbing for Beltran, slugged home runs on consecutive second-inning pitches from D.J. Houlton to stake the Mets to a 2–0 lead. Later, Jose Reyes beat out an infield single, got caught in a rundown on a pitchout, yet managed to advance on an error. Reyes scored on Wright's single after Miguel Cairo sacrificed him to third base. Randolph loved the situational hitting, the practice of having productive outs. Three times the Mets pushed a teammate from second to third base with their first out of the inning. Twice that runner scored—in the fifth inning with Reyes, and in the eighth inning when Floyd scored on Diaz's sacrifice fly. Williams stole third base and scored on ex-Mets catcher Jason Phillips's throwing error, for a ninth-inning insurance run. Cesar Izturis, a Gold Glove shortstop, was intimidated by Reyes's speed and committed two errors on ground balls during the game.

Afterward, a satisfied Randolph maintained that Seo was not on trial. He insisted he was planning to give Seo another start regardless of Trachsel's impending availability.

It was a remarkable vote of confidence for Seo, given his tenuous relationship with the organization in recent years. Seo's status had been so shaky at one point that the techno remake of Gloria Gaynor's hit "I Will Survive," which played at Shea Stadium before his home starts, could not have been a more appropriate anthem.

In the spring of 2004, after the Cleveland Indians battered him for five runs in four and one-third innings in his final spring-training outing, Seo had been blindsided by then-manager Art Howe's decision to drop him from the rotation without warning. Howe had made public proclamations earlier in the spring that Seo had ensured himself a spot in the rotation based on his rookie success the previous year.

Devastated when the demotion to Norfolk became official, Seo declined to speak with reporters. Jay Horwitz, the team's vice president of media relations, thought it would be an appropriate gesture to bring back the usually ultra-respectful Seo to the major-league clubhouse two days later so he could apologize for failing to address reporters. That backfired. An emotional Seo blasted the organization through his close friend and interpreter Daniel Kim, snapping: "What I was told was very inconsistent. If I don't pitch well for two or three games in Norfolk, will they send me down to Binghamton?"

Kim wasn't with the organization much longer, though he remains close to Seo. He was in Los Angeles as a spectator to watch Seo's stellar outing against the Dodgers.

Now twenty-eight, Seo had returned from the minors in 2005 with a full array of pitches, having picked up split-finger and cut fastballs under Triple-A pitching coach Dan Warthen's tutelage. Growing up had helped him evolve to the point where he was willing to work on improving his arsenal.

Within a year of his professional debut in 1998, *Baseball America* had tabbed Seo as the organization's fourth-best prospect, behind Alex Escobar, Octavio Dotel, and Grant Roberts. Seo set a St. Lucie Mets record for scoreless postseason innings and led the Class A team to the Florida State League title his first season, beating the Tampa Yankees in a winner-take-all Game 5 by tossing eight innings of one-hit ball while pitching with a torn ligament in his right elbow that later required surgery.

Seo experienced so much early success in 2003 as a rookie while relying nearly exclusively on a fastball and changeup—including a 4–1 stretch with a 3.05 ERA in May and June of that year—he had become blinded to the need for complementary pitches. His stubbornness irked former pitching coach Vern Ruhle, and then his successor, Rick Peterson. Ruhle once screamed at Seo in the dugout at Olympic Stadium after the first inning of a game in Montreal, imploring him to challenge hitters. Seo had become too cutesy and fine with his pitches instead of challenging batters to hit the ball. The nibbling cut down on his fastball's velocity. This made Seo's changeup that much more hittable because of the lack of difference in speed.

"No one hangs on to what they've always done," said Peterson, who transformed from a Seo critic to a fan. "That's why Fortune 500 companies put 25 to 40 percent back in research and development. They're already successful, but they're trying to become more successful. That's the evolvement it takes at the big-league level. Taking those two steps back has allowed him to take three or four steps forward."

Seo partly credited maturity for his new outlook. He had married Joo Hyun during the previous off-season, and the couple had their first child, daughter Haelin, seven weeks before Seo's start at Dodger Stadium.

"In the past I thought I could do a lot with my fastball and changeup," Seo said through Edgar Lee, his new interpreter. "From last year on I've been a little more open. I realize to be a very successful pitcher in the league, I should develop a few more pitches. I feel great. I'm a father, and I have a family to take care of. My thinking has changed. I really realized I have to go out and bring home the bacon and do the best I can."

*Bring home the bacon* wasn't a literal translation from South Korean, Lee acknowledged. Horwitz had only wished his predecessor Kim wasn't so literal that day during spring training, either.

Horwitz celebrated his sixtieth birthday the day of the series finale against the Dodgers. The PR guru really did bleed orange and blue. Hired in 1980 despite spilling orange juice on Frank Cashen during the interview, which Horwitz has always laughed about, he celebrated his 4,000th game with the club earlier in the season. He had missed only five games in the twenty-six seasons—two after his mother's death and three for the chicken pox.

Horwitz's favorite game occurred on July 22, 1986, when the Mets ran out of position players in extra innings against the Cincinnati Reds after the ejections of Ray Knight and Kevin Mitchell following a brawl. Relievers Roger McDowell and Jesse Orosco finished the game by alternating pitching and manning the outfield, swapping positions depending on whether a lefty or righty batter was at the plate.

In Horwitz's tenure, however, he had never been treated to a no-hitter. Stars Nolan Ryan (seven times), Tom Seaver, David Cone, and Dwight Gooden were among the Mets to record no-hitters while donning other uniforms. But, in fact, no Met had performed the feat in the forty-four-year history of the organization. Only Seaver had even taken a no-hit bid into the ninth inning as a Met.

Pedro nearly remedied that drought at a time when the Mets could have used the uplifting performance. If Pedro needed inspiration to accomplish it, there was Beltran at Dodger Stadium, in uniform in the dugout only three days after the collision, even though he was in no shape to play.

The effects of the concussion had worn off, but Beltran's left biceps remained sore. His fractured cheekbone had been modestly displaced, too. Beltran had gone stir-crazy at the team's hotel watching Seo's effort on television and had decided to join the team for the series finale, over the objections of the trainers. They preferred that he remain at the hotel, in a more sedate environment, before accompanying the Mets on the five-hour, cross-country flight to New York after the game.

"They probably want me to stay inside, but I don't want to stay inside," Beltran said from the dugout that morning. "They're treating me like I'm crazy, but I'm not crazy."

Beltran flashed a sense of humor, too. With three-day-old stubble on his face, and Randolph's policy against facial hair still in effect, Beltran ended the conversation by saying, "I'm going to shave right now."

Beltran attended the Sunday chapel service with his teammates at the stadium, his normal practice. Then something special nearly occurred.

The Mets had every reason to believe this was the day. For one, the Dodgers started a less-than-imposing lineup: Cesar Izturis, Oscar Robles, Milton Bradley, Olmedo Saenz, Ricky Ledee, Antonio Perez, Jayson Werth, Dioner Navarro, and Brad Penny. More importantly, the stars seemed to have aligned. Pedro was on the Dodger Stadium mound for the first time in exactly eight years.

Pedro had made his major-league debut in relief here in 1992, forming a battery with Mike Piazza—another native Dodger, who had been drafted as a favor to Tommy Lasorda in the 62nd round in June 1988, and who learned to catch once he turned pro.

Pedro was separated from his brother Ramon and Piazza when the Dodgers, concerned about his frail frame, traded him to Montreal after the 1993 season for second baseman Delino DeShields. Pedro, who worked out of the bullpen in Los Angeles, turned into a starter the next season with the Expos and went 11–5 with a 3.42 ERA.

"I'm a big fan of the stadium. I think it's one of the prettiest stadiums you're going to find," Pedro said. "The fans, the atmosphere here, I still remember those things, a lot of nice people. But I have no regrets. There's nothing negative that I can think of. There's nobody there—except for maybe Manny

Mota—out of the people that were here back then. I'm just proud I'm able to come here and show the fans what I didn't have enough time to show [then]."

Ten years before this outing, Piazza caught a no-hitter by Ramon at Dodger Stadium. Ramon retired the first twenty-three Marlins he faced on July 14, 1995, losing the perfect-game bid when he walked Tommy Gregg with two out in the eighth inning. Pedro, still with the Expos, legitimately deserved a perfect game that season. He was 27-for-27 retiring batters through nine innings against the Padres on June 3 of that year. Instead, the game remained scoreless, and Pedro surrendered a leadoff double to Bip Roberts in the tenth inning.

Pedro, for all the accomplishments in his distinguished career, had never come closer to recording a no-hitter than that game in San Diego. Piazza had caught one other no-hitter as a Dodger, when Hideo Nomo performed the feat against the Rockies at hitter-friendly Coors Field, of all places, in 1996.

Earlier in the current season with the Mets, Pedro carried a no-hit bid into the seventh inning against the Astros at Shea Stadium, before Chris Burke launched a one-out solo home run. Pedro never let the thought of a no-hitter enter his mind that day. This time he did consider the possibility beginning in the fourth inning, as the Dodgers flailed at his changeups.

Pedro carried the bid one out into the eighth inning before surrendering a triple to Perez off the wall, just to the left of dead-center, on a 1–1 cut fastball. Perez had idolized Pedro as a youngster in the Dominican Republic, identifying the ace as his favorite pitcher. The shot narrowly eluded the glove of the retreating Williams, Beltran's replacement in centerfield, who had shaded the other way.

Williams thought he might have a chance at the drive when it left Perez's bat. Unforgiving talk-radio callers were sure he did. They skewered Williams the next day, suggesting Beltran would have made the catch, though it probably would have been an extraordinary feat for anyone.

The venom probably would have been lacking had the ensuing batter not produced a devastating result. On the third pitch after Perez's triple, with the count an identical 1–1 on Werth, Pedro tried to coax a pop-up with an inside fastball. Werth, looking for the pitch, deposited the baseball into the left-field stands for his first home run at Dodger Stadium all season.

"He's just good," Werth told the *Los Angeles Times*, referring to Pedro. "His fastball was registering only 86–88 mph, when years before it was 98. To pitch the way he does and do what he did today tells you he is special."

In the ninth inning, with Penny still pitching and the Mets now trailing by a run, Anderson delivered a one-out double to the gap in left-centerfield and stole third base. Diaz, however, got jammed with a full-count pitch and sent a half-swing tapper to Perez, who was playing in on the grass at second base. Anderson didn't break on contact, but read the play and thought he could reach the plate. Perez double-clutched. He still caught Anderson, whom Navarro blocked from the plate.

"I tried to slide around, stick my hand in, but I didn't really have anywhere to go," Anderson said.

After Matsui struck out as a pinch hitter to end the series finale, the Mets watched with blank faces from the dugout. Once they had retreated to the clubhouse to change into suits, they eventually trudged across the outfield to board their buses for the airport.

"With the effort that he gave, he only needed a little bit, and we were unable to give it to him," Williams said about Pedro. "Obviously it's not about one guy. Obviously. But you'd like to see, after one guy gives an effort like that, some of his teammates—including me—do something. We didn't do that."

Randolph thought Williams had a chance at Perez's shot. But the manager, making sure not to assign blame, noted that looks can be deceiving from a distance.

"It's easy looking back and saying he should have caught it," Randolph said. "It was a very difficult play. It would have been a great play if he caught it. That's the way I look at it."

Floyd wasn't second-guessing Williams, either. He noted that an everyday player, such as Beltran, would have had a better chance. Williams had made only three starts in centerfield for the Mets—the three games of the Dodgers series. Baseballs travel out quicker at Dodger Stadium during day games like this one, Floyd added.

"He ran out real quick," Floyd said. "You're asking a guy who is very, very talented—very athletic—but who doesn't play as much to get a good read on the ball over his head off the wall. Your normal centerfielder has a slightly better chance because he's out there every day. But I would never put anything past

GW. He's one of those guys—if you're going to miss somebody, you definitely want him to be a part of helping us. And he has."

What did Pedro think?

"If Gerald didn't catch it, I don't have to think that Carlos would catch it," Pedro said. "I think it was meant to happen that way. I just thank God for the show we put on out there and the way we played the game. The fans actually got what they wanted. We're all healthy and we're all thankful."

Not only did history elude the Mets once again, but so had the win. The score was identical to three days earlier in San Diego, the day of the collision: *Los Angeles 2, Mets 1.*

Through 6,943 games of the organization's existence, the team had yet to record a no-hitter. Twenty-eight one-hitters in the franchise's history, including Heilman's in April 2005, didn't quite offset the deficiency.

"I don't think I'll need it," Pedro said about a no-hitter capping his stellar career. "But if it comes, I'll take it. When is it coming? I have no idea. I've been flirting. I've been up to nine innings perfect. I don't know when it's going to come. I think those just show up. You don't get them, they show up. I don't go out there expecting no-hitters or anything like that. I go out there trying to make things happen—actually expecting them to hit the ball—but where *I* want, not precisely where they want to. That's what happened today, and I was lucky enough to be flirting with a no-hitter."

Piazza suggested that maybe the organization was cursed. Not Pedro. Not after the Red Sox had won the World Series for the first time since 1918 the previous season.

"I don't believe in curses," Pedro said. "I believe in execution. What we have to do here is execute like we did in Boston. Believe me, there's no bigger obstacle than eighty-six years losing in a row. I was able to be part of it, and I'm really proud of it, and hopefully I'll be part of something special that happens here."

Somehow, the Mets had lost the fourth straight game started by Pedro. They had dropped to a pedestrian 13–11 for the season in his starts. Randolph dismissed the statistics as oddities of the game that cannot be explained. As the Mets left the West Coast, Randolph was simply proud of how his team had responded to the adversity, even if the trip ended at 2–4.

"I don't think you guys realize how devastating that can be when you have a couple of your guys go down on the field like that, going out there and

[Cameron] was laying in blood and they're both in pain," Randolph said. "I think the guys on this team deserve credit for getting through the last couple of days and going out and continuing to stay focused and play. I'm really proud of them for that. It's not easy. It's really scary, actually."

"That was nostalgic, but also frustrating," Piazza later recalled about Pedro's effort. "Maybe I made that mistake of grasping it too tightly, because some things you can't force. Go back to the eighth inning there—I really, *really* wanted that one. I look back at that, I just try to suppress it memory-wise, because it *is* frustrating. That's when the fan in me comes out. I enjoy watching a no-hitter. It would have been fun. Well, I've been able to catch two. I didn't get three that time."

Beltran had his own issues to consider as the Mets flew cross-country. Team brass had downplayed the severity of his injury, but the bone that formed the shape of the cheek had been displaced by six millimeters, and doctors wanted Beltran to consider surgery. After the flight, during the Mets' off-day, Beltran headed to the Hospital for Special Surgery to get examined by the team's own doctors. He knew he only had a seven-day window to have the surgery before it would turn into a major procedure.

"I really feel in my heart I don't want to go through surgery," Beltran said before he left Los Angeles. "This is part of the game. I just feel happy that I'm alive, that I feel good, and that I'm going to be back on the field."

Doctors told Beltran the initial consequence of foregoing surgery would be possible cosmetic issues, although they warned him that he might experience problems with his jaw in the future. Correcting this potentially serious condition would require a more intense procedure.

When the Mets returned to Shea Stadium for a six-game home stand against the Pirates and Washington Nationals, Beltran ended any suspense by announcing he would not undergo surgery. With a minimum of two weeks lost if Beltran underwent the procedure, Beltran decided he could not leave his teammates at this critical point in the season. The Mets had a 59–58 record entering the Pirates series and trailed Houston by four and a half games in the wild-card race. They had remained in last place in the National League East since the series against the Astros at the trading deadline, nearly three weeks earlier.

The decision to play brought respect from teammates.

"A lot of guys who aren't having the kind of season they'd like to have would have said, 'You know what? It's been a rough year, I'll see you in spring training,'" Floyd said.

With Cameron's jersey hanging in the dugout and the right fielder still hospitalized in La Jolla, Kris Benson got things started on a positive note with a 6–2 win against the Pirates. He even had two RBI in the victory.

Benson had not faced his former employer in Pittsburgh during the tumultuous series at PNC Park just before the All-Star break, when the Mets lost the opener in extra innings despite the four-run lead with two out in the ninth inning. Yet Benson had performed well off the field in Pittsburgh, making sure not to escalate tensions with Lloyd McClendon, considering the Pirates manager's inflammatory remarks earlier in the season.

McClendon, no fan of Benson's, was led to believe the pitcher had criticized the quality of teaching by Pirates coaches in a spring-training column by Jay Greenberg in the *Post*. Benson had actually said that as a Met, he was reaping the benefits of learning from veteran pitchers such as Pedro. Benson had lacked this opportunity in Pittsburgh, where *he* had been the veteran, despite the fact he had yet to turn thirty. With Benson's words seemingly misrepresented to McClendon by a Pittsburgh reporter, the manager fired back in the *Pittsburgh Post-Gazette* in May: "I'd just like to know whose fault it will be when he doesn't get it done this season. You know it won't be his fault." McClendon also said Benson didn't have the "heart of a lion. They'll find that out in New York."

By now, though, the situation had mostly been defused. Though Greenberg did not misreport what had been said, he felt awkward about leaving out a quote from Benson because of space limitations—one that had been complimentary to Pirates pitching coach Spin Williams. So when McClendon's remarks came out, Greenberg offered to send an e-mail to Williams to ensure he understood Benson's comments weren't meant to be disrespectful. Benson agreed that this might be a good idea, and Greenberg complied.

In Game 2 of the series, Beltran returned, still experiencing some discomfort with his left biceps. There had been talk of Beltran wearing a mask to protect the fractured cheekbone, but that didn't occur. Instead, the padding in his helmet was adjusted. Beltran did not alter what he wore in the field.

That day, Cameron was released from Scripps Clinic and flew cross-country with his family to New York in a plane provided by chief operating officer Jeff Wilpon. Randolph spoke with him before the trip and indicated Cameron sounded like he had marbles in his mouth. Cameron would make a surprise, unannounced visit to the clubhouse before the series finale the following day, though media did not learn about it until the day after Cameron departed.

Of course, the Mets had suffered another bad break. Piazza could not play. A fouled pitch off the bat of Freddy Sanchez in the series opener had struck Piazza on the glove hand, just below the mitt's coverage area, breaking the pisiform bone. Though the Mets would wait five days to place him on the disabled list, hoping the injury would not be a major one, Piazza ultimately landed there. He missed twenty-three games. Piazza would only return when the Mets desperately needed him in St. Louis—experiencing the same desperation Beltran felt now in deciding to forego surgery to make himself available against the Pirates in the second game of the series.

Beltran had a highlight-filled return. He scored twice, including from first base on Floyd's single to right-centerfield, as he had done in the Cubs series against centerfielder Jose Macias ten days earlier, before the collision. Fortunately for Beltran, Jack Wilson's relay throw, which might have resulted in contact at the plate that could have further damaged the injured cheek, was wide and late. Beltran later scored the go-ahead run in the 5–1 win after bunting for a single and stealing, as the Mets moved within two and a half games of the wild-card lead.

Afterward, Lisa Olson was among the columnists applauding Beltran. Under the *Daily News* headline, FOR A NIGHT, SHEA FAITHFUL DO AN ABOUT-FACE, Olson wrote:

> *Beltran clearly feels an obligation to make good on the seven-year, $119 million contract the Mets bestowed on him over the winter. He has always been a quiet, sensible, somewhat sensitive man, one who takes his faith seriously without feeling the need to proselytize. The fans' derisive boos and media's harsh criticism over his hardly spectacular season (13 homers, 59 RBI) were echoed loudly by Beltran whenever he looked in the mirror. But then he crawled away from that gruesome crash with Cameron, a crash in which the eulogy of the Mets' season appeared to be written in blood. Beltran doesn't remember much*

*of that day. He doesn't remember Tom Glavine sinking into the mound in silent prayer, or Cliff Floyd crossing himself, or the woozy conversation with reporters in the clubhouse. "All I know is it changed me," Beltran said the other day. "I always thought it was a cliché when people said stuff like that after an accident, but it's true. I'm living proof."*

Glavine, returning to the mound for the first time since the collision, earned career win No. 271, passing Burleigh Grimes for sole possession of thirtieth on the all-time wins list. It was the eighteenth anniversary of Glavine's big-league debut.

Beltran was wildly applauded throughout the game. Maybe there was a moral, albeit a twisted one: Apparently, all you have to do to transform jeers to cheers is be involved in a horrific accident.

"Every time you hear the fans cheering for you, it makes you feel great," Beltran said. "I'm here because I want to win. You give me the opportunity of being here or having the surgery, of course I want to be here with my teammates. I just want to be here and help the team win."

# ACHES AND GAINS

PEDRO MARTINEZ OFFERED A COLORFUL, though unrealistic, solution to the problem of overcrowding in the Mets' rotation.

"I'll go with T.O. to the Bahamas," Pedro joked, suggesting he and Terrell Owens might just head off together to the Caribbean, where they could drink El Presidente beers and watch baseball by satellite.

"You take care of my locker. I have two phones and an iPod," Pedro then instructed Steve Trachsel, who had undergone surgery exactly five months earlier to repair a herniated disc in his back.

Owens, the temperamental Philadelphia Eagles receiver, had just been suspended by football coach Andy Reid for insubordination after a heated argument between the two. When a camera crew caught up with T.O. at Philadelphia International Airport, Owens suggested he was en route to the Bahamas for a respite, though he actually was headed home to Atlanta for his team-imposed suspension.

A healthy but inactive Trachsel, who was addressing reporters when Pedro interrupted, was in limbo as far as entering the rotation because of Jae Seo's success during what was supposed to be a temporary assignment replacing Kazuhisa Ishii.

· Chiming in with the Owens reference was the latest in an endless string of examples of Pedro's keen ability to read situations and interject humor. When the crowd of reporters dispersed from Trachsel's locker, Pedro explained the reasoning behind butting in: The ace said he felt a responsibility to keep the mood light in the clubhouse. Things were becoming too tense, in Pedro's estimation, with Trachsel ready to return from spring-training back surgery but having no defined role.

Still, Pedro did in fact need the rest, kidding or not about the Bahamas.

The next day, Pedro felt discomfort between his shoulder blades as he pitched against the Washington Nationals. Pedro, who earlier in the season had dealt with hip issues that required cortisone, had experienced the back trouble before the Nationals outing—and even acknowledged it in Port St. Lucie, Florida, in March. Only now was the issue of the trouble resurfacing being revealed to the media and the fans, when Pedro spoke about it during a postgame interview session. Still, Pedro, a consummate pitcher who relied on changing speeds and pitch movement, did not need eye-popping velocity, or even to hit 90 mph on the radar gun with his fastball, to succeed. Despite the barking back, Pedro blanked Washington for six innings during the August 20 game.

Behind three-run home runs by Ramon Castro and David Wright and a two-run home run by Jose Reyes, all against Nationals ace Livan Hernandez, the Mets had built an 8–0 lead. So manager Willie Randolph felt comfortable conserving Pedro by yanking him after only seventy-eight pitches. The crowd erupted in boos when Randolph pinch-hit for Pedro, though it may have been the presence of unpopular Kazuo Matsui in the batter's box in Pedro's place that prompted the bulk of the jeers. Nationals skipper Frank Robinson had pretty much conceded anyway, having pulled his most potent bats—Jose Vidro, Jose Guillen, and Vinny Castilla—from the game.

The Mets should have coasted to a win.

"It seemed like it was going to be an easy day at the office for the whole team," Pedro said. "It seemed like it was only easy for me."

The Nationals posted a six-run seventh inning against relievers Danny Graves, Dae-Sung Koo, and Aaron Heilman. Washington then completed its rally from an eight-run deficit against Braden Looper on Brian Schneider's two-RBI double, after the closer had comfortably retired the ninth inning's first two batters.

The Mets salvaged a 9–8 win in ten innings and avoided a monumental collapse on sold-out Hispanic Night at Shea Stadium, when Chris Woodward's ground-ball single to the left of second base scooted through the infield and scored Gerald Williams with the winning run. Curiously, it was also the organization's inaugural "Dog Night" at the park. At least four hundred pooches attended the game in the picnic area, which led to the predictable jabs in the newspapers the next day.

"On 'Dog Day at the Park' at Shea, the Mets' bullpen was the biggest bow-wow of all," Lenn Robbins wrote in the *Post*.

"The night started with a parade of pooches on the field as the Mets held their first annual Dog Day at the Park. Then it got weird," Anthony Rieber wrote in *Newsday*.

Had the Mets lost, they would have matched the biggest blown lead in franchise history: an April 19, 1980, defeat at Wrigley Field, when a 9–1 advantage turned into a 12–9 defeat after reliever Neil Allen allowed seven runs in the eighth inning—including home runs to the Chicago Cubs' Carlos Lezcano and Dave Kingman, the latter a grand slam.

Woodward enjoyed his second walk-off hit of the season. He also delivered a pinch-hit home run July 19 that resulted in a 3–1 win against the San Diego Padres in eleven innings.

"This one's better because it was today," Woodward said.

Said Randolph: "We've had our share of tough losses, so I'm not going to apologize for anything."

Randolph was prepared to receive modest flak for removing the ace after such a light workload. During his postgame session with reporters, the manager took responsibility for the lead being lost after Pedro's removal in order to keep the ace's injury private. When Randolph learned that Pedro had subsequently volunteered the information about his aches and pains, the manager seemed genuinely surprised at his star's openness.

"I didn't feel that good, to be honest, but it was good enough to hold it for six innings," Pedro said.

Easy or not, the Mets snapped a four-game losing streak in Pedro starts, though the ace remained stuck on win number twelve, which he posted on July 23. The Mets, at 63–59, also moved to within two games of the new wild-card leader, the Philadelphia Phillies.

Afterward, no one was overly panicked about Pedro's health, including the ace himself. Pedro even attended the postgame Hispanic Night concert, which featured popular Dominican acts Frank Reyes and Aventura, the latter a boy band that hailed from the Bronx. Pedro would not sing the *bachata* music for the crowd when invited by the entertainers, but he was persuaded to perform a brief dance on the mound. Pedro swirled his hips as those in attendance erupted in cheers, so his back must not have been too troublesome. Jose Reyes would not sing the *bachata* music, either. Asked why not, the suddenly shy shortstop born in Villa Gonzalez in the Dominican Republic indicated his preference for merengue or reggaeton.

After completing a 4–2 home stand against the Pittsburgh Pirates and Nationals the following day, with a 7–4 loss to Washington, the Mets jetted to Phoenix. Once there, Pedro acknowledged the full extent of how banged-up he had become. The Mets, no road warriors, had arrived in Arizona for a four-game series against the Diamondbacks to kick off a grueling stretch that included seventeen of twenty games away from Shea Stadium. The ace noted that both his upper back, between the shoulder blades, and the right foot he uses to push off the mound were in less-than-prime condition. Alarmingly, he also showed up in the visitors' clubhouse in Arizona one day with two patches attached to his pitching arm and wires running to a rehabilitation device that delivered electrical stimulation. Pedro did nothing to conceal the device from reporters, apparently with good reason. Head trainer Ray Ramirez had sent the device back to the hotel with Pedro for the ace to use on his back. A curious Pedro had stuck the gizmo's patches on his right arm, figuring that what helps a back could not hurt there.

Pedro had already reached 176 innings after completing his outing against the Nationals, which put him on pace for 232⅓ innings for the regular season—a level he had not reached since his first season with the Boston Red Sox in 1998. Because he tossed 244 innings in 2004, including the postseason, and then had a shorter-than-normal, twenty-one-day layoff before beginning to tune up for the '05 campaign back home in the Dominican Republic, Pedro's weight had dropped to 178 pounds, its lowest level in years. Pedro's overworked body simply had not been given enough time to recharge.

"I'm a little more beat-up this year than the previous three years," Pedro acknowledged. "First of all, it was the playoffs with the Red Sox. I pitched a lot. I think I led the team in innings in the playoffs."

Pedro also complained about the Mets' unforgiving schedule. In a five-week span, the Mets had made three separate trips out West—Colorado–Houston, San Diego–Los Angeles, and now Arizona–San Francisco. By contrast, the

Atlanta Braves were able to make their Colorado, Los Angeles, and San Diego stops all on one West Coast swing in mid-May. The Braves then had a leisurely trip to San Francisco and Arizona in July, with an off-day between those series. Pedro could not figure out why the Mets' trips would not be spread out, or at least merged into two swings to minimize the air travel.

"When you wake up, you go *Aargh*," Pedro said. "You feel your fingers. You feel your toes. Your arms. On the plane your back hurts. Your arm gets numb. That's totally getting older. You know whenever you lean on that shoulder you're going to wake up numb."

Despite that, Pedro had an ability to tune out injuries while on the mound through his intense concentration on the task at hand. At one point earlier in the month, pitching coach Rick Peterson had pulled out a newspaper clipping from a black book he uses to record his staff's pitch counts. It contained a photo of Pedro delivering a pitch. Peterson showed this picture to Seo, hoping to emphasize to the pitcher how Pedro is able to lock in on the catcher's target as he is completing his delivery. After Peterson showed him Pedro's picture, Seo retired the Cubs in order the next two innings during that game.

With his hip pain, Pedro had never realized how poorly it actually felt until after he had received a cortisone shot, and the pain substantially subsided. Pedro, who had received a cortisone shot in his right foot the previous year with the Red Sox, had no interest in more injections, however; he was concerned about the negative health consequences of too much anti-inflammatory medication.

"When I'm in the game, my mind changes," Pedro said. "I'm just there to get you out."

Pedro was not scheduled to pitch until the final day of the Diamondbacks series. And with an extra starting pitcher available, the Mets could have pushed the ace back a day to the series against the San Francisco Giants and inserted the idle Trachsel ahead of him. Historically, Pedro had benefited from the extra rest. In his final season with the Red Sox in 2004, he had a 4.77 ERA when pitching on standard rest, and a 2.98 ERA with an extra day or more of rest between starts. But Randolph was no fan of a six-man rotation, even for the short term, so Pedro started on turn. However, the manager did decide to have Trachsel start the San Francisco opener to give Kris Benson an extra two days off. Benson had skipped a start at this point in '04 to rest a sore shoulder. He had held the Florida Marlins and Braves scoreless for the next fifteen innings in his two subsequent starts that season.

"It will refresh my shoulder," said Benson, though he maintained, "I would be fine if I didn't take the two days."

Marty Noble from MLB.com reported that Benson had a more serious shoulder issue than he was letting on, quoting an insider as saying: "There is something. But it's just not as bad as last year."

Benson dismissed it. "False," he insisted, before throwing a between-starts bullpen session at Bank One Ballpark in Arizona.

The Mets entered Pedro's start rolling, with their youngsters leading the charge. They pounded the Diamondbacks in three straight games to open the series, winning 4–1, 14–1, and 18–4.

Reyes and Wright, the twenty-two-year-old anchors of the infield for years to come, had career games—even though their careers had barely started—in the 18–4 victory, which made them 3–0 on the road trip. Reyes smacked his National League–leading thirteenth triple, belted a three-run home run, walked, and scored three times. He fell only a double shy of hitting for the cycle. Wright had solo home runs in consecutive innings, a walk, scored four times, and raised his average to .314 with a 4-for-4 performance. He nearly had three home runs, but his shot to left field in the third inning hit off the top of the wall in a deeper-than-normal section where a quirky crevice existed. Still, Wright produced his third career multi-homer game.

Even when Wright did wrong, it made for a light moment. Mets players were watching the Little League World Series in the clubhouse before the eighteen-run outburst, and got a kick out of one déjà vu play. A Maitland, Florida, player in the United States semifinals against Vista, California, had taken an arc-like route while approaching first base. The elongated path to the bag allowed the third baseman to retire him after making a diving stop.

"Watch this kid!" Woodward announced to teammates as a replay flashed on the television screen. "He's running the bases like David Wright."

Woodward was referring to Wright's June 23 gaffe in Philadelphia. That day, Wright thought he had a clean single. So he took an arc-like route into foul territory while approaching first base, preparing to round the bag and make a turn toward second base. However, Phillies third baseman David Bell had caught the ball. An unaware Wright was thrown out before touching the base, an embarrassing mistake. At the time, teammates Doug Mientkiewicz and Tom Glavine joked that they were going to take up a collection and buy the universally admired Wright the Tom Emanski base-running video that is always advertised on television as a teaching aide.

With his performance in Arizona, Wright won the National League Player of the Week honor for the first time in his career. The surging Wright ended the San Francisco leg of the trip with a ten-game hitting streak and was the Mets' leader in batting average (.314), RBI (83), and walks (58). For the week, Wright hit .481 with 3 home runs, 10 runs scored, a .926 slugging percentage, .533 on-base percentage, and 2 steals. Wright's week beat out solid performances by the Cincinnati Reds' Ken Griffey Jr. (.407, 4 home runs), the Braves' Tim Hudson (2–0, 2.00 ERA, 2 complete games), and the Marlins' Juan Pierre (.407, 5 steals).

"I think it's cool," Wright said. "It will be nice to tell my kids and grandkids one day that with guys like Albert Pujols and the rest of the All-Star players in the National League, there was one week where I won Player of the Week."

Wright now had more hits than any National League player since the All-Star break. He already had moved within 17 RBI of 100 for the season, despite having been placed seventh in the batting order forty times. Wright deflected credit to minor-league coach Howard Johnson, hitting coach Rick Down, and even Mike Piazza, whom he had leapfrogged in the order.

"When you have guys getting on base and driving you in, you're going to see a lot more pitches," Wright said. "A lot of credit goes to our coaching staff that sat down for countless hours and talked to me about the mental side of hitting. I'm beginning to understand a lot of what they're talking about. I'm being more patient. It's been instilled in me through talking to HoJo and Rick Down and Mike Piazza. Especially with runners in scoring position, I'm learning how to handle myself and be patient and not be overaggressive."

During the rout in the third game of the series, Reyes and Wright had company in what became a sudden youth movement. While Carlos Beltran struggled, twenty-three-year-old Victor Diaz had two doubles, a steal, and scored twice. Rookie first baseman Mike Jacobs, using Diaz's bat, outdid that. Jacobs slugged two home runs, giving him four in his first thirteen major-league at-bats.

The four home runs in the four days from his debut made Jacobs the first player in Major League Baseball history to accomplish that feat. When Jacobs smacked his first home run of the 18–4 win—a two-run shot in the second inning off right-hander Russ Ortiz—Jacobs's Double-A manager, Jack Lind, let out a gleeful yelp that could be heard throughout Binghamton's stadium. Staff had remained there to watch the Mets game on television after the B-Mets' 4–3 win against the Harrisburg Senators. Jacobs's second long ball came in the ninth inning. He scored five times, falling a triple short of the cycle while also walking.

Until his promotion, Jacobs had unexpectedly spent the entire season with Binghamton. A catcher as he rose through the Mets' minor-league system, Jacobs saw the path opening for him to reach the majors as a backstop when the Mets traded catching prospect Justin Huber in the Benson deal on July 30, 2004. Then, they shipped out Vance Wilson during the winter for minor-league shortstop Anderson Hernandez, and Jason Phillips near the end of spring training for Ishii. With Piazza's contract expiring at the end of the '05 season, and the club seemingly not inclined to re-sign him, the twenty-four-year-old Jacobs could not help but envision himself as the future in Flushing behind the plate. Then came a spring-training double-whammy: Not only was Jacobs told to repeat Double-A, but he would also be asked to focus on playing first base.

"*What?*" he admitted thinking to himself.

Said Jacobs: "That was like putting the carrot in front of your face and then taking it. But it's worked out."

Jacobs, a San Diego native with his nickname JAKE tattooed in Gothic lettering on his back, had earned the Sterling Award as the organization's top minor-league player in 2003, after hitting .329 with 17 home runs and 81 RBI at Binghamton. But team brass did not view him as a capable defensive catcher, eventually prompting the introduction to first base.

There was a funny story surrounding that Sterling honor. Not to diminish Jacobs's outstanding season, but organizations occasionally use their year-end awards to inflate their second-tier prospects' trade values, which is what the Mets were doing with Jacobs. The Mets had learned that lesson from the Cleveland Indians. When the Mets obtained Roberto Alomar via a trade in December 2001, they could not believe the Indians were willing to include their organizational pitcher of the year, Mike Bacsik. At least, they could not believe it until they saw the nice-guy Bacsik, a soft-tosser with braces on both knees, in their own spring-training camp. Mets officials, learning a lesson from the hype of Bacsik, named Dicky Gonzalez the Mets' organizational pitcher of the year. They then traded Gonzalez and Bruce Chen to the Montreal Expos for Scott Strickland and Matt Watson, when Omar Minaya was general manager there. Gonzalez never pitched for the Expos. He had a 6.14 ERA with the Tampa Bay Devil Rays in four appearances in 2004 before getting released.

Jacobs had undergone season-ending surgery on June 14, 2004, to repair a torn labrum and remove a cyst in his right shoulder that was pinching a nerve, costing him the rest of that season. He had been playing at Triple-A Norfolk at the time. So back in Double-A, he overmatched opponents at the plate. That was exactly what the organization had hoped for, figuring that Jacobs could hone his first-base skills without the pressure of facing higher-caliber Triple-A pitching. He left Binghamton with an active twenty-two-game hitting streak, and seven RBI shy of 100. He was ultimately named the Eastern League's Most Valuable Player.

"Wherever they put you, you have to go out and play and do well," said Jacobs, who had seven errors, nine passed balls, and threw out 18 percent of base stealers in forty-three games behind the plate at Binghamton in 2005—a chunk of the duty occurring after the Mets had mostly abandoned the first-base experiment because of defensive struggles there, too. "The bottom line is, if you do well, they can't hold you down. A quote my mom always likes to say is, 'The cream always rises to the top.' I truly believe that. If you take care of yourself and do what you have to do, then you're going to get your shot."

"Jake is getting his feet wet, not to get crazy, crazy," Randolph cautioned, noting Jacobs had not been forced to throw to second base or home plate in his first three starts. "But it's nice that he's doing well. . . . That's why I like fresh blood, young blood. When the adrenaline starts flowing, sometimes good things can happen. The kid deserves a lot of credit coming up here and keeping his poise and making a contribution to what we're doing right now."

The 18–4 rout became a rare feel-good night for the Mets' player-development staff. Five of the starters, none older than Seo at twenty-eight years old, came from the system. Seo took a scoreless effort into the seventh inning before allowing two runs. He had now posted a 0.89 ERA in four games since his promotion.

Seo even added a double and a walk as a batter. It seemed his only problem was an issue with his contact lenses that needed to be remedied before he stepped to the plate in the sixth inning, when he delivered an RBI groundout.

The Mets' eighteen-run output somehow outdid their performance the night before in the 14–1 rout. By outscoring Arizona 32–5 over two nights, the Mets just missed the franchise-record thirty-four runs scored in back-to-back wins against the Cubs in June 1990. The Mets had not scored eighteen runs in a game since that series, fifteen years earlier. They also produced a season-high hit total with twenty, and set franchise records for total bases with forty-four, and extra-base hits with thirteen, in the third game of the series.

The road had not exactly been kind to the Mets up to that point. They entered the Diamondbacks series with the third-fewest road wins in the National League. But with the three straight wins leading into Pedro's start, the Mets moved into a third-place tie with the Marlins and Nationals in the division, their highest spot in the standings since July 21.

"This is like an offensive dream, being a part of this lineup the past couple of days," Wright said.

Said Jacobs: "I don't even know how to explain it. I don't know if I'm sleeping with angels or what."

Pedro's body might have needed a rest, but his results did not reflect it. After the wires and pads that provided electrical stimulation had been detached from his cranky upper back, Pedro performed a high-wire act against the Diamondbacks, walking four batters and hitting another with a pitch. Yet, once again, the ace flirted with a no-hitter—as he had done against the Houston Astros in June, before Chris Burke's seventh-inning solo home run, and then against the Los Angeles Dodgers, when the no-hit bid reached the eighth inning before Gerald Williams was unable to run down Antonio Perez's shot to the wall.

This time, Pedro carried a no-hit bid into the sixth inning, when Luis Gonzalez singled to right field with one out. The hit came just after Arizona television commentator and ex-Diamondback player Mark Grace shouted from the booth, trying to jinx the ace, though that was probably more a coincidence than a hex.

"He better not pick up a bat again," Pedro playfully warned.

Ex-Met Tony Clark followed Gonzalez's hit with a single, but Pedro stranded a Diamondback in scoring position for the third time in the game by striking out Troy Glaus looking on a curveball—not his customary out pitch. Pedro then retired Shawn Green on a soft grounder to Jacobs at first base. Jacobs flipped the ball to the ace, who covered the bag to complete the play, ending his outing at six scoreless innings.

After a combined thirty-two runs and thirty-seven hits the previous two nights, a pair of second-inning runs proved adequate. Cliff Floyd and Wright opened the inning with consecutive singles against ex-Yankee Javier Vazquez. And after Jacobs—labeled Roy Hobbs by Looper—plated Floyd while grounding into a double play, Diaz followed him with a solo home run.

This time, the Mets would hold on. Heilman took over for Pedro in the seventh inning and surrendered a triple on a low-and-away, full-count offering that Royce Clayton slapped into the right-field corner. He then hit Quinton McCracken with an 0–2 pitch. Randolph summoned Roberto Hernandez, refreshed with a four-day layoff since his last appearance, and Arizona ran itself out of the inning. Alex Cintron grounded to third base, and Wright threw to the plate, freezing Clayton. Clayton did an about-face and retreated toward third base, where Wright tagged him out. Randolph actually preferred that Wright turn a double play rather than try to catch Clayton, but the young third baseman's decision worked out. Craig Counsell then lined out to second baseman Miguel Cairo, and McCracken was doubled off second base.

Hernandez surrendered a solo home run in the eighth inning to Chad Tracy, but Diaz answered with a sacrifice fly after a walk to Wright and Jacobs's single. After Looper picked up save number twenty-six, the Mets completed their first four-game road sweep since September 6–9, 2002, at Philadelphia, with a 3–1 win. It was only their second sweep of a four-game road series in sixty opportunities since 1992.

When Pedro recorded his fourth strikeout, fanning Vazquez to strike out the side in the second inning, he passed Mickey Lolich for fifteenth on the all-time strikeout list. Pedro struck out six Diamondbacks, raising his career total to 2,835. He surrendered only two hits and shaved his ERA to 2.77 as he improved to 13–5. Pedro, who had been stuck on twelve wins since July 23, threw 100 pitches. Randolph was prepared to send him out for the seventh inning if the ace had not been due to lead off the previous half-inning.

Pedro's victory drought had not exactly been his fault. Two starts earlier at Dodger Stadium, he lost the no-hit bid, and then the game, 2–1. He departed

PEDRO, CARLOS, AND OMAR

the Nationals outing after six innings and only seventy-eight pitches because of discomfort between his shoulder blades and the luxury of an 8–0 lead—only to have that evaporate and end in a no-decision.

"He was effectively erratic," Randolph said. "That's probably the most erratic I've seen him in a while. The thing is, he made pitches when he had to make them."

As for his back, Pedro offered: "It felt a little tight, but it's better than the other day."

Inside the visitors' clubhouse, the music, which had slowly increased in volume during the season, reached its loudest decibel level yet. Randolph, who had loosened the reins since the spring-training edict against any music sans headphones, jokingly speculated that it must have been the quality speaker system.

"It feels good to me that we're climbing. We don't want to keep doing the moonwalk," said Randolph, suggesting the Mets had pretty much been treading water at the .500 level for most of the season, expending energy without seeing movement. "We've been through a lot of adversity. A lot. The fact we're still in the mix—I'm proud of these guys. Very."

The Mets were rolling despite a minimal contribution from Beltran. The $119 million free-agent acquisition went only 1-for-13 in Arizona as the Mets soared to seven games over .500 and never trailed in the four-game series. The Mets also stood only one and a half games behind the wild-card–leading Phillies and trailed the National League East–leading Braves by five games.

"I don't think he's happy. He's not pleased with his overall numbers," said Minaya, who met the team in San Francisco. "These are not numbers he's accustomed to. But he's had some things along the way."

At least Beltran was only twenty-eight years old. In past years, some of the imports with big-name reputations came to the organization in their mid-thirties and ended up collecting fat paychecks while getting fat themselves. Minaya noted that the Mets and Beltran had a seven-year commitment, and that the centerfielder—along with Wright and Reyes—would form the core of the team for years to come.

"We're winning without him being the player he's capable of being," Minaya said. "After seven years he's going to be thirty-four. We knew he was not going to be the player he was in the playoffs. That's inhuman."

Pedro, on the other hand, truly was The Man. In fact, the *Daily News* sports staff, along with 8,438 of the newspaper's readers who responded to a poll, anointed him with that title. The tabloid's definition of The Man:

*The athlete who symbolizes the times and both inspires and reflects his generation. The Man is more than a great athlete. The Man has charisma and style that transcends his game. Joe Namath was The Man. Walt Frazier was The Man. Reggie Jackson was The Man. Mickey Mantle was The Man.*

Pedro won the fan voting by a sizable margin, claiming 38 percent of the ballots cast. Yankees captain Derek Jeter finished second at 30 percent, followed by teammate Alex Rodriguez at 18 percent, incoming Knicks coach Larry Brown at 6 percent, and Yankees closer Mariano Rivera at 3 percent. Yankees skipper Joe Torre, Nets guard Jason Kidd, Jets running back Curtis Martin, Giants running back Tiki Barber, and Piazza each received 1 percent.

"That's a great compliment, you know?" Pedro said "That's a really great compliment for such a short period of time. I'm very thankful you guys see me that way, along with the fans. I'm really thankful for the way they've embraced me so far. I hope I can continue to give them whatever they expect, and God is going to help me do that, to please them the way they should be pleased."

*Hoy* and *Diario Libre*, Dominican newspapers, even carried news of the award.

"That the New York Mets are in the basement of the National League [East] . . . has not affected the big city's affection for the Dominican as The Man of the moment," *Diario Libre* wrote.

In the *Daily News*, Michael O'Keeffe offered: "Martinez hasn't even been with the Mets for a full season, but his presence has turned Shea Stadium—which had the pizzazz of a morgue last year—into a funhouse this season. Pedro's energy and humor rejuvenated the Mets, turning the team from unlovable losers to exciting contenders."

Not consumed by his ailments, Pedro was always looking out for teammates, as he had done for Trachsel by interrupting the right-hander's session with reporters to interject his humorous comment about Terrell Owens.

Some believed Jacobs might never have been in Arizona to have the monster series without Pedro's influence. After Jacobs had delivered a pinch-hit three-run home run in his first major-league at-bat in the series finale against the Nationals at Shea Stadium, Mets brass—needing to make room for relief help and Trachsel—called the rookie into the manager's office to inform him he had been demoted to Norfolk. Jacobs's belongings were even pulled off the Mets' bus, which was soon departing for the airport. When Pedro learned about Jacobs being shipped out, he loudly vocalized his disappointment in the clubhouse. Fifteen minutes later, Jacobs was back on the trip, though insiders claimed factors other than Pedro's vocal objection were responsible for the reversal.

"It's just not right," Pedro said about demoting Jacobs. "I was a victim of that. I did what I was supposed to do, and it stayed with me my whole career—how I was treated. I couldn't help it. I told Mike, and I said it loud. I guess a lot of people heard it. It could frustrate a kid, when you have a top prospect like that and you bring him up and he hits a three-run homer that puts us back in the game, and you send him back down. As a person that's been there, it's frustrating. He's got all the tools to be a great hitter—power—and without a doubt, could be a .300 hitter."

The day before Jacobs's major-league debut—the Saturday game against the Nationals, when the Mets squandered Pedro's 8–0 lead—Koo had raised eyebrows during his first relief assignment in eleven days by insisting on throwing seven straight fastballs to Ryan Church, the final of which became a two-run single. Then, the next day, only a couple of hours before Jacobs learned he was to be demoted, Koo had angered teammates and earned the ticket to Norfolk instead by telling coaches he was available to pitch, then declining to warm up once the call came to the bullpen. As a result, Heilman had to pitch an extra inning, and an overworked Hernandez was forced to warm up.

The Mets also had roster complications that helped change Jacobs's fate. They could delay activating Trachsel another day, but Mets officials did not want to add left-handed reliever Tim Hamulack to the forty-man roster if he was just as quickly going to be sent back to the minors when the Trachsel move was made. (It did not stop team brass from dragging Hamulack to Phoenix, only to ship him straight back to Norfolk without ever coming to the ballpark. The only consolation: The southpaw should have cleaned up on Delta SkyMiles.)

As for Jacobs, he would not relinquish the position for the rest of the season, at least against right-handed pitching, which effectively benched Mientkiewicz.

The Mets had only called up Jacobs in the first place because they did not want to add catcher Mike DiFelice to the forty-man roster if Piazza was going to miss only a handful of games because of the broken bone in the base of his left hand. In fact, Randolph had all but said he had no intention of using Jacobs. The rookie was even listed among the prospects slated to play in the Arizona Fall League when the roster was released the same week.

How inexperienced was Jacobs at first base? He was using a first-base glove from minor-league teammate Craig Brazell, whose name was embroidered on the mitt.

Jacobs repeatedly labeled the whole experience surreal. How else could he describe the aftermath of belting a pinch-hit three-run homer in his first major-league at-bat, getting told he was being demoted and having his luggage pulled off the team bus, then having it placed back on fifteen minutes later and slugging three more home runs in Arizona? His sudden prominence and Jewish-sounding name led to more calls to the Mets offices inquiring about his religious faith than anybody since David Cone. (Neither is Jewish.)

Pedro seemed to take an instant liking to Jacobs. During a September game against the Braves, in the fourth matchup of the season between Pedro and Smoltz, Jacobs belted a two-run home run in Pedro's 4–0 victory. In the clubhouse afterward, Jacobs told Pedro, "Thanks, man. That was awesome. I've never been a part of anything that exciting before."

Afterward, Pedro joked with reporters that Jacobs probably called his family in San Diego to share his excitement.

"Mommy, I just took Smoltz out," Pedro said in a child's voice, re-creating the probable conversation.

Jacobs's playing time came at the expense of a disgruntled Mientkiewicz. Never pleased with his usage by Randolph and always more talkative than his production warranted, Mientkiewicz lashed out at the end of the year. The first baseman, lobbying to return to the Minnesota Twins, his original organization, told the *Minneapolis Star-Tribune* of the Mets: "I don't know why they would pick up my option, but if they do, I might quit. I'm serious. I don't want to be back there. . . . I always thought Minnesota was a great place to play. After a year with the Mets, an organization that doesn't have a clue, I know that for sure."

Not to worry. The Mets swiftly declined the $4 million option.

After sweeping the Diamondbacks in the four-game series, outscoring them 39–7, the Mets extended their winning streak to five games. They took the opener against the Giants, 1–0, in Trachsel's triumphant return. With the victory, the Mets reached their high-water mark for the season at eight games over .500. It also marked their highest plateau since finishing the 2000 Subway Series season at 94–68.

Trachsel also took a no-hit bid into the sixth, a third of an inning beyond Pedro's. In his first start of the 2005 season, Trachsel surrendered his first hit when Randy Winn sent a two-out groundball single under his glove and into centerfield.

"Glav might go a little further," a giddy Pedro predicted about the next no-hit bid, alluding to Glavine's start the following game. "Stay on your toes. That's how we do it over here."

"I give it up in the first inning," Glavine said. "Then nobody worries about it."

In five games on this trip, Mets starters had allowed only four runs in thirty-seven innings, good for a 0.97 ERA. They scored the lone run to hand Trachsel a win on Wright's mammoth solo home run off Kevin Correia. This long ball landed a few rows from the back of the stands in left field, a shot that measured 426 feet, falling twelve feet shy of another titanic shot by Wright in Phoenix.

"The fan that threw that back probably has a sore arm," Giants manager Felipe Alou said. "It was so far up in the stands, there was probably a relay."

Trachsel, a huge wine collector, celebrated the successful return by going wine-tasting in the Napa Valley with Piazza and their wives that Saturday night. The next morning Trachsel got sobering news: He was out of the rotation, despite tossing eight scoreless innings against the Giants in his return to the big leagues five months after surgery. Trachsel had limited the Giants to two hits as the Mets improved to 5–0 on the road trip.

Trachsel was informed during a less-than-discreet meeting with Randolph that he would not start at least through the September 5–7 series at Atlanta, after which the Mets might reevaluate Zambrano's status. But Trachsel came away from the closed-door session pessimistic about pitching much even after that.

He was in a prickly mood, and seemingly rightfully so; he had busted his butt to get back during the season, and then, despite his delayed opportunity, had managed to achieve extraordinary success.

"I guess I should have pitched a no-hitter," said Trachsel, with biting sarcasm that did not sit too well with Randolph. "The impression I got is my next start is going to be quite a while from here."

Zambrano had looked like the logical choice to get bumped from the rotation. But Randolph noted that he had challenged Zambrano before the start in Arizona, and that Zambrano responded by limiting the Diamondbacks to one run in eight innings—even if the manager omitted that left fielder Cliff Floyd had to make a diving catch to ensure a positive outing. Zambrano also had a lifetime 2–0 record and 0.82 ERA in three appearances against the Marlins at Dolphins Stadium. Peterson loved that kind of data, which suggested why Zambrano would get his next start when the Mets headed to Florida that week.

Trachsel's agent called Minaya, but no trade was requested, and the Mets intended to hold on to the right-hander.

"It's pretty good to have that experience going forward," Minaya said.

Minaya added that the rotation decision was left to Randolph and Peterson.

"At least that proved I'm healthy. The last pitch I threw of the game was the hardest pitch I threw," Trachsel said.

Trachsel had recently expressed hope that the Mets brass would pick up his 2006 option, which included a $2.5 million base salary. But now, Trachsel, who was 51–47 with a 3.86 ERA as a Met, could see the writing on the wall. He strongly suspected he would be pitching elsewhere in '06, even if the option was picked up, because he figured the team would trade him. Trachsel would have five years with the Mets after the season, and the requisite ten in the big leagues; so, he could not be traded without his consent.

Randolph, who consistently expressed a desire to go with only five starters to maximize his marquee pitchers' usage, said he would only use Trachsel out of the bullpen in an "extreme emergency," since the right-hander had only one major-league relief appearance. That meant Trachsel essentially had no role.

"He's got too many good pitchers," Trachsel said.

Though he did not realize it then, Trachsel would end up with more chances—including one during the back end of the stretch of seventeen games on the road in a twenty-game span. After a three-game series against the Phillies at Shea Stadium that would take them into September, the Mets still had to embark on a ten-game trip to face the Marlins, the Braves, and the National League Central–leading St. Louis Cardinals.

The Mets lost the final two games of the Giants series, but they had set themselves up for a wild-card run during the season's final month, with a banged-up but upbeat Pedro leading the charge.

The morning after Trachsel's performance had made the Mets 5–0 on the trip, Pedro popped into the visitors' clubhouse in San Francisco, buzzing about the Eagles exhibition game against the Cincinnati Bengals. On the first play from scrimmage, the reinstated Owens caught a sixty-three-yard touchdown pass from Donovan McNabb, the quarterback with whom the receiver had openly feuded.

"Hey, you see T.O. last night?" Pedro said. "Straight from the Bahamas."

# MEANINGFUL GAMES

DURING THE SPRING OF 2004, in what had become an annual state-of-the-team address to beat writers in Port St. Lucie, Florida, Fred Wilpon defined the goal for that season as "meaningful games in September." It was a somewhat nebulous ambition, but after back-to-back last-place finishes—in Bobby Valentine's final year, then Art Howe's first season as manager—everyone sort of knew what the mild-mannered principal owner meant: Just remain close enough to postseason contention so the fans feel good and keep buying tickets and ownership doesn't see red . . . ink, that is.

Wilpon's seemingly innocuous remark ultimately haunted the organization as the team floundered late in the season. *Meaningful games* became a recurring punch line, fodder for ridicule such as Mike Vaccaro's whack in the *Post*: "They guaranteed us some meaningful games at Shea this year. And as I recall, Opening Day was very, very meaningful to me. Was it for you?"

In 2005, The New Mets were poised to realize Wilpon's goal, albeit a year late. By winning the first five games of a trip to Arizona and San Francisco to buck a season-long road funk, the Mets returned to Shea Stadium on August 30 only one and a half games behind the wild-card-leading Philadelphia Phillies, with manager Charlie Manuel's crew scheduled for a Flushing visit.

General manager Omar Minaya could not recall the last time the Mets had such an important stretch of games so late in the season, the last time the organization was playing *meaningful games* as September approached. Yes, Minaya called them meaningful games without prodding.

It had been a while.

In 2001, the Mets had their emotional return to Flushing ten days after the September 11 terrorist attacks. That day a Marine Corps honor guard fired a twenty-one-gun salute, and virtually all of the 41,235 spectators joined Marc Anthony in singing the national anthem. Liza Minnelli planted a kiss on star-tled outfielder Jay Payton before performing "New York, New York" during the seventh-inning stretch. Mike Piazza then produced one of his signature New York moments. The slugger belted a two-run homer in the eighth inning to lift the Mets to a 3–2 win against perpetual tormentor Atlanta, a victory that gave the hard-charging Amazins their tenth win in eleven games and moved them to within four and a half games of the division leader. The next night the Mets, who had trailed by twelve and a half games a month earlier, again gained on the Braves before the bubble burst. Atlanta scored three runs in the ninth in-ning of the series finale against foil Armando Benitez, and won, 5–4 in eleven innings, to scuttle the Mets' pennant push.

Of course, there was also the previous season, when the Mets rode the wild card all the way to a 2000 Subway Series matchup with the Yankees. Yet Mi-naya believed even that season didn't have the same feel as '05, given the youth-ful energy provided by twenty-two-year-old infielders David Wright and Jose Reyes, plus Pedro Martinez's electricity and the adversity created by Carlos Bel-tran's collision with Mike Cameron.

"I think this team is so much younger than those teams," said Minaya, a deputy to general manager Steve Phillips during those earlier seasons. "It's dif-ferent. A different excitement."

The Mets needed no motivation against the Phillies, but they did have in-spiration. Cameron, less than three weeks after his head-to-head collision with Beltran, rejoined his teammates for the day, donning his No. 44 uniform, which looked tremendously oversized considering his pronounced weight loss.

"He's lost some booty," Willie Randolph said in describing Cameron, who was transferred to the sixty-day disabled list during the series to clear a roster spot for a September call-up, ensuring he would not play again in '05.

Cameron—with titanium plates in both cheeks and above his right eye, which had caused him to set off an airport metal detector—presented the lineup card at home plate before the game, as he had during an interleague homecoming in Seattle earlier in the season, also to cheers. The man who pushed Cameron to right field then had a rare glorious night in what otherwise had become a disappointing inaugural season in New York.

After Jae Seo allowed three first-inning runs in his first subpar outing in five starts since replacing ineffective Kazuhisa Ishii, Beltran delivered a solo homer in the bottom of the first against Robinson Tejeda. Beltran reached base four times, also delivering an RBI single that snapped the Mets' 0-for-24 funk with runners in scoring position. He had not homered since August 4, against Milwaukee Brewers left-hander Doug Davis, sixty-four at-bats earlier and a week before the collision. Beltran even threw out speedy Kenny Lofton trying to score from second base on a single to centerfield.

The final heroics, though, belonged to catcher Ramon Castro, who capped the rally with a three-run homer off Ugueth Urbina, his former Florida Marlins batterymate. The two-out shot in the eighth inning sent the crowd, and Castro's teammates, into delirium. Reyes, on-deck, jumped up and down like an excited child. Reyes then reached over the dugout railing to high-five an equally ecstatic Randolph. Castro received a curtain call from the fans, which he gladly answered, triumphantly pumping his right fist in the air.

*Mets 6, Phillies 4.*

The deficit in the wild-card standings now stood at only a half-game behind Philadelphia and the victorious Marlins. Four teams, the other the Houston Astros, were bunched within a half-game of each other in the congested field. Even the Washington Nationals stood only one and a half games off the wild-card lead.

The Mets were engaged in more than meaningful games. They were in a bona fide dogfight. And the Mets had Pedro on the mound the next night, their premier free-agent acquisition, whom they had handed a four-year, $53 million contract during the winter to win big games like this one.

"This is the first time it's great to be a Met fan since *Teddy Roosevelt* was in the White House," host Steve Somers declared on WFAN with his charming hyperbole as the lines opened to callers on the team's flagship radio station. ". . . It's meaningful game number one, with thirty-one to go."

Castro arrived in spring training with more recognition for jurisprudence than catching. During an August 2003 road trip with the Marlins to Pittsburgh, he was arrested and charged with felony rape, involuntary deviate sexual assault, and unlawful restraint after a former flight attendant alleged he had raped her in his hotel room. Castro, married with three daughters, professed his innocence and ultimately pleaded no contest on November 29, 2004, to a misdemeanor indecent assault charge, receiving one year of probation. Less than a month later, two days before Christmas, he had a contract with the Mets, though his job only became secure when Minaya shipped Jason Phillips to the Los Angeles Dodgers.

"When he was there," Castro said about Phillips, "I was thinking I had to do my job. That was really pressure. I was a little bit nervous about making the team. When they traded him, I was pretty sure I had made the team."

Castro became a savior, really. Piazza had suffered the fracture at the base of his glove hand on August 16. The injury, which Piazza had reexamined by a New York hand specialist the day before the Phillies series, was originally thought by team brass not to be overly serious. In reality, the broken pisiform bone threatened to end the All-Star's season, and with that, his Mets career. After all, Piazza—days away from his thirty-seventh birthday and in the final weeks of a seven-year contract—appeared headed to an American League team in 2006 where he could split time between catching and serving as a designated hitter.

Castro had been signed as a catch-and-throw specialist, a defensive complement who could replace Piazza in the late innings with the Mets leading. Yet Castro, a lifetime .212 hitter entering the season, contributed at the plate, too. In thirteen starts, from Piazza's injury through the deciding homer to open the Phillies series two weeks later, Castro produced thirteen RBI and scored eight runs, even if Randolph quibbled with his assertiveness calling pitches and fielding bunts. The manager also dinged Castro's base-running instincts, which Randolph suggested rivaled his lack of speed—not an ideal combination.

One of the most popular players in the clubhouse, Castro often injected himself into the middle of the antics. During the season, he had already conspired with the usually reserved Beltran to draw a face on a watermelon and leave it in Cliff Floyd's locker, placing Floyd's hat on top for maximum effect. He had repeatedly pretended to trip, alarming unsuspecting onlookers. He even used flatulence for humor. Reliever Dae-Sung Koo instructed interpreter Edgar Lee to write up Castro at least twice in the team's reinstituted kangaroo court, presided over by judge Tom Glavine, for malodorous clubhouse emanations. (Mr. Koo by now had been banished to Triple-A Norfolk. The South Korean southpaw was eventually dumped in mid-September when the Mets needed to free up forty-man-roster room for promising young infielder Anderson Hernandez.)

Like Castro, the departed Phillips had a keen sense of humor, though it was mostly self-deprecating. More damning, Phillips's mood always seemed to be dictated by his personal success or failure rather than the team's state. Phillips had actually been as unpopular among teammates as Castro was popular.

Even when Phillips offered a compliment, it backfired. When the Dodgers arrived at Shea Stadium in late July—the day after Piazza matched Johnny Bench for forty-sixth on the all-time home-run list—Phillips sent congratulations through an intermediary to his former teammate. Phillips's message included the addendum that Piazza better watch out, because he was only one RBI behind the future Hall of Famer for the season. A disapproving Piazza noted that Phillips ought to keep quiet until he approached the veteran's Cooperstown-worthy career total.

The afternoon after the series-opening win against the Phillies, as Game 2 neared, the clubhouse was as loose as one could imagine, considering the stakes. It was the kind of carefree mood that suggested The New Mets might go far because they weren't placing added pressure on themselves.

Castro and Pedro were in the middle of the zaniness.

The catcher, looking to demonstrate his humor, called over to second baseman Miguel Cairo, who was seated at a table in the middle of the clubhouse with his back to Castro, watching video of Phillies pitchers.

"Dumbo! . . . *Dumbo!*" Castro hollered.

Cairo, fully familiar with the reference to the size of his ears, turned around.

"See," Castro said, satisfied at Cairo responding to the call. "Dumbo. He looks like Dumbo. You know the movie *Dumbo*?"

Pedro then popped out of the training room wearing a white T-shirt that read RAMON CASTRO FAN CLUB. APPRECIATE DAT!—one of the twelve tees assistant trainer Mike Herbst had arranged to have made. The garment also had a picture of a bulldog, which players said resembled Castro. A thrilled Castro excused himself to get one. When he returned, he called over to Wright.

"*David!* The best joke I made this year?" Castro asked the emerging star.

"Yolk?" Wright replied, playfully giving the Puerto Rican–born Castro a hard time about his pronunciation. "I don't think you're very funny. I don't think you have any funny jokes."

Truth is, Wright thought Castro was a riot.

"You know the way I am," Castro said. "I'm a happy guy. I'm a positive guy. I like to keep everybody loose. I like to joke. I'm a fun guy. I like to win, especially."

That night, Castro slugged his second homer in two days, a 410-foot solo shot into the back rows of the bleachers in left field, staking the Mets to a 2–0 lead. Cameron, wearing sunglasses during the night game because of continued sensitivity to light, and with his face still numb, was among those cheering in the dugout. Why not celebrate? With Pedro pitching, the Mets seemed poised to take over first place in the wild-card race as the calendar flipped to September, assuming the Florida Marlins would cooperate and lose, too.

Yet even with their ace on the mound, the Mets could not hold the lead. Pedro allowed four homers, including two to Chase Utley, darkening what had been an electric atmosphere that only the combination of Pedro and a pennant chase could create.

*Phillies 8, Mets 2.*

The Mets, on June 5, 1998—the day Pedro plunked Piazza on the left hand, leading to a heated verbal war—had ripped four homers against Pedro at Fenway Park, on shots by Bernard Gilkey, Alberto Castillo, John Olerud, and Luis Lopez. Five days after that game, the Braves also homered four times against him, the only other instances in Pedro's career when he had allowed that many long balls.

Pedro, still experiencing back discomfort and trouble pushing off the mound because of big-toe pain on his right foot—and by now rarely hitting 90 mph on radar guns—indicated that he had long ago divorced himself from emotions teammates and fans might feel because of higher stakes. He didn't once check the out-of-town scoreboard for the Marlins update, though he knew about them trailing because it was mentioned on television during a trip to the clubhouse. Eventually, he learned the final score: St. Louis 10, Florida 5. The Mets, it turned out, would have been the National League's wild-card representative—at least, if the season had ended on September 1—had Pedro won.

"Believe me, I was fully aware, and I tried as hard as I could," Pedro said about the stakes. "There was no one moment when I let up, when I gave up on what I wanted to do. I just couldn't execute. I'm human. No excuses. It was just, 'Hey, they got to me'; that's all."

Randolph confessed that he checked the out-of-town scoreboard during lulls in the action throughout the second half, noting it was better than picking his nose. Pedro's teammates, like the ace, almost uniformly said they did not, figuring they controlled their own destiny.

"I very rarely look at it, unless the fans are yelling, '*Yankees suck!*' Then I try to see what they're doing," Floyd said after Pedro's loss.

That comment by Floyd, more lighthearted than controversial, nonetheless prompted vice president of media relations Jay Horwitz—once the clubhouse had mostly cleared of reporters—to approach the left fielder and request he avoid such inflammatory remarks. Horwitz probably just anticipated a 5 A.M. call from Jeff Wilpon seeking an explanation for the comment. The chief operating officer religiously reads the morning newspapers on the Internet at an early hour.

Floyd often got a raw deal because of his candor and openness to print reporters. During the next home stand, one article mentioned how Floyd was prematurely packing his belongings into boxes, the suggestion being he was resigned to the season being lost. That wasn't the image the organization wanted to project with three weeks left, so, after reading the report, Jeff Wilpon called Horwitz to prevent additional packing. Truth is, the report proved inaccurate. Floyd was filling a box with items for victims of Hurricane Katrina, which had recently flooded New Orleans and ravaged the rest of the Gulf Coast.

An upset Floyd boycotted the media, though his silence didn't even last twenty-four hours. "It's that time of year I say something stupid," Floyd said half-seriously, regarding his scoreboard-watching comment.

Told it was a lot tamer than his claim the Mets had "no light at the end of the tunnel" from the previous year, Floyd good-naturedly replied: "A little bit." That statement had drawn the ire of the front office, and, combined with him calling Port St. Lucie "that hole" during the 2004 season, nearly fueled a winter trade.

The next day, in the rubber game of the series, Glavine reached 164⅓ innings for the season by retiring Philadelphia's Jimmy Rollins on a groundout to open the first inning. That vested the southpaw's contract for 2006 at a minimum base salary of $8 million. But Glavine's hard luck continued: He fell to 10–12 with the Mets' 3–1 loss, a terrible defeat considering the Mets had now dropped their lone home series during a twenty-game stretch.

Worse yet, the next ten games, all away from Shea Stadium, featured a daunting group of opposing pitchers that would begin with Florida's Dontrelle Willis, Josh Beckett, and A.J. Burnett, followed by John Thomson, John Smoltz, and Tim Hudson in Atlanta. Finally, they would play four games at Busch Stadium against the juggernaut St. Louis Cardinals, who had the National League's best team ERA.

To their credit, the Mets didn't panic, even as they underperformed.

Buoyed by the confidence-building 5–2 trip to Arizona and San Francisco to start the stretch of seventeen of twenty on the road, and by their manager's even-keeled nature, the clubhouse remained loose.

Infielder Chris Woodward, Wright, and first baseman Doug Mientkiewicz—who had just rejoined the team following a disabled-list stint to recuperate from the lower-back injury—tossed a football around the visitors' clubhouse before the opening game of the Marlins series. The Venezuelan-born Cairo examined the football, too, trying to learn the proper grip.

Wright needled Mientkiewicz, making fun of the first baseman for continuously telling and retelling the story of his prep football career at Westminster Christian High School in South Florida, catching passes from Alex Rodriguez. The next day Wright and Mientkiewicz traded the football for lacrosse sticks. When Wright couldn't scoop a bounced throw from Mientkiewicz, the first baseman turned the tables, making fun of Wright's erratic throws and lofty error total by saying, "Now you know what it feels like to play first when you play third."

Dolphins Stadium, renamed the previous winter for the facility's National Football League tenant, still had the yard lines visible from the previous night's exhibition game, a 20–17 Atlanta Falcons win. The carved-up outfield served as a clear reminder of what the Mets would be watching in October if they didn't produce a string of victories soon.

The pressure on, the focus quickly shifted to Randolph, whose honeymoon had ended. Decisions affecting back-to-back games exposed the rookie skipper to scrutiny he had mostly skirted during his rookie season—with the exception of talk-radio callers' relatively harmless quibbling about Wright's position in the batting order or Aaron Heilman's role with the pitching staff.

Randolph—or, more precisely, pitching coach Rick Peterson (though the buck stops with the manager, regardless)—selected Victor Zambrano to oppose eventual twenty-two-game winner Willis in the series opener. The Mets had six capable starting pitchers, with Trachsel having returned from back surgery to toss eight scoreless innings against the San Francisco Giants. But Randolph chose Zambrano for Game 1, trying to capitalize on his 2–0 record and 0.82 ERA in three career appearances in Miami—even if Zambrano's erratic tendencies made him a suspect selection for such a critical game.

Zambrano, who had not pitched since August 23 at Arizona, allowed eight hits and nailed Alex Gonzalez with a pitch during the opening three innings. He suggested that a longer-than-normal layoff between starts might have affected his control. Yet the Mets somehow trailed only 2–1 into the sixth inning. They could thank Floyd, whose one-hop throw to the plate in the second inning nailed Gonzalez. The Mets nonetheless fell short. Resurgent Marlins closer Todd Jones struck out Castro to end the game. The 4–2 loss dropped the Mets three and a half games behind the wild-card–leading Phillies and seven and a half games behind the National League East–leading Braves, with twenty-eight games left.

The next afternoon, Randolph wasn't second-guessing his decision to start Zambrano. In fact, he spoke about how secure he was in his managerial skin.

"I feel like I'm playing as far as the feel I'm getting," the longtime Yankees second baseman said. "During the game I'm just not swinging the bat or fielding ground balls. I feel so comfortable. It's because I've been in these types of situations so many times. It doesn't feel like I'm managing, even though I am."

A violent storm was raging outside, causing the lights to flicker ominously as Randolph spoke. Randolph then set himself up for the ultimate second-guess. Actually, *second-guess* would be a misnomer. After all, everyone in the press box pretty much was startled even before former White Sox closer Shingo Takatsu threw his first pitch as a Met.

Randolph decided Takatsu, released by the White Sox a month earlier, should make his Mets debut at a critical point in the season. The bases were loaded. The feared Miguel Cabrera was at the plate. And the Mets' two-run lead was in serious jeopardy in the seventh inning.

"He had seventeen saves last year, I believe—right?" Randolph asked, actually understating Takatsu's total with the White Sox in 2004 by two saves. "He's been in situations like that where he's pretty comfortable. If you're in the bullpen, for the most part, I'm going to use you."

Cabrera won the matchup, sending a screaming liner over Floyd's head and off the base of the left-field wall, clearing the bases. The Marlins rallied to beat the Mets, 5–4. The devastating defeat, the Mets' fourth straight, dropped them into fifth place in the wild-card standings.

What made the decision to use a newcomer—albeit an experienced, thirty-six-year-old newcomer—so out of character for Randolph was that he had been steadfastly loyal all season. He had leaned on the veterans, players such as Cairo, who had taken him this far even if the prominent role sometimes seemed undeserved. At the same time, Randolph had babied young players such as Wright, who batted seventh forty times early in the season, despite the fact that he would ultimately possess the team's highest on-base percentage and RBI total. Just that afternoon, in explaining his decision to start Mientkiewicz at first base over rookie Mike Jacobs, Randolph offered, "He's been with us all year."

Randolph figured the advantage swung toward Takatsu against Cabrera because they had never met. He presumed the right-hander's funky sidearm delivery was quirky enough to be disruptive to those unfamiliar with it—especially a youngster like Cabrera, whom Randolph had admitted scared the crap out of him.

Afterward, even the most outspoken players weren't about to criticize their manager, though their reticence strongly hinted at what they really thought about his using Takatsu.

"You can turn around and walk away with that one," veteran reliever Roberto Hernandez said when approached.

Told it must be tough to rely on a newcomer with the season at stake, Floyd offered: "I'll plead the fifth on that one."

Complimented on his diplomacy, Floyd added, "Well, I put my foot in my mouth a lot before."

Even Takatsu admitted surprise at getting the call.

Had Randolph still been employed in the Bronx, he might have been crucified—or worse—by Yankees owner George Steinbrenner. The aging Boss mostly relied on press releases issued through PR man Howard Rubenstein of late, rather than the off-the-cuff, inflammatory comments of his younger days, which had generated many tabloid back pages. Nonetheless, Steinbrenner had erupted at manager Joe Torre less than a month earlier for a pitching decision. Torre had let southpaw reliever Alan Embree pitch to Chicago White Sox slugger Paul Konerko to open the ninth inning at Yankee Stadium on August 9. Konerko responded by launching a homer in a 2–1 White Sox win, prompting Steinbrenner to bark to reporters: "I'm not pleased with the manager. I don't know why they kept the left-hander in there. . . . He should never have pitched to Konerko. Konerko's their best hitter." So what that Konerko had a .209 average against lefties and a .284 average against righties?

Luckily for Randolph, talk-radio callers couldn't vent, either. The Mets' radio team, headlined by Gary Cohen, had stopped taking calls weeks earlier because of the vitriolic nature of some comments, even though they were not specifically directed at Randolph. After the Mets' postgame show concluded, WFAN went directly to the Notre Dame–Pittsburgh college football game as scheduled, rather than call-in programming.

The Mets' loss also meant career win No. 1,000 for Marlins manager/noted cigar aficionado Jack McKeon. Whereas Randolph had to wait days before lighting up the cigar given to him by Piazza in Cincinnati to smoke after his first managerial win, McKeon could puff away without delay. On ESPN the next morning in the visitors' clubhouse, an old clip of McKeon smoking a stogie prompted one person in uniform to yell at the TV: "Fuck that cigar."

The season slipping away, Randolph again refused to acknowledge reservations about his managerial decisions, especially inserting Takatsu for Juan Padilla. While displeased with Takatsu's pitch selection, Randolph initially even stopped short of faulting the Japanese reliever. "He should have probably . . ." Randolph said, before censoring himself.

Takatsu had fallen behind 2-and-1, and then threw a fastball rather than the funky, sidearm slider or changeup Randolph eventually admitted he preferred. (Takatsu's "funk" sometimes approached the plate as slow as 58 mph.) When *New York Times* beat writer Ben Shpigel informed Randolph the following morning that Takatsu threw a fastball because the reliever knew as early as his warm-up session that he didn't have command of his breaking pitches, the disappointed manager tried levity.

"I wish he had told me that *before* I put him in," Randolph said. "Next time I'll call down and say, 'Do you have the funk?' The bottom line is that I felt good about the funk that Takatsu brings there, with a kid like Cabrera, who is a great young hitter, having never seen anything before like that. I thought in my gut it was the right thing to do. 'Hey man, take a shot here.' I would have loved for him to throw the funk. He didn't throw the funk. I don't know why. He threw him a fastball. I could have left Padilla in there to throw him a fastball."

Randolph had often spoken about how he doesn't toss and turn at night, reliving and wrestling with each decision made during the just-completed game. Given the magnitude of this ill-fated decision, Ed Coleman from WFAN naturally asked, "How'd you sleep?"

"I slept good again, Eddie," Randolph said. "I slept great again, man. I didn't say *when* I went to sleep. But once I closed my eyes, I was out."

Turning more serious, Randolph said he reviews games in his mind briefly afterward, analyzing his decisions. He then added: "I went to sleep on time. Maybe it will be different next year. This year I've been so involved in what I'm doing that I put everything I have into what I do every day, so that's why I'm so exhausted at night."

Their backs against the wall, the Mets salvaged the series finale with a 7–1 win behind seven solid innings from Seo. And with losses by Philadelphia and Houston, the Mets somehow—despite occupying last place in the National League East—moved back to within two and a half games of the wild-card lead, while snapping a four-game losing streak. They even pulled to within seven and a half games of the first-place Braves.

"That's why you don't panic," Randolph said. "That's why you don't overreact."

To the pessimist, however, the victory only meant one thing: The Mets had stayed their execution until arriving in Atlanta—an all-too-appropriate setting, considering how many previous editions of the Mets had had their seasons unravel there.

The Mets entered the series with a 20–48 record against the Braves at Turner Field since the stadium had opened after the 1996 Summer Games, and with a 1–5 mark in 2005. The later it was in the season, the worse they performed. They had a 4–19 record at the stadium in September and October, including the 1999 National League Championship series, which Atlanta won in six games.

A sampling of the heartache, courtesy of the *Daily News*'s Bill Price:

◆ July 3–5, 1998: The Braves sent the Mets stumbling into the
   All-Star break with a three-game sweep that included a controversial series-ending play. Atlanta's Michael Tucker appeared out

at the plate, but was ruled safe with the winning run in the eleventh inning by umpire Angel Hernandez. "It's the most ridiculous call I've ever seen in ten years of professional baseball, and twenty years of baseball, period," said Piazza, who suffered a concussion a night earlier when nailed in the head by the follow-through of Gerald Williams's swing.

♦ September 25–27, 1998: Jockeying with the Chicago Cubs and San Francisco Giants in the wild-card race, the Mets were swept and missed the postseason. Game 1 featured rookie Jay Payton's eighth-inning base-running gaffe. Payton, pinch-running, was nailed by Andruw Jones by five feet, going from first to third. "Rule number one is you don't make the third out at third base with Mike Piazza coming up," manager Bobby Valentine lamented after the 6–5 loss.

♦ October 19, 1999: Kenny Rogers issued a bases-loaded walk to Andruw Jones in the eleventh inning of Game 6 of the National League Championship Series, ending the Mets' season. Earlier, after Al Leiter had surrendered five first-inning runs, the Mets rallied on Piazza's homer against Smoltz, only to see John Franco and Armando Benitez each blow saves.

♦ September 29, 2001: With the Mets up 5–1 in the ninth and poised to move to within three games of first-place Atlanta, Franco and Benitez combined to undermine the Mets. The Braves posted seven runs in the ninth, including a walk-off grand slam by Brian Jordan.

The New Mets professed not to care about the history. In some cases, they professed to not even being aware of it.

"It's a new team, a new year," Randolph vowed.

"This team has a lot of confidence," Floyd said. "We believe in ourselves."

Said Wright: "I don't think anybody here except Mike (Piazza)—and who's got the second most time, Trax?—know about the struggles in Atlanta. It's not like the younger guys in this clubhouse come here scared of these guys. I mean, they're a great team. Don't get me wrong. They have a lot of talent, and they find ways to win. But we don't come in here scared, and we don't come in here putting pressure on ourselves, because a lot of these young guys probably have no idea about the struggles that the Mets have had in the past in Atlanta."

It sounded good in theory, anyway.

In the series opener, Randolph visited Trachsel on the mound after the right-hander's 102nd pitch, inquiring whether Trachsel could continue against longtime Mets tormentors Chipper and Andruw Jones with the score tied.

"I don't know if I want to go after Andruw," Trachsel replied, fully aware of the Most Valuable Player candidate's career .400 average against him, which included a 452-foot homer in the fourth inning, the longest ever by a Brave at Turner Field.

"Well, get this guy here," Randolph replied.

Two pitches later, Chipper Jones sent Trachsel's offering over the centerfield wall for a two-run, eighth-inning homer, and the Mets lost to the Braves, 4–2.

"He seems to always be the one to drop the hammer," said Wright, more acquainted with the Mets' failures in Atlanta than most of his teammates because he had grown up a Mets fan in Norfolk, Virginia, the longtime home of the organization's Triple-A affiliate.

The next afternoon, Trachsel came out early to run, as is the custom of starting pitchers the day after their outings. He noticed the wind blowing in, and, reflecting on the homers he had surrendered to Chipper and Andruw Jones, exclaimed in frustration: "Why couldn't the wind be blowing in like that last night? We'd still be fuckin' playing."

The Mets had taken a 1–0 first-inning lead in the series opener when Reyes singled, stole his National League–leading forty-ninth base, and scored on Beltran's RBI double. But they went 0-for-8 with runners in scoring position from that point, even failing to score in the seventh with the bases loaded and Beltran at the plate with one out.

Beltran had catapulted himself into the national spotlight with an eight-homer postseason that began with the National League Division Series in Atlanta in October 2004. He had parlayed that success into a $119 million contract. He had also prevented The New Mets from heading home with an 0–6 record at the start of the season by launching a two-run homer against Smoltz at Turner Field in the eighth inning of the finale to the season-opening road trip. Overall, however, his season had been a profound disappointment, and this night in Atlanta illustrated it perfectly.

Beltran got the full-count fastball he expected from reliever Kyle Davies, but lifted a fly ball with backspin to shallow right field. Jeff Francoeur, a strong-armed rookie, fired a strike to catcher Johnny Estrada, who blocked the plate with his shin guard, then tagged out Victor Diaz to end the inning.

"I just got under it and didn't come through," Beltran said. "Being honest, I thought we were going to win today."

During the series, Beltran continued a frustrating, season-long propensity to attempt sacrifice bunts, even though Randolph had gently tried to dissuade him because of his responsibility as the No. 3 hitter to drive in runs. He was also inexplicably thrown out trying to steal third with Wright at the plate, which happened again once the Mets returned to New York. Beltran was booed by the fans at Shea Stadium but treated relatively tamely by the media; Mike Lupica finally took the gloves off in the *Daily News* that weekend:

> *For this one season, he has been as much of a free-agent disappointment as any big hire either the Yankees or Mets have ever made. A thinner Mo Vaughn.*
>
> *Jason Giambi, whose contract is almost identical to Beltran's, looked completely washed up earlier in the season, and his contract, with three years to go after this, looked to be one of the worst in sports history. Whose bat would you rather have in your lineup now, Giambi's or Beltran's? The Yankees expected nothing from Giambi. The Mets expected everything from Beltran.*
>
> *You kept thinking that he was too talented to play like this the whole season. But he has. He has, in his quiet way, seemed to be completely overwhelmed by the circumstances of playing in this city, for this kind of money.*

On Beltran's failed sacrifice fly, Francoeur recorded his eleventh outfield assist, tying Floyd—the on-deck batter—and Florida's Cabrera for the National League lead. Francoeur's total was remarkable considering he had only joined the Braves from Double-A Mississippi on July 7. More remarkable was how the Braves continued to promote players such as Francoeur from their loaded minor-league system and not miss a beat as they steamed toward their fourteenth straight division title.

"There's a reason they do it *ev-er-y sin-gle year*," Wright said. "They do the small things right."

At the start of the trip, as the Mets were arriving in Florida, Minaya had reassigned vice president of player development and scouting Gary LaRocque and had fired or demoted at least nine scouts for a failure to produce even a fraction of the young talent Atlanta annually turned out. When the Mets had their rookie hazing event later in the month, a paltry three players were required to wear costumes—Jacobs (who had to dress as Daisy Duke), the young second baseman Hernandez (a cheerleader), and reliever Tim Hamulack (Elvira). Truth is, the Mets didn't have much in the minors to promote.

While LaRocque took the hit for the farm woes, third-base coach Manny Acta also had some explaining to do for sending Diaz on Beltran's relatively shallow fly ball.

"I know he's tied now for the outfield lead in assists, but that doesn't mean you can't run on him," explained Acta, the former Montreal Expos third-base coach, who was a finalist for the Arizona Diamondbacks' managerial job the previous winter. "You take a chance and the guy made a good play, and what are you going to do? . . . I think the guy has a better chance percentage-wise scoring on a play like that than a guy on-deck to hit with two out."

Randolph wouldn't criticize Acta after the game, saying: "I coached third base for ten years, and I don't second-guess my third-base coaches." But as was the case when he did not initially question Takatsu's pitch selection, Randolph ultimately let his feelings be known. One needed only to reflect back to one of Randolph's comments during the preceding series in Florida to understand the manager's point of view. "This time of year, you have to minimize your mistakes," Randolph said. "You have to minimize taking chances and not executing."

When told that Acta thought Diaz had a better chance to score on a tag-up than with the cleanup hitter Floyd batting, Randolph later asked, with a mixture of disappointment and disbelief, "*He did?*"

In Game 2 of the series, the Mets needed Pedro to top Smoltz, as he had done at Turner Field with Beltran's aid on April 10 in a victory that sparked a six-game winning streak. Beltran couldn't even remember that opening-week homer against Smoltz. Truth be told, the thought of the Mets in the postseason was becoming something to forget, too. Randolph had Code Red–flavored Mountain Dew resting on his desk, a perfect metaphor.

Just as it happened with his four-homer outing at Shea Stadium against the Phillies, Pedro couldn't deliver. Actually, he *did* deliver—just not well enough to outdo Smoltz. The Mets lost, 3–1, to drop nine and a half games behind the first-place Braves. They also fell four games behind wild-card-leading Houston, and the legitimacy of that pursuit was fast becoming open to debate with only twenty-four games left.

With the defeat, the Mets dropped to 15–13 in Pedro starts, though the ace could hardly be faulted. Andruw Jones, named National League Player of the Month for August the day of Pedro's start, staked Atlanta to a 2–0 lead with a run-scoring fielder's choice in the first inning and a sacrifice fly in the third inning as the Braves—schooled from the minor leagues in fundamentals—manufactured runs the Mets did not. Hitless in their final eight at-bats with runners in scoring position in the series opener, the Mets went 0-for-9 in those situations in Game 2. They had runners in scoring position with fewer than two out in each of the first three innings—on Kazuo Matsui's double and triple, and on Mientkiewicz's double—and, each time, they failed to score.

"Look at the way they scored their runs," Randolph said. "They scratched them out."

The Mets didn't do the little things.

The final of the three runs scored against Pedro came when Marcus Giles, running on the pitch, reached home from second base on a slow roller fielded by the ace just to the left of the mound. Mientkiewicz pointed toward home and Castro tried to alert him, too. Pedro didn't notice and threw to first to retire Julio Franco. Randolph insisted that Castro, with a full view of the developing play, should have been more assertive. Pedro, as accomplished as any pitcher in the majors, had never seen anything like it, saying it was something to file away in his "coconut."

Said Pedro: "I never expected Giles to actually take a chance on that play. We're facing a good team, a smart team, a very difficult team. They're on top of their game and, obviously, we're not."

Matsui also had a less-than-stellar fielding play. With a chance to turn an inning-ending double play on Andruw Jones in the first inning, Matsui couldn't get a firm grip on the ball and never let go of the throw as Rafael Furcal scored.

Afterward, there was no room for levity.

Mientkiewicz had doubled in the second inning on a shot that hit the yellow stripe atop the right-field wall and bounced back into play, narrowly short of a home run. The base hit moved Mientkiewicz temporarily to .250 for the season, the point at which a months-old bet with Wright kicked in, forcing Mientkiewicz to shave his head. Even Mientkiewicz had the sense not to get the crew cut at that point, given the somber mood.

Inside the gloomy clubhouse, Cameron—who lives in an Atlanta suburb and was attending the series—rummaged through Floyd's locker. He found a Chipper Jones bat that had been given to his teammate and swung it ever so lightly.

"I've got one more day to put a uniform on," lamented Cameron, who remained in Atlanta when the team moved on to St. Louis.

The Mets missed Cameron desperately, and not just his on-field contribution. The New Mets clearly lacked a Keith Hernandez from the 1980s, or a Robin Ventura from the '90s—the player who led the charge behind the scenes, chewing out a teammate when necessary and carrying the team on his back if need be. They didn't have a Chipper or an Andruw Jones for that matter, either. The Atlanta tandem made sure the young Braves stayed on track. After scolding the youthful players during a September 11 game at RFK Stadium, the Joneses belted consecutive two-out homers against saves leader Chad Cordero in a three-run ninth inning to lift the Braves to a 9–7 win against the Nationals.

While Pedro and Castro could keep things loose, Cameron truly was the guy who could keep the energy level up and the frame of mind positive. Sure, Beltran had given a half-hour base-running tutorial to Reyes in spring training after the young shortstop twice was picked off in an intrasquad game, but Beltran was reserved and quiet and seemingly not comfortable as the focal point or rah-rah leader.

Instead, Cameron was taking baby steps in the recovery from his collision with Beltran. At this point, he was still a week away from eating solid food, though he was salivating at the prospect of soon being able to wolf down an entire pizza with a six-pack of beer.

"I have the best weight-loss plan of anybody in the world—get your mouth wired shut," quipped Cameron, who had roughly forty screws inserted into his face in addition to the titanium plates.

Inactivity had drastically altered Cameron's appearance. Whatever his actual weight loss, his face appeared considerably thinner, like it belonged to another person. Teammates kidded him that he should be wearing lightweight Gerald Williams's pants.

"Beat me while I'm down," Cameron replied, clearly enjoying the banter at his expense because at least it meant he was surrounded by his teammates.

Resigned to not playing the rest of the season, Cameron said he might play winter ball in Puerto Rico to make up for the lost at-bats, though he later rethought that idea. He had nearly attended a Cincinnati Reds game against the Braves the previous weekend with his son Dazmon, to visit former teammate Ken Griffey Jr., but had changed his mind, deciding it would have been too emotionally painful.

"It's hard for me to sit in the stands if I can't sit in the dugout," Cameron said.

With the Mets in danger of being swept, Cameron did what he could to loosen the tension before the series finale. He donned a Pedro-like wig with curly black hair on the last day in Atlanta and headed toward the dugout, even performing Pedro's signature point with both hands.

"Chipper almost fell down laughing," Pedro said.

In the end, Chipper and the Braves had another laugh at the Mets' expense.

Asked to preserve a one-run lead in the ninth as the Mets tried to salvage the finale for a second straight series, closer Braden Looper failed. Twice. And the free-falling Mets experienced another agonizing defeat, suffering a sweep with a 4–3 loss to the Braves in ten innings.

Even the unflappable Randolph admitted to being stung by this setback.

"We're gluttons for punishment, I guess," Randolph said. "This is probably as tough as it gets this year."

Takatsu surrendered the game-deciding blow, a two-out, two-strike, two-RBI single by Ryan Langerhans in the tenth that plated you-know-who—Chipper Jones and Andruw Jones. But it was Looper who loaded the bases with no out on a single, hit batsman, and walk.

Takatsu, who became the goat of the middle game in Florida when he allowed a three-run double to Cabrera, had nearly escaped this impossible situation, getting a pair of infield pop-ups. Then, after Langerhans fouled off one full-count offering, the sidearm-throwing right-hander threw a fastball, the same pitch Cabrera had beaten him on in Miami. Langerhans's liner fell in left-centerfield.

"I thought we had it, man," Randolph said. "He came in there and did a pretty good job. After the full count he had to challenge him, I guess."

The Mets fell five games behind wild-card leader Houston, with twenty-three games left, though at 70–69, remaining over .500 seemed a more appropriate goal for the final three-plus weeks.

In the ninth, Looper—handed a 2–1 lead after a stellar outing by Glavine against his former employer—had blown the save as Langerhans delivered a one-out double to plate Francoeur, who had doubled on a shot that kicked up chalk on the right-field line. Woodward's single to center in the top of the tenth scored Beltran from third base and restored the Mets' one-run lead, though the Mets failed to add on as Wright was doubled off second base on Castro's one-out liner to shortstop.

Randolph insisted he had no reservations about sending Looper back out for redemption after what had transpired in the ninth.

"We have to win the game, and he's my closer," he said.

Randolph did admit, however, that he had planned to have Hernandez, who recorded two outs in the eighth inning, attempt the save rather than Looper. But the Mets had not double-switched when Hernandez entered the game, and the reliever was replaced by pinch hitter Marlon Anderson after Diaz doubled with one out in the ninth.

Worse yet, the Mets had to travel to St. Louis, home of the defending National League champion Cardinals, who again had the league's best record.

"We're going to miss Mulder," Randolph said, referring to Mark Mulder, the former Oakland A's ace. "That's good, I guess, *huh*?"

The true pain was about to come.

In the series opener, Albert Pujols belted two solo homers against Kris Benson, more than enough scoring as Chris Carpenter beat the Mets, 5–0. Wright, who struck out three times, said Carpenter would get his Cy Young vote. As for the rest of his ballot, Wright added, "I'll go Andruw Jones MVP, but Pujols is no slouch, either."

Their season slipping away, the Mets experienced one more indignity the following night, when they fell below .500.

Larry Walker's two-out solo homer in the eighth spoiled a stellar outing by Seo as the Mets lost their fifth straight game, 3–2, to the Cardinals. Walker's shot traveled 457 feet, hitting the edge of a scoreboard. The Mets, meanwhile, were in the midst of a profound scoring drought. They had scored more than three runs only three times since a season-high eighteen-run outburst in Arizona nearly three weeks earlier. The Mets had not had a losing record since July 16.

Looking for a spark, Randolph privately spoke with Piazza after the game. They agreed his twenty-three-game absence from the lineup would end the following day, even if his left hand might take months to fully heal.

Piazza had not even faced game-speed-type pitching since suffering the injury. The closest to it: a batting practice session with Randolph, seemingly not sufficient, even if the manager always took pride in his ability to throw BP. Randolph even noted how he won the home-run derby with Jason Giambi one year at the All-Star Game.

Piazza's knack for timely magic quickly resurfaced. His night began with a rocket over the right-field wall in his first at-bat. But Piazza later took a jolt flush to the head on a pitch from reliever Julian Tavarez, eerily reminiscent of a one-time beanball from Roger "The Rocket" Clemens during a regular-season matchup with the Yankees.

Piazza fell to the ground after getting nailed with the 92 mph fastball in the eighth inning, his helmet flying as he landed. Soon afterward, he was able to walk to the dugout under his own power, allaying some fears, though he suffered at least a mild concussion. The Mets suffered their season-high sixth straight loss, 4–2, though the result almost became an afterthought.

"I think I'm all right," Piazza said at his locker in brief, measured comments after the game, while clearly seething.

Aaron Heilman plunked Cardinals shortstop David Eckstein on the left thigh the following half-inning, a welcome sight for an organization that notoriously had let opposing teams get away with hitting batters as far back as when Clemens beaned Piazza on July 8, 2000. Heilman's pitch brought a warning from plate umpire Bill Hohn, but St. Louis expected the retaliation. It took the Mets two years to finally get back at the Yankees for Clemens's action. And Shawn Estes, not around during the original incident, threw behind the Rocket's backside in the batter's box at Shea Stadium as manager Bobby Valentine visibly reacted with disgust.

Piazza never shared his true feelings—and not everyone was pleased with the nature of Heilman's retaliation. One person in a Mets uniform expressed disappointment, noting that plunking the lightweight Eckstein was tantamount to hitting the bat boy. There was no guarantee Pujols or another slugger was going to bat in the eighth, but that should have been Heilman's target in the person's view.

"You have to be able to pitch inside," Heilman said, wisely professing no premeditation. "Sometimes you're going to miss."

Said Cardinals manager Tony La Russa: "All I know is if you pitch down, all you do is sting guys."

La Russa had immediately confronted Tavarez after the reliever returned to the dugout, trying to find out if there was any malice.

"I jumped Tavarez," La Russa said. "I asked Tavarez, 'Fuck, you're a sinkerball pitcher—you missed by *that much?*'"

Tavarez told his manager he hadn't intended to hit Piazza, and La Russa accepted the explanation. Still, Trachsel—the only Met other than Piazza on the team since July 4, 2002—couldn't help but recall Tavarez, then with the Marlins, beaning Edgardo Alfonzo in the head that day after giving up three runs.

La Russa, who conducts his postgame media interviews directly outside the home clubhouse, intercepted Piazza and met with him afterward. Their meeting was held in an adjacent office belonging to the traveling secretary, right after Piazza walked down a hallway to the side where the St. Louis clubhouse is situated. Cardinals closer Jason Isringhausen, Piazza's former teammate, also met with him.

This time, a calmer Piazza did not try to enter the opposition's clubhouse, as he had done during spring training in 2003, looking for then-Dodgers reliever Guillermo Mota. An enraged Piazza—shouting "Where's Mota? *Where's Mota?*"—narrowly missed catching him. Mota had just sped off in Brian Jordan's vehicle. Piazza received a five-game suspension for that incident, which included an on-field brawl during which Mota backpedaled away from the charging slugger. (Interestingly, after that incident, Pedro—a friend of Mota's—criticized Piazza's reaction, telling SI.com: "Maybe he felt like he had to show off his testosterone. But this may be more embarrassing than the one before. Why do you go after skinny Guillermo Mota in spring training and do nothing to Roger Clemens in the World Series?")

Tavarez never came out of the clubhouse to talk to Piazza, though word filtered back to New York that Pujols confronted the reliever in the clubhouse, as La Russa had done on the bench. Pujols probably was into self-preservation, not wanting to get killed by a Pedro pitch in the series finale. Pujols and Piazza are both represented by the Beverly Hills Sports Council and are relatively close, too.

"I told Mike, 'Listen, it looks like shit, but I checked with Tavarez and there's nothing there,'" La Russa said. ". . . The whole incident where somebody gets hit in the head, whether it's Mike Piazza or anybody, spoils the whole night for me. It's been my number-one pet peeve because it's scary, it's dangerous. I'd trade him not getting hit and we lose the game. Anybody who knows me knows that's sincere. They have guys on that club who have played for me who know that. In twenty-some years I've managed, I bet we've hit a half-dozen guys. We just won't pitch up and in."

Despite La Russa expressing remorse and publicly proclaiming his annoyance with pitches like Tavarez's—regardless of the intent—Piazza was still bristling the following day. Asked if he still had any ill will toward the Cardinals, Piazza fiddled in his locker with a pinstriped suit and waited several seconds before declining to comment.

Piazza indicated that the symptoms of his concussion had mostly cleared up by the next morning, though headaches persisted into the week.

Pedro took the mound, with the Mets again trying to salvage the last game of a series—and some dignity—their record now 1–8 on the trip. Pedro's role as stopper seemed like it would take on another dimension—that of enforcer. After all, Pedro indicated during spring training he would blow the head off anybody who tried to harm Piazza. The ace was not known for being shy about hitting batters, either. He finished 2005 ranked sixth among active pitchers in career batters plunked.

Yet Pedro had no desire to escalate any hostility with the Cardinals in what turned out to be an incident-free game. In fact, the ace pronounced the case closed with Heilman hitting Eckstein.

"Nothing happened in my game," Pedro said. "It wasn't my duty to do it today. We did it obviously yesterday, it looked like, protecting Mike the best way possible. It wasn't my duty to do any of that. . . . But I do take pride in protecting."

Surprisingly, Pedro claimed he found relaxing easier during his previous start at Busch Stadium, which happened to be Game 3 of the World Series. Then Pedro had margin for error, with the Red Sox having won the opening two games—wiggle room he couldn't afford, given the Mets' dire situation.

"I had space to actually make mistakes," Pedro said, referring to his seven scoreless innings in October 2004. "The way we're losing right now, it seems we're not going to last very long if we continue to lose games the way we were."

Pedro took a scoreless effort into the eighth inning as the Mets snapped a season-high six-game losing streak with a 7–2 win. They had finished a devastating road trip to Florida, Atlanta, and St. Louis with a 2–8 record, but at least they could fly home on a positive note. Pedro picked up only his second win in nine starts.

Mets brass, who had tried to hawk "pennant pack" tickets for the remaining games at Shea Stadium—which also required a nonrefundable $200 deposit toward 2006 season tickets—by now had yanked the advertisement off the team's Web site.

Pedro said he could easily put the Mets' plight into perspective just by watching the televised scenes of tragedy in a flooded New Orleans, with hungry people, needing medical attention, crowded into the Superdome, and bodies in the submerged streets. The tragedy reminded Pedro of trouble in May 2004, when rivers on the border between the Dominican Republic and Haiti had overflowed and 2,000 people drowned. Pedro had flown in medical supplies from Miami during that tragedy and had arranged for a team of medical professionals to help out.

"You know how lucky we are to be losing games here? What about those people in New Orleans? They're not losing games; they're losing lives," Pedro said. "That's why you have to smile every day regardless of what happens in the game. I hate looking at the TV and seeing those people. It makes you want to cry. That's the reason I take having fun and being happy so seriously."

Randolph tried to keep the Mets upbeat, too, particularly trying to ensure his young players didn't get demoralized. Walking with Wright across the street from Busch Stadium to the team's hotel after the second game of the Cardinals series, Randolph—trying to gauge Wright's mind-set—asked, "What are you thinking right now?"

Wright explained that it was good preparation for the future to be exposed to a pennant race, even if it didn't translate into a berth in a National League Division Series in 2005. That's just what the manager wanted to hear.

"I'm glad we're going through this at this particular time for guys like Reyes and Wright, guys like that, so they can get a taste. I remember Jeter and

Bernie and Mariano and Posada, back in '95, they all went through it," Randolph said, reflecting on his Yankees days. "They would sometimes be spectators. Jeter was a spectator in '95. And I thought the experience was invaluable for him. This is how you learn. This is how you grow. This is what professional sports is about—learning how to win. It's a good experience for everyone here. It's important to know what it feels like to play in September."

Said Wright: "It's a great experience for the younger guys on this team. Hopefully we're in this type of situation year in and year out. We need to get used to playing meaningful games in September."

# THE DIRECTION OF WINNING

THE FLAT-SCREEN TELEVISIONS in the visitors' clubhouse at Citizens Bank Park were tuned to the final inning of the Houston Astros–St. Louis Cardinals game on September 27. Yet no players were paying significant attention as Astros closer Brad Lidge struck out John Rodriguez to officially eliminate the Mets from postseason contention.

With a 3–2 victory against the Philadelphia Phillies earlier that night, the Mets had won their fifth straight game, even with Pedro Martinez scratched from the start. They improbably had remained mathematically alive in the wild-card race into the final week of the season. And Willie Randolph was simply proud that The New Mets had answered his challenge—preventing the 2–8 trip to Florida, Atlanta, and St. Louis from devolving into a month-long funk that would have eroded the season's accomplishments and the winning attitude the first-year manager had instilled.

"The satisfaction is that I challenged these guys a couple of weeks ago to keep playing—to play hard and play for each other—and that's what we've done," Randolph said.

Beginning with Pedro's shutout of the Atlanta Braves that reinvigorated the Shea Stadium faithful, the Mets closed the season by winning twelve of sixteen games. They finished with an 83–79 record, their first winning season in four years and their best mark since reaching the Subway Series in 2000. Despite coveted first baseman Carlos Delgado and agent David Sloane maintaining the Florida Marlins offered a better opportunity than the Mets to reach the postseason—with or without Carlos Beltran in Flushing—the teams tied for third in the National League East. Naturally, Atlanta's reign continued, with its fourteenth straight division title.

"We had times where we were in similar positions in years past, and you didn't see the same vibrancy on the field I think you do now," principal owner Fred Wilpon said about the Mets' finish. "I think it's progress. I'm not sure it's success unless you are in the playoffs, and we're not in the playoffs. So that part is a disappointment. I think the guys have responded very well."

General manager Omar Minaya had handed Pedro a four-year, $53 million contract, and the ace had done everything to justify the commitment. Not only did Pedro go 15–8, with a 2.82 ERA and 208 strikeouts in 217 innings, but he had also energized his teammates and the crowd. The Mets averaged 5,266 more fans per home game when Pedro pitched, while the 2.83 million attendance at Shea Stadium marked the organization's highest total since 1989.

Who knows how many VOTE FOR PEDRO T-shirts the Mets had sold at $24 a pop? Tom Glavine's son Peyton even had one, though the six-year-old was booed when he ended up on the scoreboard at Milwaukee's Miller Park wearing the shirt. (The slogan originated in the 2004 comedy *Napoleon Dynamite*, starring Jon Heder, when his character was trying to get his best friend elected as student-body president. But it certainly fit in Flushing upon Pedro's arrival.)

Pedro enjoyed the New York experience, even if the Mets fell short of the postseason, while his former employer, the reigning champion Boston Red Sox, earned the American League wild card on the season's final day before getting swept in a division series by the eventual-champion Chicago White Sox. Pedro pledged to again report early for spring training in 2006. He even thanked the media for maintaining a positive working relationship, something he had lacked in Boston. Pedro passed out business cards to beat writers that read PEDRO J. MARTINEZ, #45, 123-01 ROOSEVELT AVENUE, FLUSHING, NY 11368. On these he handwrote a private number so he could be reached in the Dominican Republic if anything pressing came up during the winter—such as, say, trading for Manny Ramirez.

Obtaining Ramirez hardly seemed unrealistic. A graphic designer employed by the Mets even created an advertisement in mid-November featuring Ramirez to hawk tickets, presuming the slugger would be acquired. The problem? Ramirez still was with the Red Sox at the time, despite again demanding a trade. So, high-level Mets executives were mortified when they learned a second employee had e-mailed the concept to someone at ESPN. With the speed of cyberspace, the advertisement, which read MANNY'S ON BOARD: METS ON THE RISE, quickly made its way to the *Daily News*, where it appeared underneath a breaking story that Delgado would be traded to the Mets by Thanksgiving the following day.

Yes, Delgado became a Met, despite the hostility during the previous winter's recruitment. The inferior offer he had signed with the Marlins lacked the no-trade protection the Mets had offered at the time. Florida, forced to dump salary as it had after winning the 1997 World Series, this time because of its failure to secure a stadium, accepted rookie first baseman Mike Jacobs, pitching prospect Yusmeiro Petit, and Class A third baseman Grant Psomas for the slugging first baseman. Florida even kicked in $7 million to cover the $48 million guaranteed to Delgado through 2008. Delgado's backloaded deal in Florida had paid him only $4 million in 2005. Mets special assistant Tony Bernazard, who had somehow particularly upset Delgado, was the official who called the slugger to welcome him to the organization. Bygones were bygones.

"I *want* to be here," said Delgado, who pledged to abide by the team's request to stand for "God Bless America" rather than put his own political views ahead of the organization's wishes. "I *want* to become part of the New York community, and I *want* to try to help the Mets go to the next level. I've never had the opportunity to be in the playoffs. I've never had the opportunity to be in a playoff race. So, I'm really looking forward to this."

The same week as the Mets obtained Delgado, the Marlins sent ace Josh Beckett to Boston for prospects because the Red Sox were willing to take on the remaining $18 million owed to third baseman Mike Lowell as well.

Pedro had detached himself from Boston. With four days left in the season, and the Red Sox trying to avoid falling two games behind the Yankees in the American League East standings, Mets players—including Cliff Floyd, Mike Piazza, and Glavine—gathered around a television in the clubhouse to view the final two innings of Boston's game against the Baltimore Orioles. The Mets' 11–0 rout of the Colorado Rockies already complete, Pedro did not stick around with his teammates to watch David Ortiz's game-tying home run in the eighth inning, much less Ortiz's walk-off RBI single an inning later that won the game, 5–4.

"You see how worried I am?" Pedro asked. "I'm leaving."

Added Pedro: "Competing, I miss. I miss the competitiveness that's out there between those two teams, because they're probably the best two teams in the American League. Just the hostile atmosphere between the two teams and the fans, and the media attention, I don't miss at all. I'm glad I'm here and I'm off of it."

Pedro mentioned how he was not eagerly awaiting the Mets' 2006 inter-league schedule, which called for a June 27–29 series in Boston, with an off-day in Beantown before the opener, no less. He had already started speculating about the content of what promised to be an unforgiving column by the *Boston Globe*'s Dan Shaughnessy. Pedro even suggested he might ask pitching coach Rick Peterson to align the rotation so he could avoid the Red Sox and instead pitch against the Toronto Blue Jays, then at Yankee Stadium.

Rarely the stressed type, Pedro likely wasn't consumed during the winter with his impending return to Fenway Park. His mind figured to be elsewhere anyway, like his planned off-season marriage to ESPN Deportes reporter Carolina Cruz. Claudia Julissa Cruz Rodriguez, her sister, was the 2004 Miss World first runner-up. Elvis Cruz, her brother, hit .148 in thirty-eight games for the Mets' Class A affiliate in Kingsport, Tennessee, in 2005.

Pedro's season ended on September 22, when he left a matchup against the Marlins' Dontrelle Willis after only seventy-five pitches. Afterward, Pedro acknowledged the severity of the injuries that had nagged him for months. Not only had Pedro suffered stiffness between his shoulder blades, but he'd also had the hip trouble that required a cortisone shot on May 17. In addition, the right foot he used to push off the mound was badly beaten up, the result of the foot violently grinding into the ground as he followed through on his delivery. The eroded exterior of his cleat offered clear evidence of how much pounding the foot had taken. The nail on Pedro's big toe was completely blackened by season's end. His trouble pushing off the mound helped explain why he rarely hit 90 mph with his fastball any longer, though his pinpoint control and pitch movement allowed him to maintain mastery of opposing batters regardless. Even in December, Pedro mentioned he was still unable to run.

"I think I pitched fine, right?" asked Pedro, who had not exceeded 217 innings in the regular season since 1998, his first year with the Red Sox.

Team brass maintained during the season's final weeks that Pedro would be scratched once the Mets became mathematically eliminated from the wild-card race. When the Mets swept the Washington Nationals, and the Astros stumbled the same weekend against the Chicago Cubs at Wrigley Field, Victor Zambrano took Pedro's September 27 start in Philadelphia anyway, plus the season finale at Shea Stadium. There was no compelling reason to risk injury to Pedro by throwing him against the Phillies. A borderline miracle would have been required to reach the postseason. The bottom line: Pedro needed the rest. His weight had dropped to the upper-170s because of the taxing season, down fifteen pounds from when he had arrived before spring training.

"We have to look at the big picture, and we have to be wise in how we handle not only him, but any player," Minaya said. "The big picture is, we want Pedro pitching for us the next couple of years."

Shut down, Pedro still bubbled with energy. During the final weekend, with the only compelling reason to attend Shea Stadium to celebrate what appeared to be Piazza's final days as a Met, Pedro donned an inflatable orange football helmet emblazoned with a Jägermeister logo in the dugout. After Marlon Anderson homered, Pedro head-butted him, to the delight of onlookers and cameramen. Teammate Steve Trachsel joked that a shipment of the herb liqueur ought to arrive from the German company for all the buzz Pedro's antics generated.

Pedro still had the blue boxing gloves from spring training in his locker on the final day, the ones he had used in Port St. Lucie, Florida, to playfully jab at reliever Bartolome Fortunato.

"He's been a great citizen," Fred Wilpon said. "He's been a great pitcher. With a little break here and there, he might have won twenty games this year. Everything we've asked him to do, he has done 120 percent. He's a man of his word. He's a man of character."

Wilpon also kept true to his word, lying low, as did his son Jeff, the team's chief operating officer. The principal owner had barely been seen, much less quoted in newspapers, all season. He finally surfaced in late September at a news conference in the Time-Life building, at the Avenue of the Americas and 51st Street in Manhattan, in an old CNN studio with a view of Radio City Music Hall. He was there to celebrate the announcement of the name, logo, and studio designs of SportsNet New York. The new regional sports channel, which the Mets' parent company, Sterling Equities, had partnered with Time Warner and Comcast to create, was scheduled to carry 125 regular-season games in 2006 when it debuted. It would provide another vehicle for the Mets to brand their name and increase revenue. Popular radio announcer Gary Cohen would shift over to the network to perform the play-by-play role, though television requires fewer words.

The future seemed bright on virtually every front. Wilpon beamed when he announced that ground would be broken for a new Ebbets Field–influenced stadium the following spring. Better yet, third baseman David Wright would be only twenty-six years old when the 45,000-seat stadium opened in 2009. Jose Reyes would be only twenty-five.

"One of our players just said to me, 'Where have you been, Freddy?' " Wilpon said. "I've been at every game. I just don't go down to the clubhouse, and I'm not on the field. Frankly, I like it better that way. We have very good baseball people and it's their job. There's no need for me or Jeffrey to be out there that way. When there was, we had to be out there. Now we don't."

If there was one overriding disappointment, it had to be Beltran and it was unlikely that the centerfielder would quibble much with that assessment. Handed a seven-year, $119 million contract, Beltran hit .266 with 16 homers, 78 RBI, and 17 steals, his lowest totals in each category since 2000, when he had missed two months of the Kansas City Royals' season due to a bruised right knee.

Beltran frustrated fans with his insistence on sacrifice bunting, despite occupying the third slot in the batting order, which carries the responsibility for driving in runs. Even Randolph mentioned to Beltran on multiple occasions a preference for him to swing away. Beltran also had a pair of ill-timed, ill-fated steal attempts of third base late in the season that warranted criticism.

Curiously, nine of Beltran's ten first-half homers came in Pedro-pitched games, including the long ball off John Smoltz in Atlanta on April 10 that allowed the Mets to arrive at Shea Stadium at 1–5 rather than 0–6. Beltran's production for Pedro led the ace to playfully suggest: "Maybe I need to write my name in the lineup and then, as the game is going to start, erase it." Maybe Pedro should have. Impact moments were few and far between for Beltran.

Quiet and respectful, Beltran never emerged as the team's leader on or off the field. During spring training, he had pulled Reyes aside for a thirty-minute chat after the speedster was picked off first base twice in the same intrasquad game. But Beltran's reserved personality made him a complementary component rather than the commanding presence his $119 million salary suggested he ought to be.

He certainly didn't have the temperament to stand up in the clubhouse during tough times and rally the Mets with a resounding go-get-'em address.

"I'm realistic enough to know that's not going to be him. Not right now," Randolph said. "That's not going to be him. He's not going to do it. He's been here all year and he's spoken up a couple of times in meetings, but nothing big. Hopefully, eventually he will. I understand that it's going to take him time to be that way, and maybe it will never happen. I've been around great players who never stand up and say anything. That's just my idea of what I wish he was a little bit more like. But that's fine."

"I'm quiet. And I always will be quiet," Beltran said. "When I see something wrong, I will always, maybe not show people up, but I will always maybe call him to the side and let him know, 'Hey, you should do it another way.' There's a lot of different leaders. There's leaders who like to show up people. I'm not like that."

When players arrive in New York, most notably with the Yankees, they initially seem to struggle while experiencing an adjustment period, though it rarely takes a full year. In the Bronx, Alex Rodriguez and Jason Giambi went through rough times while pressing early in their pinstriped careers as they tried to justify exorbitant salaries and hype and fan demands.

"I think Carlos is going to continue to get better here and get more comfortable here," Piazza predicted. "This is definitely a shock for him."

With a new home still under construction in Sands Point, Long Island, Beltran lived in three different locations during his inaugural Mets season as his wife Jessica tried to find a place that suited her. The couple spent the season's first month in Long Island City, then moved to Glen Cove in Nassau County, and finally, to Manhattan.

Beltran, repeatedly the target of boos from the home crowd, though seemingly shy of the venom dedicated to favorite target Kazuo Matsui, had another alibi. He played through pain that affected his mobility and hampered his production for a lengthy period. Beltran tweaked his right quadriceps muscle May 1 at Washington when he was caught stealing in the first inning. He thought he could play through the mild discomfort, but worsened the injury three weeks later against the Yankees at Shea Stadium, after rounding second base on Piazza's first-inning single. Beltran considered removing himself from the game at that point, but instead, applied ointment and continued. When he strode to right-centerfield to snag Randy Johnson's fly ball in the fifth inning, he told himself: "I can't go anymore." He labored getting to first base on a groundout the following half-inning, and then departed.

Rather than go on the disabled list, Beltran stayed out of the starting lineup for nine days, then returned and struggled as the injury lingered.

Speed supposedly doesn't slump, but Beltran didn't have that major facet of his game at his disposal. After exceeding forty stolen bases each of the previous two seasons, Beltran had only one steal until the final day of June, when he swiped a pair of bases three days after getting eight cubic centimeters of fluid drained.

Fans in Flushing weren't the only ones upset with Beltran. Jilted Astros followers remained consumed with Beltran into October, especially since their owner had offered what would have been a record commitment by that organization—$20 million more than Jeff Bagwell had received for a five-year deal in 2000. They never let go of their anger, even though Beltran had slugged a postseason-record–tying eight home runs for them the previous year while carrying Houston to within a game of the World Series. With the Mets' season completed, a sign was displayed in the upper deck in right field at Minute Maid Park. It was hung from a railing during Game 4 of the National League Division Series, which the Astros won in eighteen innings, 7–6, to eliminate the Braves. It read: CARLO$—HOW'S THE VIEW FROM THE COUCH? Even when the Astros marched to the World Series, the taunts continued. Ten-year season-ticket holder Joe Valentino, who had just relocated to Colorado, held up a sign at his seat behind the home dugout before Game 3. It read: TICKETS: $125.00 EACH. AIRFARE: $450.00 EACH. BELTRAN WATCHING THE WORLD SERIES ON TV: PRICELESS. If it's any consolation, the White Sox swept Valentino's beloved Astros.

"A lot of ups and downs," Beltran labeled the season. "I was a little bit frustrated when I started to feel good about my leg and [then] I had the collision with Mike and I felt like I went down again. I think what really upset me was when I had my leg injury. For two months I was feeling my quad, and that really took away a lot from my game. It was a little difficult for me because that was the first time I hurt [a muscle in] my leg.

"I hurt my leg at the wrong time and probably in the wrong city, New York, because a lot of people expect a lot from you. *A lot* of expectations. But, to me, I feel like I've done my best the whole year. I've been playing as hard as I can the whole year."

Fred Wilpon agreed and stood by his $119 million investment. The principal owner had sung the praises of playing in New York to Beltran during a face-to-face recruiting pitch at the Ritz-Carlton in San Juan. He understood the pressure to perform on the big stage.

"I certainly have been satisfied with his effort—110 percent," Fred Wilpon said. "He's not satisfied with his performance, and he knows he can do better. He knows he *will* do better. He's a real pro. I mean, he was banged up pretty badly, and there was no way he wasn't going to play."

To their credit, Beltran and his Mets teammates remained upbeat until the end. Deposed closer Braden Looper was headed for arthroscopic surgery the day after the season to repair the AC joint in his right shoulder, which had grown increasingly uncomfortable. Yet on the final morning of the season, Looper—who blew eight saves, particularly high-profile ones, in thirty-six chances—was still mischievous. He playfully dumped the clothes hanging in Wright's locker before they could be packed for the winter. That prompted an escalation in the hijinks. Suddenly, the shoes Looper needed to wear home were missing their laces. After that, the cleats Wright needed to wear during the season finale had their laces cut.

Wright professed innocence.

"Look through all that and tell me you see shoelaces," he told Looper, feigning no culpability as the closer rummaged through Wright's belongings.

They were still jostling after the game. As Looper walked down a clubhouse hallway toward the players' dining area, wearing the shoes with no laces, Wright said: "You're getting warmer. . . . Hot. . . . Hot. . . . *Hot.*"

Wright emerged as a star in his first full major-league season and had the universal appeal and displayed the grit that suggested he would one day be named the team's captain. He was so popular, even 2002 Olympic gold-medal figure skater Sarah Hughes came to Shea Stadium for a specially arranged meeting.

Wright started 160 games, finishing with a .306 average, 27 home runs, and team-high 102 RBI, albeit while committing 24 errors, tied with the Arizona Diamondbacks' Troy Glaus for the most in Major League Baseball among third basemen. He had positive relationships with all of his older teammates, who constantly ribbed him to ensure he remained grounded.

During a May trip to Florida, a profusely sweating Floyd pranced around in Wright's pink Polo shirt in the clubhouse before a game to stink it up.

"What is that, extra medium?" Cameron called out to Wright.

"They don't understand," Wright said, defending his attire's not-so-masculine color. "I can pull it off."

Wright wore the shirt back to the hotel without getting it cleaned. When he wore it again several weeks later, the shirt ended up taped to his locker with a sign that read DIANA WRIGHT—THAT'S ME.

Teammates particularly got a kick out of the media attention Wright received as the anniversary of his July 21, 2004, major-league debut neared. Infielder Chris Woodward joked he ought to recognize the occasion, too. He did just that when the anniversary arrived, taping a sign atop Wright's locker that read CONGRATULATIONS ON 1 YEAR IN THE BIG LEAGUES. Teammates Doug Mientkiewicz and Anderson both interrupted Wright's postgame interviews to needle him about wearing his Virginia Tech hat backward on camera.

"We'll see the next time I see something in your swing!" Wright jokingly fired back to Mientkiewicz. (Wright had given a batting tip to Mientkiewicz, encouraging him to start his hands moving earlier during his swing, which the first baseman credited for a home run that day.)

Wright continued to carry Floyd's luggage even after the one-year anniversary. The veterans proclaimed rookie status didn't end until one full season in the big leagues was complete—at least in Wright's case. Yet Floyd was extremely fond of Wright. Floyd even bought him an oversized grayish suit. Wright looked at himself in the mirror for a month and a half while wearing it before finally stepping out in public in the attire, not sure it was his look.

Wright had two highlight-reel catches during the season. The first came in Seattle, with a Derek Jeter–style grab, when Wright threw his body into the armrest of a chair along the third-base stands at Safeco Field to catch Raul Ibañez's foul pop. The latter came in San Diego two days before Beltran's collision with Cameron, when Wright retreated on Brian Giles's broken-bat flare to shallow left field, reached out, and caught the baseball over his right shoulder with his bare hand before tumbling to the ground.

"*Are you kidding?*" Ted Robinson said on the Madison Square Garden Network telecast. "That may be the best I've ever seen. . . . Well, David Wright just guaranteed he will be seen on scoreboards around baseball for the next twenty years."

Said Mientkiewicz: "He totally better take me to the ESPYs. If that's not Play of the Year, that's bull. He better not get a girlfriend between now and then, because I'm going."

Wright, who lived in the same Long Island City apartment building as mentor Joe McEwing during his two-plus-month introduction to the majors in 2004, spread his wings off the field, too. He moved to the East Side of midtown Manhattan for the '05 season. Not that anyone needed to worry about a reprise of Darryl Strawberry and Dwight Gooden's troubles as emerging stars in the 1980s in the city that never sleeps. Wright spent most of his time away from the ballpark sleeping and tending to a few-weeks-old puppy named Homer.

"My idea of going out is having a nice dinner during the season because I'm exhausted after the games," Wright said.

Back at shortstop after an ill-advised decision to move him to second base to land Matsui, Wright's teammate on the left side of the infield also had a season to celebrate. Plagued by assorted leg injuries during his first two seasons in the big leagues, Reyes played in a team-high 161 games. He led the National League with 60 steals and 17 triples, even if his batting remained a work in progress and he briefly slipped to seventh in the order.

Reyes's franchise-record 696 at-bats underscored how he had failed to walk enough. His .300 on-base percentage ranked 141st of 148 major-leaguers who qualified for the batting titles. When Reyes reached a full count at Shea Stadium in early May, having yet to get a base on balls all season, the fans started chanting, "Walk! Walk! Walk!" as teammates howled in the dugout. After 119 plate appearances, Reyes finally did get his first walk, ending the longest streak to open a season by a leadoff hitter since Luis Salazar went 129 plate appearances without a walk for the San Diego Padres in 1983.

"I'm so happy. I worked so hard this year," Reyes said. "I stretched a lot, more than I did before. I stretched like three times before the game. I'm running outside a half-hour before the game. That was a key for me this year. The people in the Dominican are going to feel happy, too. When they call me, they say, 'Get the title of stolen bases.'"

Said Randolph: "The main thing for me is the growth of the young players. To me that's the most positive thing about this year, that David Wright and Jose Reyes got a chance to really play a full, solid year. I think everyone had a chance to see the potential of what they can do. That's important when you have young players who are somewhat the core group of your team. You look forward to the future. When you add a few pieces, that could be really special."

The feel-good year also had its share of difficulties.

The Mets obtained the slick-fielding Mientkiewicz from the Red Sox for Class A prospect Ian Bladergroen the night Delgado committed to the Marlins. The first baseman ended up in Randolph's doghouse, contributing little.

Mientkiewicz and Randolph had polar-opposite personalities—the player outspoken and prone to shattered confidence; the manager reserved, serious, and self-assured.

One particular emotional meltdown took place in Atlanta in May, and proved to be an early warning sign. A slumping Mientkiewicz—after grounding into two double plays during an 0-for-4 night against the Braves—told reporters he had not eaten in two days, or slept in a week. He then begged for the tabloid back pages to carry his picture with the headline: I SUCK! (The *Daily News* never actually went to press with it, but the copy editors printed a couple of mock back pages using Mientkiewicz's suggestion. Mientkiewicz kept one copy in his locker. Another hung at least briefly in the trainer's room in the home clubhouse at Shea Stadium.)

Things definitely weren't going well for Mientkiewicz at the time of the Atlanta meltdown. A taxi driver who took him to Turner Field had a tire blow out. Mientkiewicz also got locked in the stairwell where the team was staying. His pregnant wife Jodi even told him she would refuse to reveal their first child's gender until he got a hit. Presumably, she was joking. Mientkiewicz even initiated a lengthy meeting with Randolph at the hotel in trendy Buckhead to discuss his troubles.

"Mentally, I'm just fried," Mientkiewicz said. "I've never felt like this. I've been bad before. Not this bad. I've been 5-for-110 and finished at .300. This is inexcusable. I apologize to every Met fan in America right now. I'm better than this. I know you guys wrote about how good defensively I am. But I can hit. I know I can hit. I'm embarrassing everybody with this. . . . A guy tonight screamed, 'Mientkiewicz, you suck.' I had to turn around and agree with him. I said, 'You're absolutely right, sir. I feel I owe you. I should pay you the admission you paid.'"

Though Mientkiewicz had a solid relationship with Wright and a self-deprecating sense of humor that attracted reporters, some Mets grew to see him as an attention hog, always the first to congratulate a teammate after a home run primarily to mug for the cameras.

Mientkiewicz had a $4 million team option for 2006, but had no doubt he was through as a Met, with the Red Sox forced to pick up the $450,000 buyout. Still, when Randolph inserted Woodward over him as a defensive replacement for Mike Jacobs at first base during the final weekend of the season, Mientkiewicz was stung. He said aloud: "Fuck, I'm a Gold Glove first baseman." He hit .240 with 11 home runs and 29 RBI in 275 at-bats and barely played in September as the rookie Jacobs emerged. Delgado hit .301 with 33 home runs and 115 RBI for the Marlins. Mets first basemen finished with the lowest average (.227) and on-base percentage (.303) in the majors, according to the Elias Sports Bureau.

Other than the Mientkiewicz move, Minaya had a brilliant run until his acquisition of left-handed pitcher Kazuhisa Ishii from the Los Angeles Dodgers late in spring training, after Trachsel's back injury. As the trade neared completion, Dodgers pitching coach Jim Colborn, asked to assess what pitch Ishii had the most difficulty throwing, deadpanned: "Strikes." It proved too true. Worse, the Mets waited too long to pull the plug and insert Jae Seo into Ishii's spot in the rotation. The control-challenged Ishii went 3–9 with a 5.14 ERA and was eventually banished to Triple-A Norfolk, then the Mets' bullpen once rosters expanded in September.

There were other disappointments.

Matsui was a bust at second base, just like he was at shortstop. He arrived in the United States having played 1,143 straight games for the Pacific League's Seibu Lions, the fifth-longest streak in Japanese baseball history, yet he struggled to stay healthy for a second straight season with the Mets. He had modest success at the plate his first year, but 2005 included difficulties there. Matsui hit .255 with 3 home runs and 24 RBI in 267 at-bats and figured to be aggressively shopped during the winter—despite the Mets owing him $8 million in '06 and the infielder having a no-trade clause to all but the Los Angeles Angels and Dodgers and the Yankees.

The Mets tragically traded flame-throwing young left-hander Scott Kazmir to the Tampa Bay Devil Rays to obtain Zambrano on July 30, 2004. Zambrano, briefly sent to the bullpen the final month, continued to be maddeningly erratic, going 7–12 with a 4.17 ERA. Randolph even coined the term "Zambrano-ish" to describe his wildness.

Looper, who struggled as closer, underwent surgery on October 3 to shave a bone in his right shoulder that had caused season-long discomfort and affected his control. He compared the sensation to walking around for months with a quarter-inch rock in your shoe. Looper had experienced trouble with the same AC joint late in the 2004 season, but the organization's former medical staff had advocated rest over surgery. When the Mets switched affiliations to the Hospital for Special Surgery and Looper was reevaluated, the new medical staff presented surgery as an option. By that time, Looper would have missed most of April. Given the Mets' less-than-stellar bullpen alternatives, with Mike DeJean and Felix Heredia as the other primary relievers, Looper opted to pitch through any trouble and take care of it after the season.

Though teammates and Mets brass knew he was pitching with an injury, Looper concealed the information from the media and fans until the final week of the season because he didn't want it to seem like he was making excuses. Lefties hit .336 against Looper, a ground-ball specialist who struggled to keep the ball down in the strike zone because the discomfort adversely affected his ability to follow through during his delivery.

His blown saves came during high-profile moments. They included Opening Day against the Cincinnati Reds (to undermine Pedro's masterful Mets debut); at Yankee Stadium with the Mets poised to sweep; at Pittsburgh before the All-Star break, when the Mets let a four-run lead with two out in the ninth slip away; and in Atlanta during the 2–8 road trip in early September, when he twice lost leads in one game.

"By no way, shape, or form is this an excuse for anything," Looper said when he acknowledged the injury in Philadelphia the final week. "You have to perform, but it is something I have had to deal with."

On balance, the season's positives vastly outweighed those issues.

Floyd, as prone to injury as Reyes in his career, responded to early challenges from Randolph and outfield coach Jerry Manuel and played in 150 games, his highest number since 1998. He repeatedly heard chants of "MVP, MVP, MVP" from crowds at Shea Stadium while batting .273 with 34 homers and 98 RBI. Floyd led the National League in outfield assists while showing the solid range he had previously lacked because of a litany of leg ailments.

Glavine, who looked washed up at thirty-nine years old during the first half, reinvented himself by introducing a cut fastball and more regularly throwing a curveball. That forced batters to become conscious of the inner half of the plate, making his signature changeup on the outside corner more effective. The south-paw evened his record at 13–13 during the season-ending series against the Rockies to post his first non-losing season in three years as a Met. He had a 2.22 ERA during the second half, making the fact that his contract vested for 2006 welcome news after all. Glavine increased his career win total to 275, making the historic 300-win plateau achievable with two more seasons of pitching, which would take him to age forty-one.

He became the MVP off the field, nearly two full months after the season ended, along with his wife Chris. The Glavines greeted Billy Wagner from the Phillies at Westchester County Airport during the coveted free-agent closer's recruiting visit. The pitchers and their wives then toured Greenwich, Connecticut, housing options, so the country-boy Wagner could feel comfortable with New York. Glavine, who himself picked the Mets over the Phillies three years earlier as a free agent, succeeded in wooing Wagner. At least, Glavine played a role, one likely secondary to Minaya's continued aggressive bidding. Wagner agreed to a four-year, $43 million contract with an option for 2010 and a no-trade clause the day Delgado was introduced with a news conference at the Diamond Club at Shea Stadium. The next day, Wagner appeared in the same location for the formal announcement of his signing.

Aaron Heilman, a former first-round pick out of Notre Dame, became one of the most pleasant surprises. He returned to a three-quarters arm angle at the suggestion of team consultant Al Jackson, a Mets pitcher during the 1960s, and blossomed in the bullpen. Once Looper lost the closer's job and eventually got shut down because of the shoulder trouble, Heilman effectively combined with Roberto Hernandez to complete games. Heilman finished with five saves. After the All-Star break, he produced a 0.68 ERA, while opposing batters hit only .175 against him. He struck out seventy-two in sixty-six relief innings.

Hernandez, at forty years old, became an unexpected eighth-inning specialist, the role originally slated for DeJean. Looper and Hernandez, in fact, were the only relievers to remain with the club from the time the Mets broke camp until the October 2 finale against Colorado. And to think that on the day the team's moving truck was set to leave Port St. Lucie, Florida, at the end of spring training, Hernandez's belongings were sitting in his Hummer because he was unsure of his fate.

"If I didn't make the team I was going home," Hernandez said.

By season's end, DeJean had been released and signed by the Rockies. Heredia had undergone surgery for an aneurysm, which had alarmingly caused his left hand to turn cold and numb. (Hernandez was the one who convinced Heredia to come clean to team officials about the extent of the hand condition, which potentially prevented the issue from becoming graver.) Among the other original bullpen members: South Korean left-hander Dae-Sung Koo had been designated for assignment. Mike Matthews was demoted to Triple-A Norfolk; May 30 at the ballpark in Pawtucket, Rhode Island, he left the game before its completion on his own after allowing seven runs, and he never rejoined the Tides. Manny Aybar had been relegated to the minors, too.

Behind the plate, Ramon Castro proved much more than a defensive complement to Piazza. Castro, who entered the season with a .212 career major-league average, had 41 RBI in 209 at-bats. Combined with Piazza's numbers, the Mets got quality offensive production from the catching position—.249, 27 home runs, and 103 RBI.

Seo returned from a three-month minor-league stint to dominate the National League. Once dependent on a fastball-changeup repertoire, the South Korean right-hander developed split-finger and cut fastballs at Norfolk, winning his first five decisions after replacing Ishii in the rotation. Seo finished the season at 8–2 with a 2.59 ERA.

Jacobs, who set a major-league record by producing four homers within three days of his major-league debut, became a viable first-base option for 2006. The rookie had been told he was demoted after a pinch-hit homer in his first big-league appearance—only to have the decision reversed fifteen minutes later and his belongings placed back on a team bus bound for the airport and a flight to Phoenix. A converted catcher, Jacobs finished with a .310 average, 11 home runs, and 23 RBI in 100 at-bats. He headed to winter ball in Venezuela to hone his skills as a first baseman under the tutelage of Mets infield instructor Edgar Alfonzo, the brother of former Met Edgardo Alfonzo. While in South America, Jacobs received the news he had been traded for Delgado, when his fiancée's brother called to let him know about New York–based reports.

The bench players performed well, too. Anderson hit .321 in 56 pinch-hit at-bats and parlayed that production into a two-year contract with the Washington Nationals. Miguel Cairo eventually overtook Matsui as the starting second baseman, though leg injuries and limited range made him best suited for a reserve role. Woodward hit .283 and started at six positions.

"Last year the Mets only won seventy-one games, and right now, we've improved," Hernandez said. "It's fun coming to the ballpark when you've got David Wright, Jose Reyes, and Mike Jacobs, the way Aaron Heilman and Jae Seo have pitched this year. Mets fans have something to be happy about this year—that these guys are getting this much experience this soon and getting good and getting better." Said Randolph:

> *I definitely think we got as much as we could out of this team, especially with the injuries we had. Think about that. Carlos didn't have the year he was supposed to have. We didn't have a right fielder or first baseman, a stable situation at the catcher's spot and second base. So when you think about this season, those guys deserve a lot of credit for what they did this year. We had more than our share of injuries and tough luck. I don't make excuses for that. That's part of baseball. But we still had to rely heavily on a lot of our bench people, who did a great job.*
>
> *We just had a certain toughness as a team that carried us through a lot. We definitely got the most out of our group, the guys who were here. The main thing for me is, we took our hits and we kept fighting back. A team could easily just roll over and feel sorry for themselves and cry over things, but we didn't do that. I'm real proud.*

Perhaps Randolph deserved the most credit. From the 0–5 start, through the Beltran-Cameron collision and the disastrous 2–8 road trip in early September, the first-year manager remained the even-keeled rudder. Players respected Randolph. They played hard for him to the end despite adversity, the clearest evidence of his imprint and the resonance of his message.

Whereas the Mets won twelve of their final sixteen games, the Marlins—arguably with more talent—lost twelve of seventeen down the stretch, as sniping between young star Miguel Cabrera and the veterans, as well as manager Jack McKeon's disconnect with the clubhouse, contributed to Florida's implosion.

It was inevitable that Randolph's moves would be scrutinized. It *is* New York, after all. There was the botched double-switch in Cincinnati in his second game as manager. There was allowing Shingo Takatsu to make his Mets debut in Florida against Cabrera at a make-or-break point in the season. There was also the decision to pitch to the Nationals' Vinny Castilla in September at Shea Stadium, with first base open and light-hitting catcher Keith Osik on deck. (Randolph insisted Nationals manager Frank Robinson would have pinch-hit with Brian Schneider had Castilla been walked. Apparently, Randolph was unaware that Schneider was unavailable because of a shoulder injury, though the responsibility for gathering that information probably belonged to bench coach Sandy Alomar Sr.; Randolph planned to flip Alomar and first-base coach and former White Sox manager Jerry Manuel's roles for the 2006 season.) Regardless, Robinson was one of the opposing managers who complimented Randolph about how hard the Mets had played down the stretch, a contrast with previous editions that swooned in September.

Randolph made sure to communicate with his players, one of predecessor Art Howe's deficiencies. Anyone around the team for even a brief period knew Randolph emphasized his connection to the clubhouse. He incessantly mentioned how he always conducted what he termed "skull sessions" with his players, how he would summon them into his office for private, one-on-one chats, which kept them on the same page and meant full-team meetings were mostly unnecessary. Randolph added:

*I take a lot of positives out of this year. I didn't come in here thinking we were going to win a World Series the first year. I just wanted to come in here and change the culture and the mentality and the focus of this team, and get these guys playing hard for these fans every day. I think for the most part I've accomplished that. That's just a first step for me.*

*It's just getting guys to believe in themselves as far as expecting to win every day. When you come to the ballpark in preparation for the game, you have to really believe that you can win, and bring that consistently every day. I lived in this town, and I've seen over the last four or five years how this team has kind of fallen off in the second half or down the stretch. Even before we got to that point, I just wanted to instill the mentality that we need to believe we can go out there and compete with anybody in the division and league. It's how you prepare yourself and feel about yourself. It kind of caught on after a while, where players started to believe, regardless of the injuries or the misfortune or the things that happened around us, that we could still continue to compete. It's really just building a winning mentality.*

*There are a lot of teams that are more talented than we are. But I don't think there's any team that plays harder than we do. That's a step in the right direction.*

Randolph remained unflappably confident, refusing to let criticism influence his decision making—even though he seemed acutely aware of what was being written in the newspapers and said about him on talk radio.

Three weeks after Floyd sat out with a twenty-game hitting streak (then had it snapped the following game when he returned), Randolph was still irritated at the chatter on WFAN, which suggested that he had somehow sent Floyd into a 7-for-60 funk by giving him a day off for no good reason. Unsolicited, Randolph brought up the topic in Atlanta. Randolph reminded reporters how he had told them Floyd had an ailing Achilles tendon when he sat out.

"According to certain people, I put him in a slump," Randolph said. ". . . That's crazy. I'm going to sit somebody down with a twenty-game hitting streak?"

As reporters departed the visiting manager's office at Turner Field, he added, "I'm not being sensitive, either. Coming in, that was one of my labels. I just want it told straight."

Pedro had referred to Randolph as being cold-blooded during spring training. The ace meant it as a compliment, and it proved an apt description. Even in dissecting the season, Randolph had only begrudgingly labeled it a success, despite all the positive occurrences. After ten straight trips to the postseason as a Yankees coach, falling short of meaningful games in October wasn't something to crow about in Randolph's estimation. IT'S THAT SIMPLE—WE PLAY TO WIN read the placard on Randolph's desk.

Randolph did have a little bend. He amended the rule from spring training about music in the clubhouse. Well, at least he didn't enforce it.

"I guess he had to get some grips on everything," Cameron said, speculating about the manager's initial motivation. "He finally broke down and let us do our thing."

Randolph could be feisty with the media, with no better example than before a July 19 game against the Padres. The manager dropped Piazza, a future Hall of Famer, to sixth in the lineup, where he had not batted since early in his rookie season in 1993 with the Dodgers. Wright jumped ahead of Piazza to fifth, an undeniable changing of the guard in which the Mets' future star was superceding the club's fading one. Randolph hoped to minimize the story. In doing so, he insisted there was none, which led to a testy exchange with reporters.

It was one thing to ensure his players didn't get too high or low by maintaining an even keel. But Randolph could not stop New York tabloids from creating a stir through simply downplaying the move. Not even Karl Rove, President Bush's brilliant and controversial strategist, would have succeeded.

"We're at the halfway point. I've learned a lot from watching my team up to this point. And after a while you make adjustments, or you do what you feel is best," Randolph said, when explaining about dropping Piazza. "I still don't understand why this is a big deal, but I'll answer the questions. I'll sit here and just play along."

"It's not a big deal," Marty Noble from MLB.com said. "We just need your words."

"No. No. It's more than that, Marty," Randolph said. "C'mon, you need my words? . . . Whatever."

"What do you think it is?" Peter Abraham from the *Journal News* of Westchester asked. "It's not personal."

"No, it's not personal. I'm not taking it as personal," Randolph said. "But what's the big deal? It's from fifth to sixth. It's putting together the team."

"We have stories to do," Abraham said. "Tell me what we should write."

"Oh, so you want to make a *story* then?" Randolph asked.

"I don't want to," Abraham said. "I *have* to."

"Oh, you *have* to?" Randolph said.

"I have to," Abraham said. "I have to write a notebook before the game."

"Tell your editor this is not a big deal," Randolph said. "It's not a big deal right now."

"Well, it was big enough that you talked to Mike about it, right?" Don Burke from the Newark *Star-Ledger* asked, noting how Piazza had been summoned into the manager's office for a meeting earlier that afternoon.

"Well, that's because I'd rather tell my player before I tell you guys," Randolph said. "If I don't, then you're going to jump him or whatever and make a bigger story. So I always make a practice of telling my player."

"Every day, no matter what happens, we have to write a story before the game," Abraham said. "Every single day. We can't tell our editors, 'You know—'"

"I understand that," Randolph said, jumping in. "But is this really a story? Is this the story, though?"

"Well, then you tell me what the story is," Abraham said. "What else is the story? *It's a sunny day?* I mean, we have to write about the lineup."

"Is this a story?" Randolph said. "Is this a story, is what I'm saying to you."

"It's part of the notebook," Abraham said. "That's all it is. It's not the end of the world."

"Okay. All right," Randolph said. "And it's not. That's why I don't understand. I mean, he's on my team. He's in the lineup. He's playing. Instead of hitting fifth, he's hitting sixth."

"But no one gives a shit what *we* think," Abraham said. "We've got to get what you think. People care what *you* think."

"I just think I'm putting together the best lineup for me," Randolph said. "I've said that from day one. Even right now, we don't need to be talking about this, because all you're going to do is make a big deal about *this*. All I'm saying to you is that I've moved my lineup around all year long. I've done it all year long, okay? To me, this is a waste of time to be talking about something as simple as moving a guy from fifth to sixth. That's all.

"Or from seventh to first," Randolph continued, making reference to the weeks-old, brief demotion of Reyes from the leadoff spot. "That's all. It's a story because you have a job to do and I understand that. But for me, it's like . . . it's part of my team."

In his last meeting of the 2005 season with the beat writers, Randolph professed with a straight face that he enjoyed his dealings with the media. "Even though some of you are assholes," he added in a playful manner.

Overall, Randolph handled well what could have been a minefield with Piazza. The manager ever so gently began to de-emphasize the aging slugger, making sure no movement was so abrupt as to embarrass Piazza or create a headline like his predecessor Howe had done. The former skipper had revealed on television—before directly telling Piazza—that he would begin taking ground balls at first base, which created a media frenzy.

Randolph first dropped Piazza from the cleanup spot to fifth in the order against right-handed pitchers, then to fifth on a more regular basis, then to sixth, and even to seventh on two occasions. Randolph also began to more liberally play

Castro, starting the backup twice in a three-game series at Pittsburgh to close the first half, even with a three-day All-Star break to follow.

The crowd anticipated that Piazza's days in Flushing were about to end and toasted him throughout September. Piazza must have set a record for curtain calls during the season's final month. He mostly felt embarrassed by the attention, which included his Mets highlights played on the new high-definition Mitsubishi Diamond Vision board during late-season home games.

"There's a certain amount of myself that's very basic and very simple and very appreciative," said Piazza, a 62nd-round pick of the Dodgers in 1988, who learned catching as a professional ballplayer and became the game's all-time home-run leader at that position. "Because of where I've come from in my career, I guess I've never taken myself too seriously. I've been able to laugh at myself. Honestly, I really don't feel like I need a tribute. When they talk about that, I'm like, 'It's really not necessary.' I've been really honored enough. I've been enriched enough by just being here. The fans know how I feel about them, with last year's ceremony with the catchers [for passing Carlton Fisk and becoming number one in homers] and all these things. Coupled with the fact I don't know what's going to happen in the future, just leave it at that. Enjoy it for what it is. Sometimes less is more."

Piazza—in the final season of a seven-year contract, and thirty-seven years old as of September 4—seemed best served by continuing his career in the American League, where he could play at least part time as a designated hitter to reduce the pounding on his body. Though neither Mets officials nor Piazza completely ruled out a return, names of free agents-to-be, such as catchers Ramon Hernandez of the Padres and Bengie Molina of the Los Angeles Angels of Anaheim, had already been widely bandied about as potential successors.

"He, in my opinion, is going to be the second Met Hall of Famer," Fred Wilpon said about Piazza, who hit .251 with 19 home runs and 62 RBI in 398 at-bats. "I think he loved being here and was certainly the star of the team. No matter who we had here, I think Mike was always the center point. But things change, which I think is good. I hope Mike goes on and plays out as long as he wants to play out."

With Pedro and Beltran on board and Wright and Reyes rising stars, The New Mets acknowledged the past on the season's final day, embarrassment to Piazza be damned. They gave a worthy tribute to Piazza that included a rousing video presentation during the seventh-inning stretch. With former Creed lead singer Scott Stapp's "The Great Divide" serving as the theme music for the highlight video, Piazza's most memorable moments—including the home run against the Braves in the first game back in New York after 9/11, and the long ball that allowed Piazza to pass Fisk as the greatest home-run hitting catcher of all time—played on the video board. Old headlines were mixed into the piece, among them tabloid staples such as PIAZZA DELIVERY, A HOT PIAZZA, PIAZZA PARTY, and MIGHTY MIKE. The raucous crowd saluted Piazza with repeated curtain calls, which he obliged as the Rockies remained in their dugout, applauding rather than taking the field for the bottom of the seventh inning.

"You have to be The Man to have a Major League Baseball game stop for you for a five-minute tribute, and then to have five or six curtain calls," Wright said. "That's when you know you've done something. That's when you know you're The Man in New York, when that happens. It's fun to be a part of. As a teammate, you go through a wide range of emotions. It's obviously sad. We saw a tear come from his eye. It's great to see the fans respect and support him the way they did. It sends a chill up your spine. If you don't get goose bumps from that, something is wrong with you."

Randolph held Piazza out of the starting lineup the day before the season finale, to the disappointment of fans at the game trying to catch a glimpse of him before he departed. In the final game, Randolph removed Piazza in the top of the eighth, after allowing him to take the field. That caused more media uproar, since Piazza was due up third in the bottom of the inning.

"The thrill meter was on empty," Piazza said, absolving his manager, even if he agreed the timing seemed awkward. "Trust me. I was out of gas."

Piazza simply was happy to be playing. He feared not too much earlier that his season might be over because of the broken pisiform bone at the base of his left hand. He missed twenty-three games, then took another painful jolt to the spot while blocking a bounced Zambrano pitch. Piazza said the second whack made the injured area turn a different shade of purple.

When Randolph pulled him, Piazza doffed his helmet as he walked toward the dugout. The crowd, initially caught off guard by the sooner-than-expected departure, noticed what was happening and responded with gradually escalating cheers. Third-string catcher Mike DiFelice, heading toward home plate to replace him, shook Piazza's hand. Piazza hugged longtime equipment manager

Charlie Samuels, then emerged from the dugout, shin guards still on, and blew kisses to the crowd in various directions.

Afterward, Piazza pledged to always maintain a relationship with New York, though he decisively indicated his primary residence following his playing days would be in a warmer climate. Piazza added:

> *I'll tell you what—if you're not up for a challenge and a roller-coaster ride, then maybe you're better off not coming here. But personally, if you can embrace it, and understand there are definite frustrations—but the positives definitely outweigh the negatives—then strap in and enjoy the ride, because it is fun. Frustrating, but I'll tell you what, to me, that makes the good times better.*
>
> *I'll always come back here. I'll always feel comfortable here. This is a huge block of my professional life. I've made so many friendships here from all over the world. I've met people from New York. I've met people from Europe. I've met people from Asia here. I have great friendships. That's the beauty of this city. It's so cosmopolitan and so worldly.*

No one figured to wear Piazza's No. 31 for a while—unless, possibly, former teammate John Franco returned as a coach one day and wanted it. Franco turned the number over to Piazza when the catcher arrived from the Marlins in a May 22, 1998, theft of a trade for Preston Wilson, Ed Yarnall, and Geoff Goetz. Told the number ought to be retired, Piazza said: "Well, I don't know." He then added with a laugh about the next person to wear No. 31, if there was one: "He better be pretty good."

Piazza had been among the final players in uniform after the season finale. Cameron, unsure whether the organization might trade him during the off-season, was the last one.

"It may be my last day in a Met uniform," Cameron explained, prophetic since Minaya sent him in mid-November to San Diego, the site of his collision with Beltran, for outfielder/first baseman Xavier Nady. The trade saved the Mets $5 million, freeing money for the acquisition of Delgado.

Piazza and Franco, released by the Astros during the season, dined together the night of the season finale. At his locker just before he excused himself from a final chat with reporters and left the home clubhouse at Shea Stadium, Piazza heaped praise on The New Mets. "There's a little frustration because this is going to be a 'what if?' year. It's the way you look at it," Piazza said. "Omar has done a really good job. He got Pedro here. He signed Carlos."

On the first anniversary of Fred and Jeff Wilpon's hush-hush flight to Montreal to court Minaya to replace Jim Duquette as general manager, September 27, the Mets had been mathematically eliminated from the wild-card race. Yet they had remained alive into the final week and finished above .500. Heck, they finished with a better record than the National League West champion Padres by a game.

Duquette left the organization after the season. He accepted a job with the Baltimore Orioles as vice president of baseball operations, which offered more responsibility than his diminished role in Flushing. Still, Duquette maintained he had a solid relationship with Minaya, who went out of his way to ensure no friction arose.

"I have a ton of respect for him," Duquette said. "It was a very difficult situation for him coming in to replace me. He handled it very well and treated me better than I expected. He's a classy guy. He's an easy guy to cheer for and root for because he's such a good guy."

When Duquette took over for fired general manager Steve Phillips in June 2003 on an interim basis, he was charged with bringing the Mets' $117 million payroll under the luxury-tax threshold. He shipped out outfielder Jeromy Burnitz, closer Armando Benitez, second baseman Roberto Alomar, reliever Graeme Lloyd, and infielder Rey Sanchez in cost-saving moves that netted Victor Diaz and left-handed reliever Royce Ring. In his one winter as GM, once the interim tag was removed, Duquette didn't have authority to lavishly spend, like Minaya subsequently had been given. The Mets had dropped their payroll to $81 million under Duquette's watch yet signed Cameron, Looper, and Matsui, though Duquette had little to do with Matsui's acquisition, which maintained the Mets' presence in Japan. Of course, Duquette also was at the helm when the Mets obtained Zambrano for Kazmir, even if it's clear the organization had other voices exerting influence at the time, particularly in overstating Zambrano's value.

"My style, and the successful organizational style of an executive, is to get a lot of opinions—educated opinions of a lot of the evaluators—and make a decision of when and if to make a trade," Duquette said, addressing the Zambrano-Kazmir swap. "Ultimately, the final responsibility falls on the general manager."

On the Mets' future, Duquette was bullish. "I think the state of the Mets is the reason why I have the opportunity I do now, the reason why my name was mentioned," he said.

During the team's winter caravan in January 2005, Pedro had expressed hope that the Mets would overtake the Yankees to dominate the attention in New York. That was a work in progress, but the Mets were no longer irrelevant. And the Yankees were no longer dominant. Their division series loss to the Angels made them another year removed from their final World Series title, five years earlier against the Mets.

Not only did Pedro and Beltran raise the profile of their new organization, their presence in Flushing rather than the Bronx arguably sealed the Yankees' disappointing playoff exit in '05. A lack of quality starting pitching and a bona fide centerfielder had haunted the Yankees all season. Pedro might have won 20 games with Mariano Rivera closing for him. Beltran could have hit second in that lineup like he did with Houston, and might have exploded with the decreased pressure of that slot; plus, he would have at least provided quality defense, which the Yankees sorely needed in their critical Game 5 ouster against the Angels. Los Angeles took the lead for good in the deciding game when centerfielder Bubba Crosby collided with right fielder Gary Sheffield on what became Adam Kennedy's two-run triple.

"I think what Omar has done and what Willie has done is they've made it attractive for players to want to play here in New York," Fred Wilpon said. "And that was not necessarily always the case. Players are now coming up to Willie and coming up to Omar, and they want to be here. When they're available, they want to be here. And that's exciting."

Said Beltran: "Since I got to spring training, I've felt like we have a lot of great guys on this ball club, a lot of young guys who can become great ballplayers. This organization, like I said before—the front office, Omar, all of those guys—they're going in the right direction. They really want to put a real good winning team in this city, and that's what I like."

As Beltran expected when he signed in January 2005: The New Mets had headed in a different direction—the right direction—the direction of winning.

# INDEX

Wilson, Mookie, 122
Wilson, Paul, 47, 50
Wilson, Preston, 208
Wilson, Vance, 7, 148
Winn, Randy, 110, 156
Woodward, Chris, 11, 166, 193
   Braves series, 178
   Nationals series, 142, 143
   season's stats, 201
Wright, David, 13, 31, 163, 166, 190
   base running, 146–47
   on Braves, 171–72, 173
   Braves series, 63, 178
   Cardinals series, 178
   Diamondbacks series, 146, 147, 150, 151
   Dodgers game, 129
   home run, 156
   Nationals game, 142
   Padres series, 114–15, 120

   on Piazza, 207
   season's stats/popularity of, 193–95
   spring training, 36–37
   on team's struggles, 182–83
   Yankees series, 75, 83–84

**Y**

Yarnall, Ed, 208
Yastrzemski, Carl, 64
Young, Cy, 98, 99

**Z**

Zambrano, Victor, 156, 157
   Braves game, 56, 57
   Dodgers game, 128
   Marlins game, 166–67
   replacing Martinez, 189
   season's stats, 197
   trade for, 4–5, 55–56, 209
Zeile, Todd, 28